ULTIMATE THOR

ULTIMATE THOR

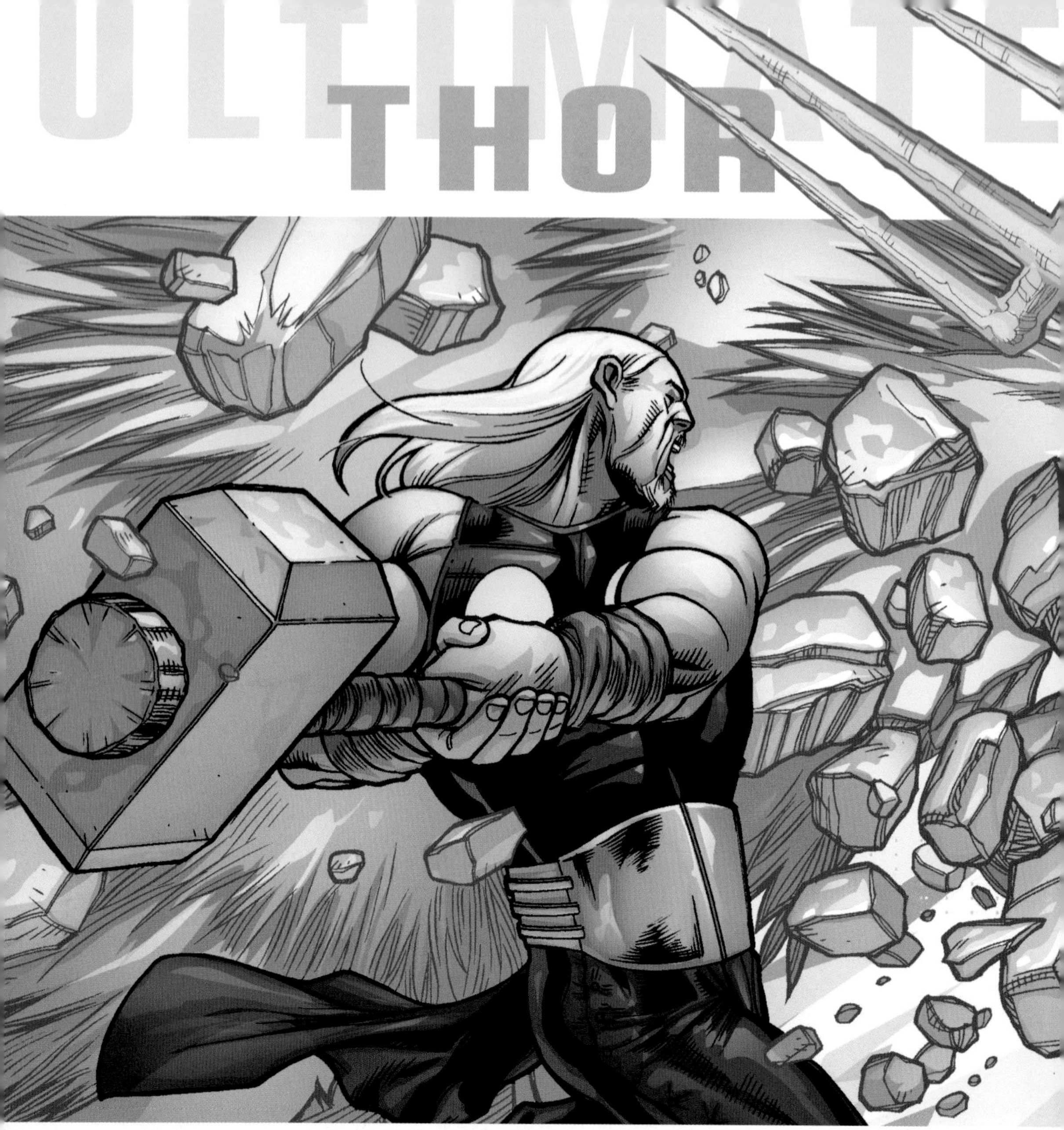

WRITER:
JONATHAN HICKMAN
PENCILER:
CARLOS PACHECO
INKER: **DEXTER VINES** WITH **JASON PAZ** & **JEFF HUET**
COLORIST: **EDGAR DELGADO** WITH **J. ABURTOV** & **JORGE GONZALEZ**
LETTERER: **VC'S CLAYTON COWLES**
COVER ART: **CARLOS PACHECO, DEXTER VINES, JASON PAZ, FRANK D'ARMATA & EDGAR DELGADO**
ASSISTANT EDITOR: **SANA AMANAT** SENIOR EDITOR: **MARK PANICCIA**

COLLECTION EDITOR: **JENNIFER GRÜNWALD**
EDITORIAL ASSISTANTS: **JAMES EMMETT & JOE HOCHSTEIN**
ASSISTANT EDITORS: **ALEX STARBUCK & NELSON RIBEIRO**
EDITOR, SPECIAL PROJECTS: **MARK D. BEAZLEY**
SENIOR EDITOR, SPECIAL PROJECTS: **JEFF YOUNGQUIST**
SENIOR VICE PRESIDENT OF SALES: **DAVID GABRIEL**
SVP OF BRAND PLANNING & COMMUNICATIONS: **MICHAEL PASCIULLO**

EDITOR IN CHIEF: **AXEL ALONSO**   CHIEF CREATIVE OFFICER: **JOE QUESADA**
PUBLISHER: **DAN BUCKLEY**   EXECUTIVE PRODUCER: **ALAN FINE**

ULTIMATE COMICS THOR. Contains material originally published in magazine form as ULTIMATE COMICS THOR #1-4. First printing 2011. ISBN# 978-0-7851-5188-3. Published by MARVEL WORLDWIDE, INC., a subsidiary of MARVEL ENTERTAINMENT, LLC. OFFICE OF PUBLICATION: 135 West 50th Street, New York, NY 10020. Copyright © 2010 and 2011 Marvel Characters, Inc. All rights reserved. $15.99 per copy in the U.S. and $17.99 in Canada (GST #R127032852); Canadian Agreement #40668537. All characters featured in this issue and the distinctive names and likenesses thereof, and all related indicia are trademarks of Marvel Characters, Inc. No similarity between any of the names, characters, persons, and/or institutions in this magazine with those of any living or dead person or institution is intended, and any such similarity which may exist is purely coincidental. **Printed in the U.S.A.** ALAN FINE, EVP - Office of the President, Marvel Worldwide, Inc. and EVP & CMO Marvel Characters B.V.; DAN BUCKLEY, Publisher & President - Print, Animation & Digital Divisions; JOE QUESADA, Chief Creative Officer; JIM SOKOLOWSKI, Chief Operating Officer; DAVID BOGART, SVP of Business Affairs & Talent Management; TOM BREVOORT, SVP of Publishing; C.B. CEBULSKI, SVP of Creator & Content Development; DAVID GABRIEL, SVP of Publishing Sales & Circulation; MICHAEL PASCIULLO, SVP of Brand Planning & Communications; JIM O'KEEFE, VP of Operations & Logistics; DAN CARR, Executive Director of Publishing Technology; SUSAN CRESPI, Editorial Operations Manager; ALEX MORALES, Publishing Operations Manager; STAN LEE, Chairman Emeritus. For information regarding advertising in Marvel Comics or on Marvel.com, please contact John Dokes, SVP Integrated Sales and Marketing, at jdokes@marvel.com. For Marvel subscription inquiries, please call 800-217-9158. **Manufactured between 8/17/2011 and 9/5/2011 by R.R. DONNELLEY, INC., SALEM, VA, USA.**

10 9 8 7 6 5 4 3 2 1

1

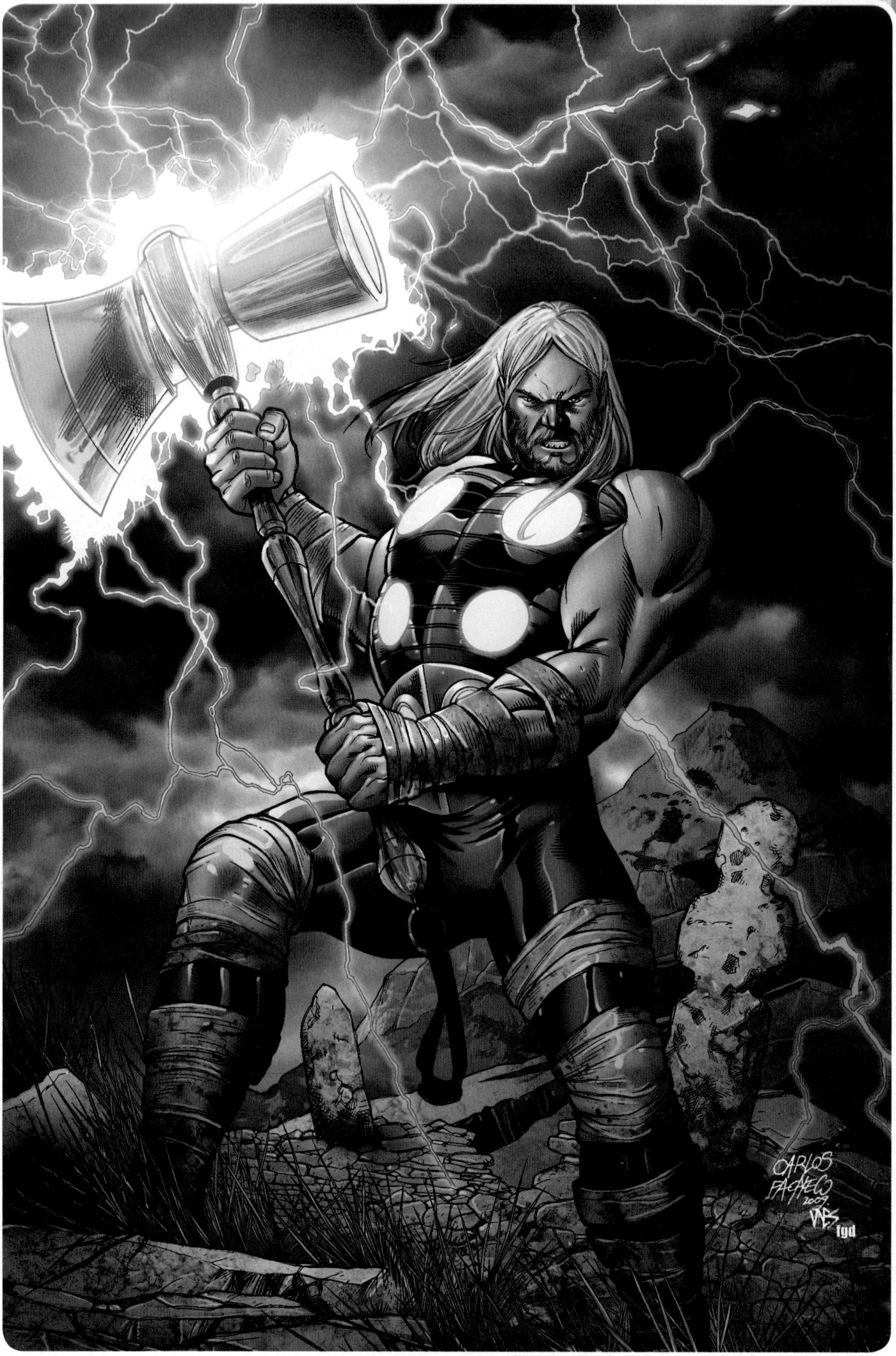
CARLOS
PACHECO
2009

DO YOU LACK FAITH, BROTHER... OR DO YOU BELIEVE?

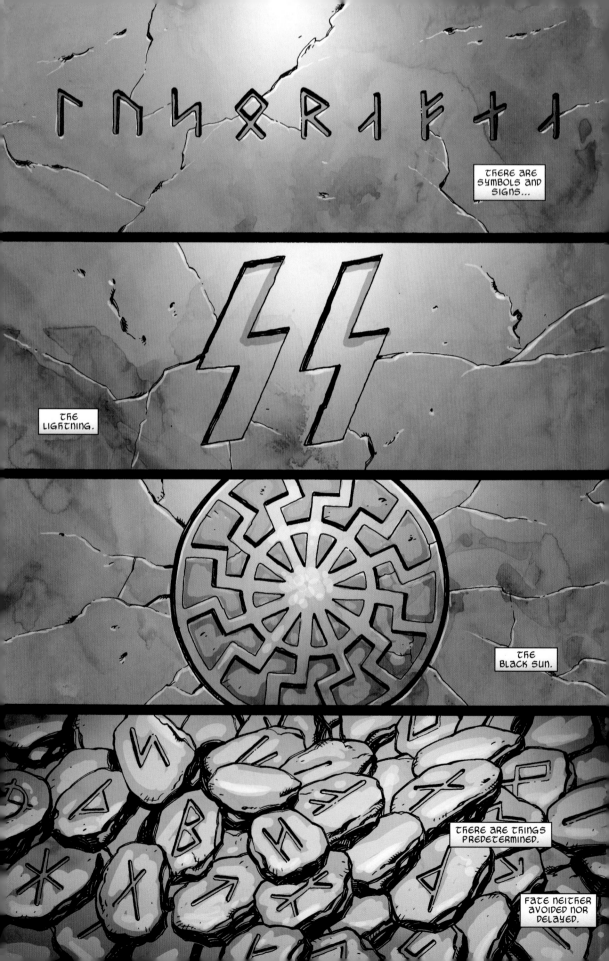

THERE ARE SYMBOLS AND SIGNS...

THE LIGHTNING.

THE BLACK SUN.

THERE ARE THINGS PREDETERMINED.

FATE NEITHER AVOIDED NOR DELAYED.

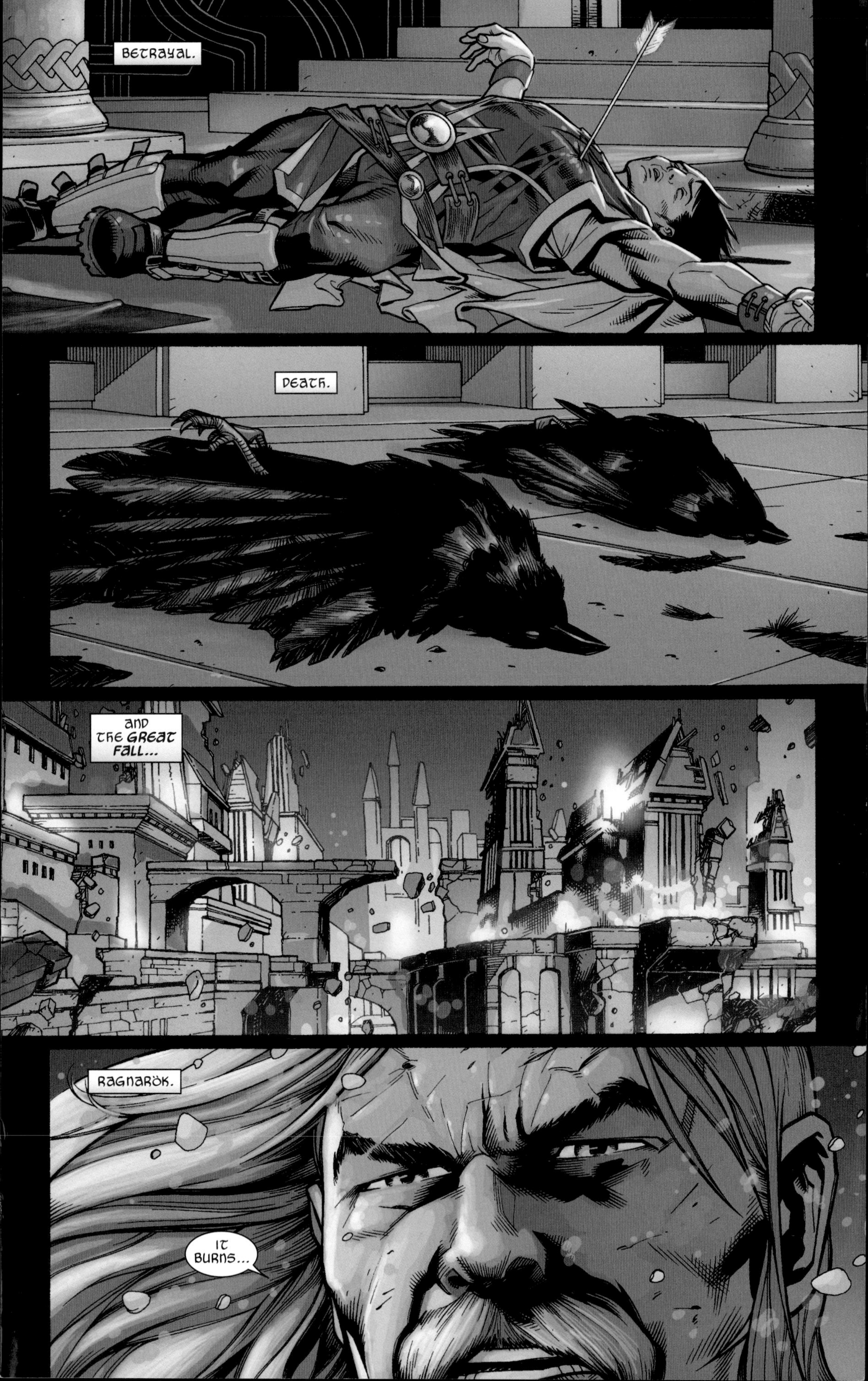
BETRAYAL.
DEATH.
AND THE GREAT FALL...
RAGNARÖK.
IT BURNS...

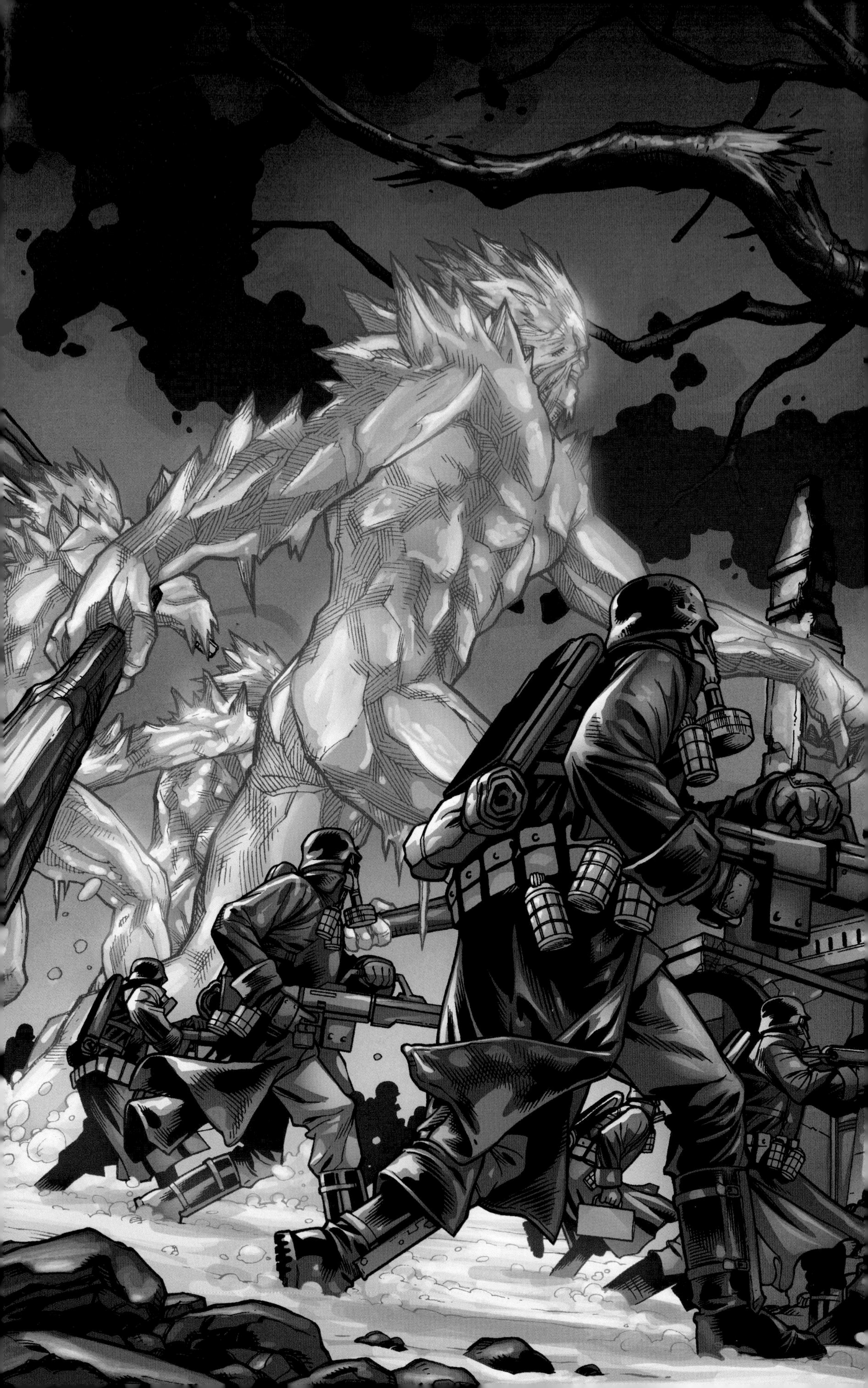

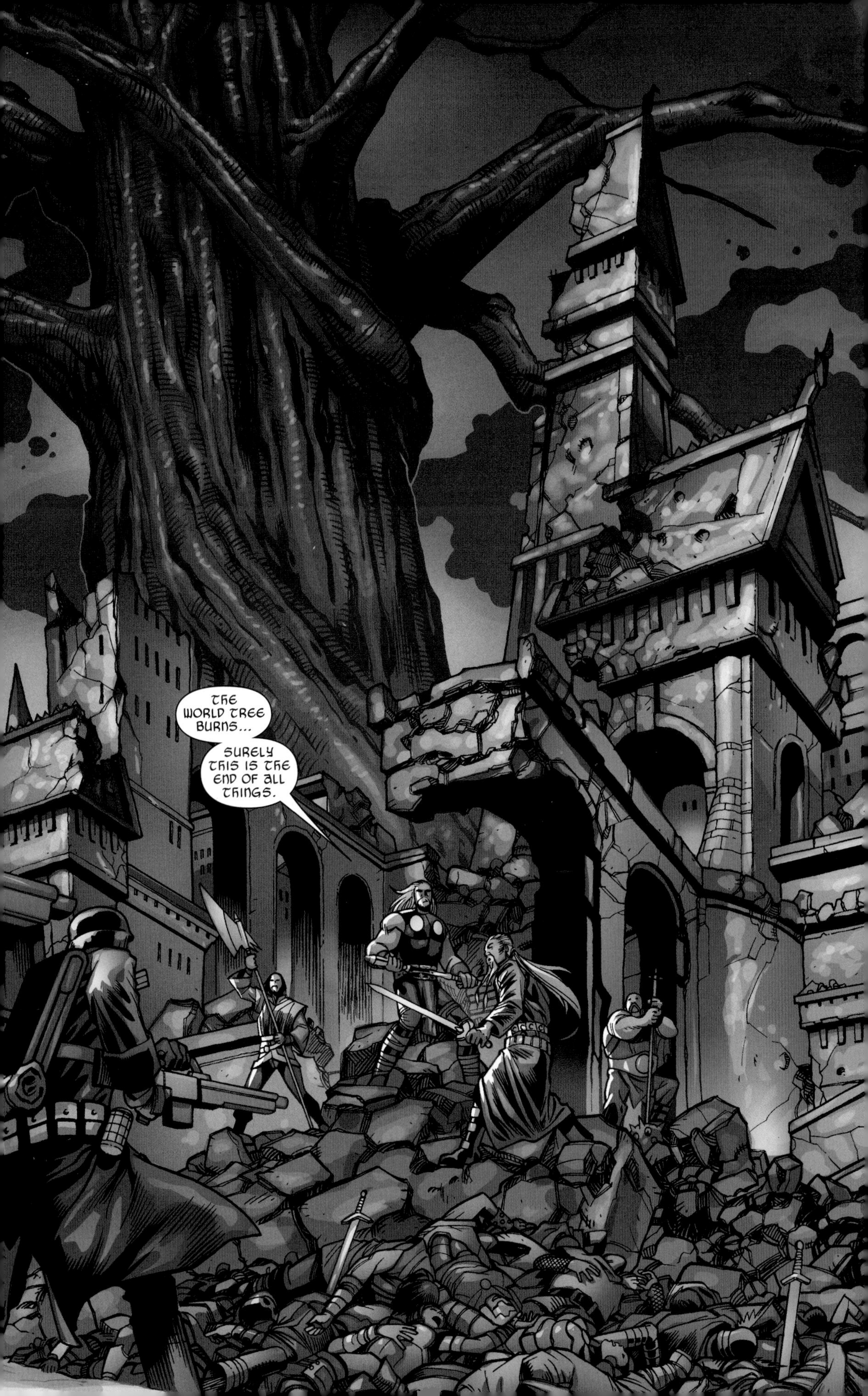
THE WORLD TREE BURNS...
SURELY THIS IS THE END OF ALL THINGS.

ULTIMATE

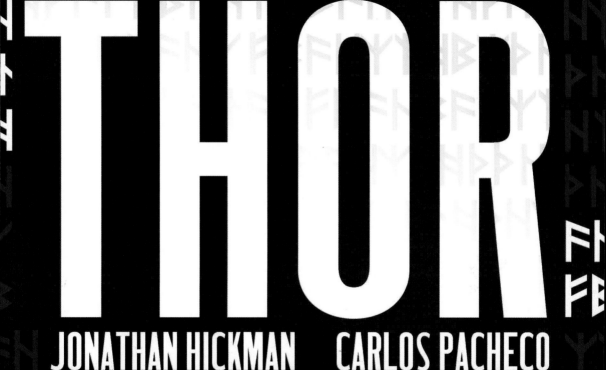

THOR

JONATHAN HICKMAN   CARLOS PACHECO

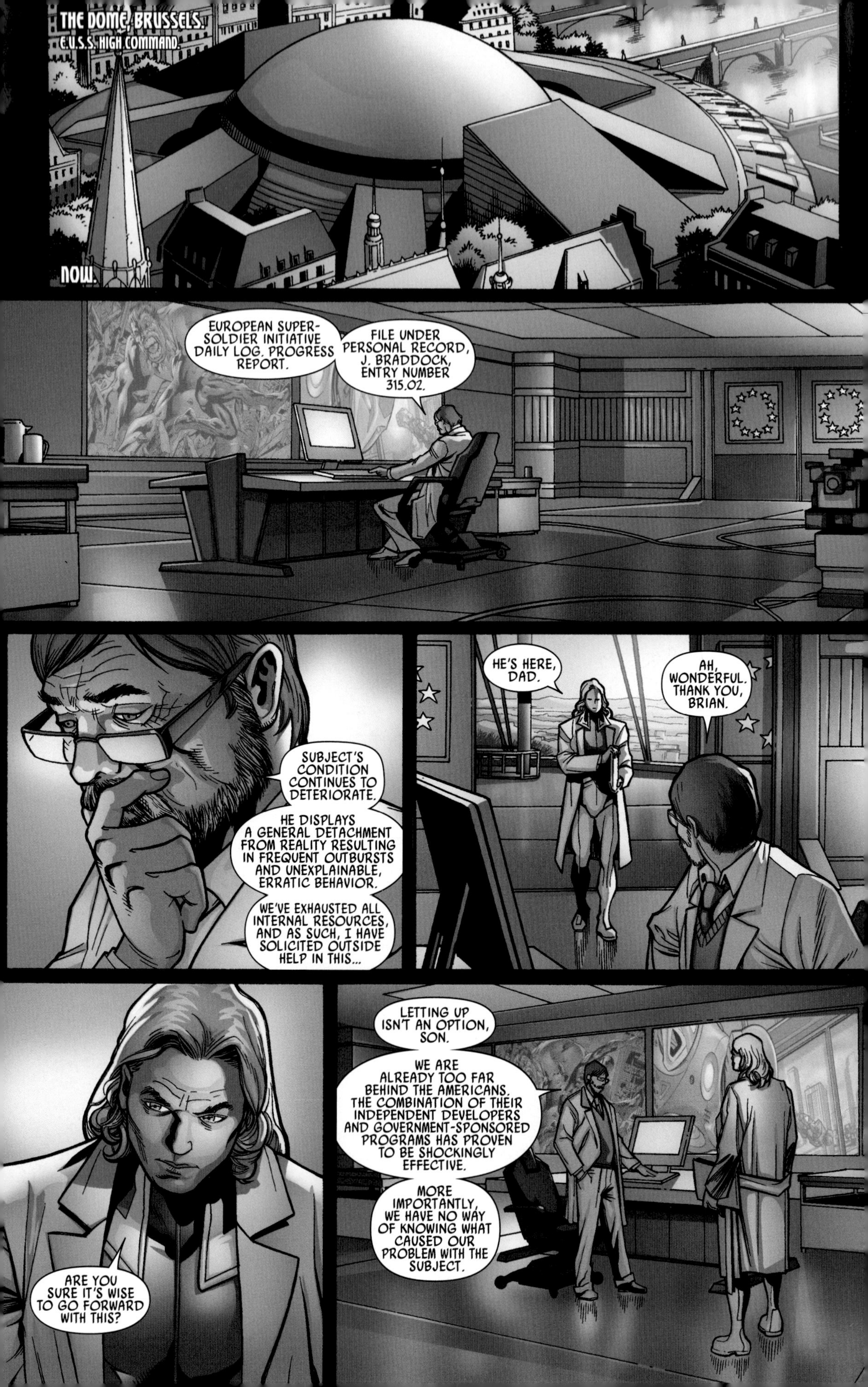
THE DOME, BRUSSELS.
E.U.S.S. HIGH COMMAND.
NOW.
EUROPEAN SUPER-SOLDIER INITIATIVE DAILY LOG. PROGRESS REPORT.
FILE UNDER PERSONAL RECORD, J. BRADDOCK, ENTRY NUMBER 315.02.
SUBJECT'S CONDITION CONTINUES TO DETERIORATE.
HE DISPLAYS A GENERAL DETACHMENT FROM REALITY RESULTING IN FREQUENT OUTBURSTS AND UNEXPLAINABLE, ERRATIC BEHAVIOR.
WE'VE EXHAUSTED ALL INTERNAL RESOURCES, AND AS SUCH, I HAVE SOLICITED OUTSIDE HELP IN THIS...
HE'S HERE, DAD.
AH, WONDERFUL. THANK YOU, BRIAN.
ARE YOU SURE IT'S WISE TO GO FORWARD WITH THIS?
LETTING UP ISN'T AN OPTION, SON.
WE ARE ALREADY TOO FAR BEHIND THE AMERICANS. THE COMBINATION OF THEIR INDEPENDENT DEVELOPERS AND GOVERNMENT-SPONSORED PROGRAMS HAS PROVEN TO BE SHOCKINGLY EFFECTIVE.
MORE IMPORTANTLY, WE HAVE NO WAY OF KNOWING WHAT CAUSED OUR PROBLEM WITH THE SUBJECT.

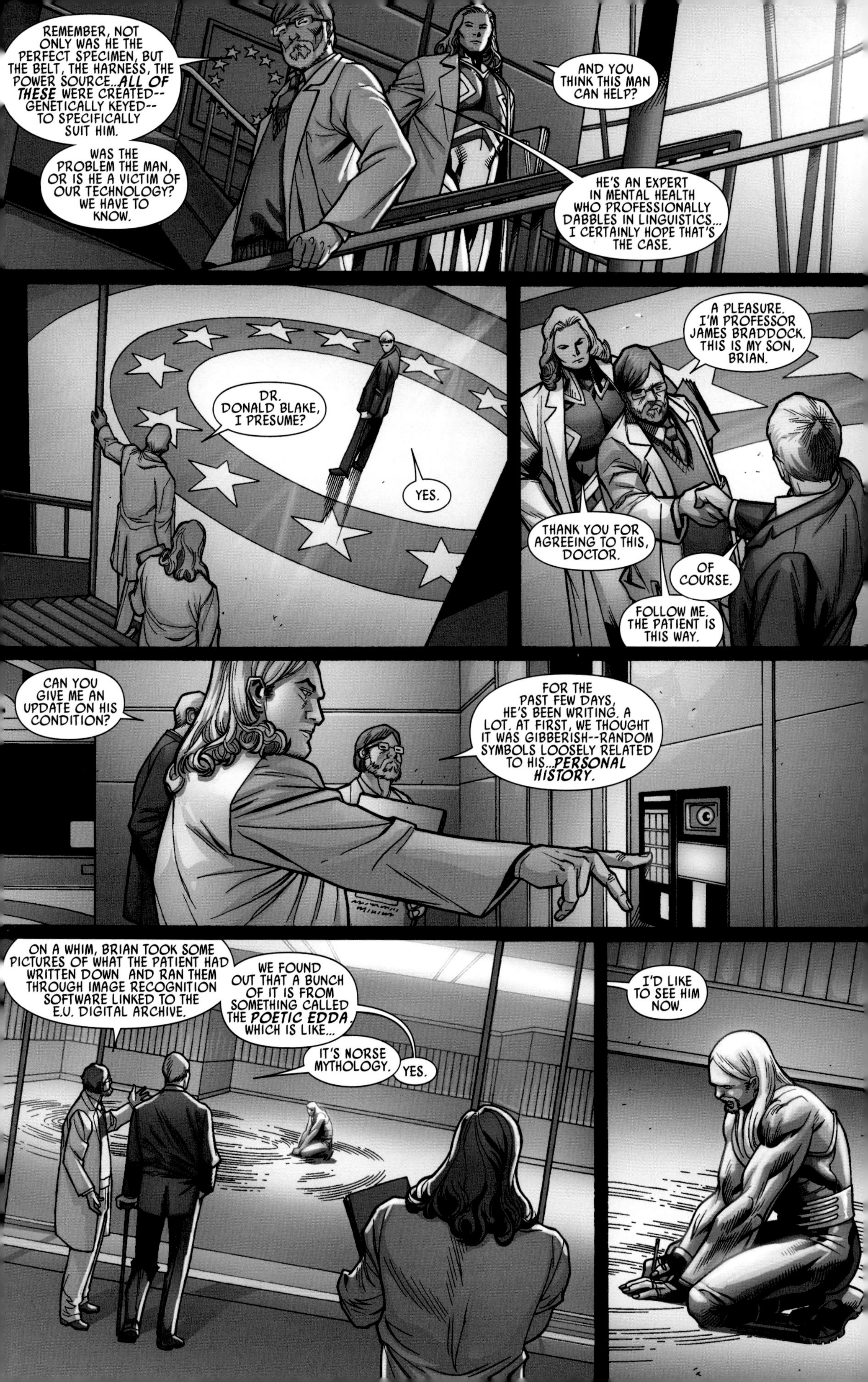
REMEMBER, NOT ONLY WAS HE THE PERFECT SPECIMEN, BUT THE BELT, THE HARNESS, THE POWER SOURCE...ALL OF THESE WERE CREATED--GENETICALLY KEYED--TO SPECIFICALLY SUIT HIM.
WAS THE PROBLEM THE MAN, OR IS HE A VICTIM OF OUR TECHNOLOGY? WE HAVE TO KNOW.
AND YOU THINK THIS MAN CAN HELP?
HE'S AN EXPERT IN MENTAL HEALTH WHO PROFESSIONALLY DABBLES IN LINGUISTICS... I CERTAINLY HOPE THAT'S THE CASE.
DR. DONALD BLAKE, I PRESUME?
YES.
A PLEASURE. I'M PROFESSOR JAMES BRADDOCK. THIS IS MY SON, BRIAN.
THANK YOU FOR AGREEING TO THIS, DOCTOR.
OF COURSE.
FOLLOW ME. THE PATIENT IS THIS WAY.
CAN YOU GIVE ME AN UPDATE ON HIS CONDITION?
FOR THE PAST FEW DAYS, HE'S BEEN WRITING. A LOT. AT FIRST, WE THOUGHT IT WAS GIBBERISH--RANDOM SYMBOLS LOOSELY RELATED TO HIS...PERSONAL HISTORY.
ON A WHIM, BRIAN TOOK SOME PICTURES OF WHAT THE PATIENT HAD WRITTEN DOWN AND RAN THEM THROUGH IMAGE RECOGNITION SOFTWARE LINKED TO THE E.U. DIGITAL ARCHIVE.
WE FOUND OUT THAT A BUNCH OF IT IS FROM SOMETHING CALLED THE POETIC EDDA, WHICH IS LIKE...
IT'S NORSE MYTHOLOGY.
YES.
I'D LIKE TO SEE HIM NOW.

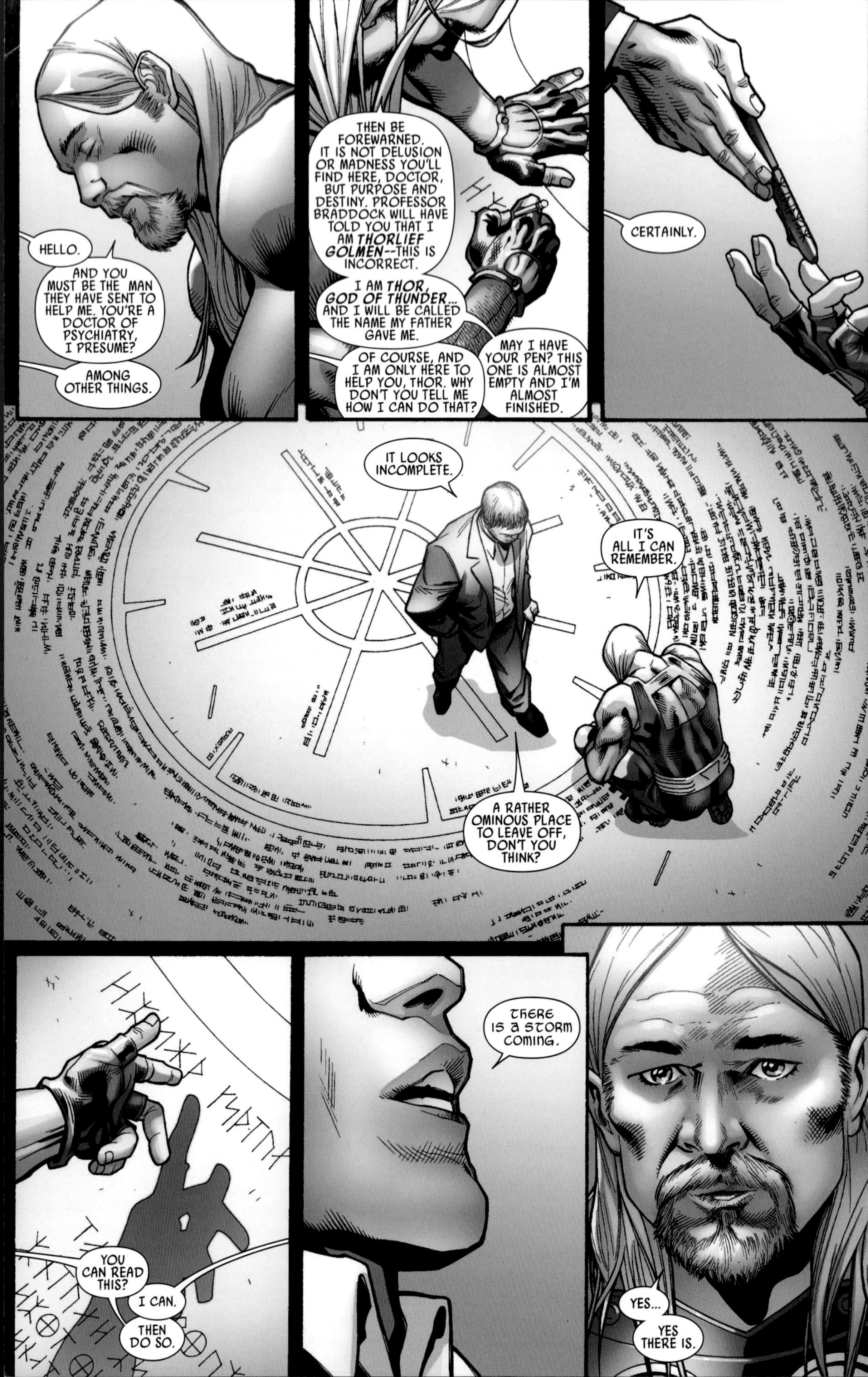
HELLO.
AND YOU MUST BE THE MAN THEY HAVE SENT TO HELP ME. YOU'RE A DOCTOR OF PSYCHIATRY, I PRESUME?
AMONG OTHER THINGS.
THEN BE FOREWARNED. IT IS NOT DELUSION OR MADNESS YOU'LL FIND HERE, DOCTOR, BUT PURPOSE AND DESTINY. PROFESSOR BRADDOCK WILL HAVE TOLD YOU THAT I AM THORLIEF GOLMEN--THIS IS INCORRECT.
I AM THOR, GOD OF THUNDER... AND I WILL BE CALLED THE NAME MY FATHER GAVE ME.
OF COURSE, AND I AM ONLY HERE TO HELP YOU, THOR. WHY DON'T YOU TELL ME HOW I CAN DO THAT?
MAY I HAVE YOUR PEN? THIS ONE IS ALMOST EMPTY AND I'M ALMOST FINISHED.
CERTAINLY.
IT LOOKS INCOMPLETE.
IT'S ALL I CAN REMEMBER.
A RATHER OMINOUS PLACE TO LEAVE OFF, DON'T YOU THINK?
YOU CAN READ THIS?
I CAN.
THEN DO SO.
THERE IS A STORM COMING.
YES...
YES THERE IS.

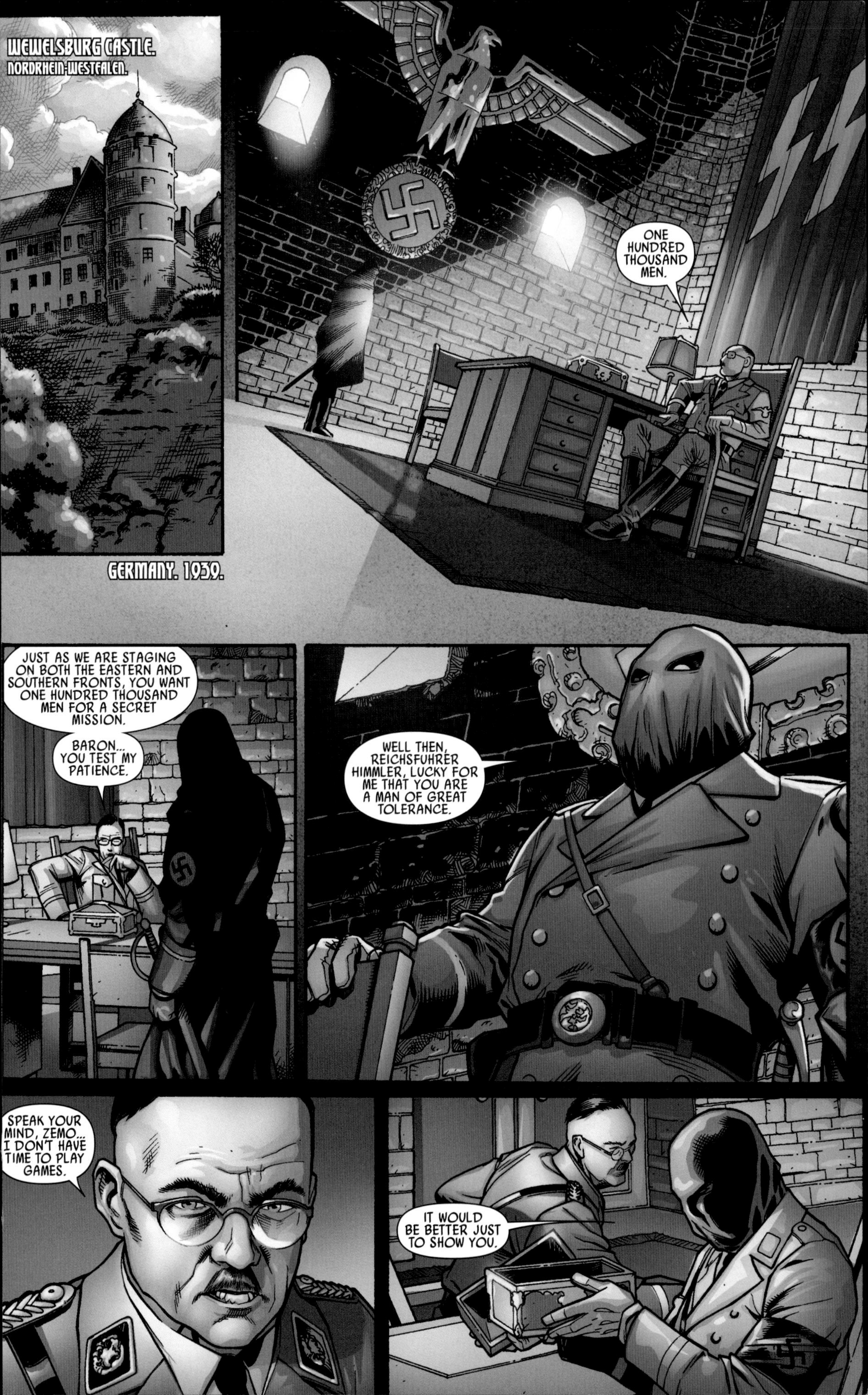
WEWELSBURG CASTLE.
NORDRHEIN-WESTFALEN.
GERMANY. 1939.
ONE HUNDRED THOUSAND MEN.
JUST AS WE ARE STAGING ON BOTH THE EASTERN AND SOUTHERN FRONTS, YOU WANT ONE HUNDRED THOUSAND MEN FOR A SECRET MISSION.
BARON... YOU TEST MY PATIENCE.
WELL THEN, REICHSFUHRER HIMMLER, LUCKY FOR ME THAT YOU ARE A MAN OF GREAT TOLERANCE.
SPEAK YOUR MIND, ZEMO... I DON'T HAVE TIME TO PLAY GAMES.
IT WOULD BE BETTER JUST TO SHOW YOU.

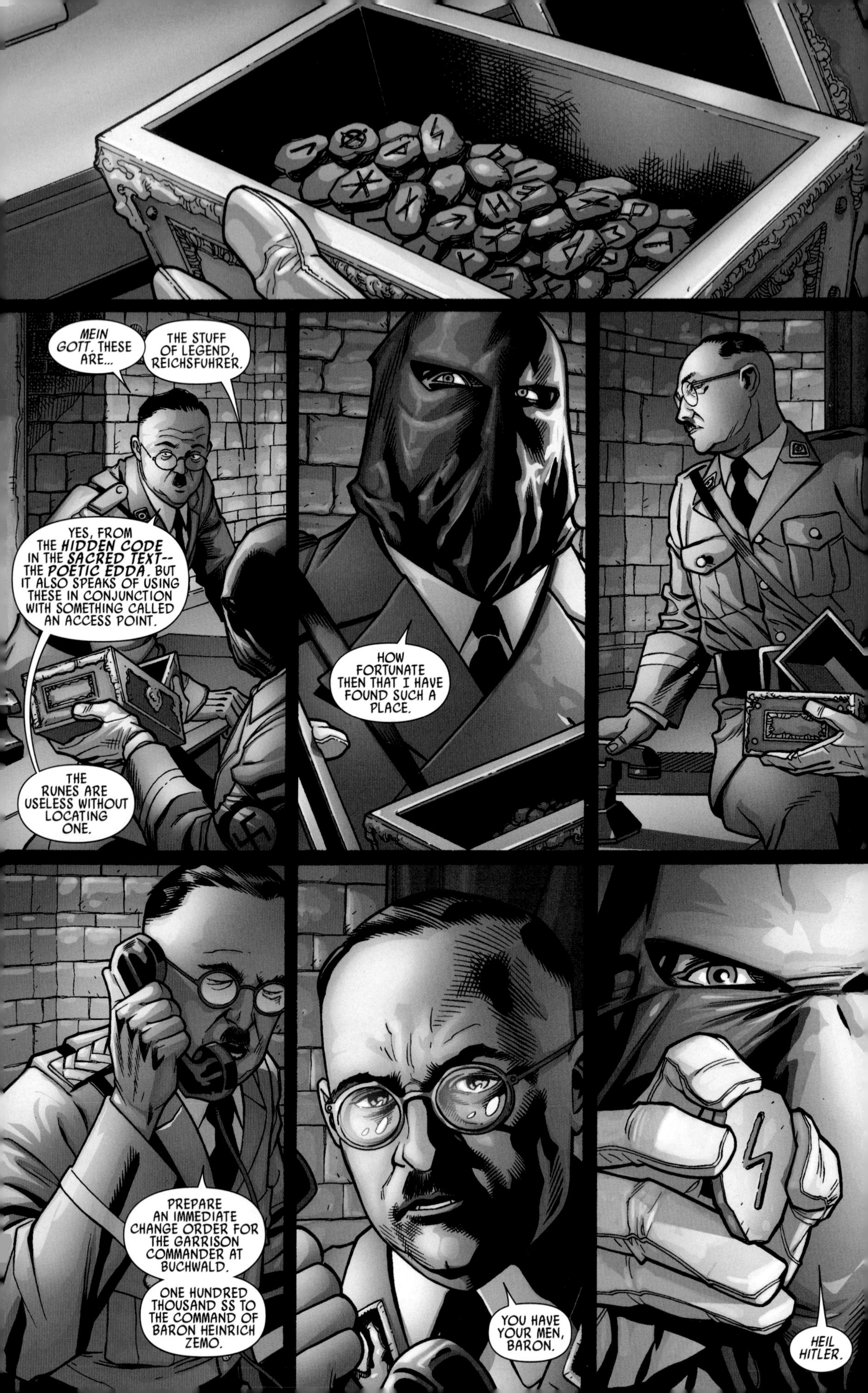

MEIN GOTT. THESE ARE...
THE STUFF OF LEGEND, REICHSFUHRER.
YES, FROM THE **HIDDEN CODE** IN THE **SACRED TEXT**-- THE **POETIC EDDA**. BUT IT ALSO SPEAKS OF USING THESE IN CONJUNCTION WITH SOMETHING CALLED AN ACCESS POINT.
THE RUNES ARE USELESS WITHOUT LOCATING ONE.
HOW FORTUNATE THEN THAT I HAVE FOUND SUCH A PLACE.
PREPARE AN IMMEDIATE CHANGE ORDER FOR THE GARRISON COMMANDER AT BUCHWALD.
ONE HUNDRED THOUSAND SS TO THE COMMAND OF BARON HEINRICH ZEMO.
YOU HAVE YOUR MEN, BARON.
HEIL HITLER.

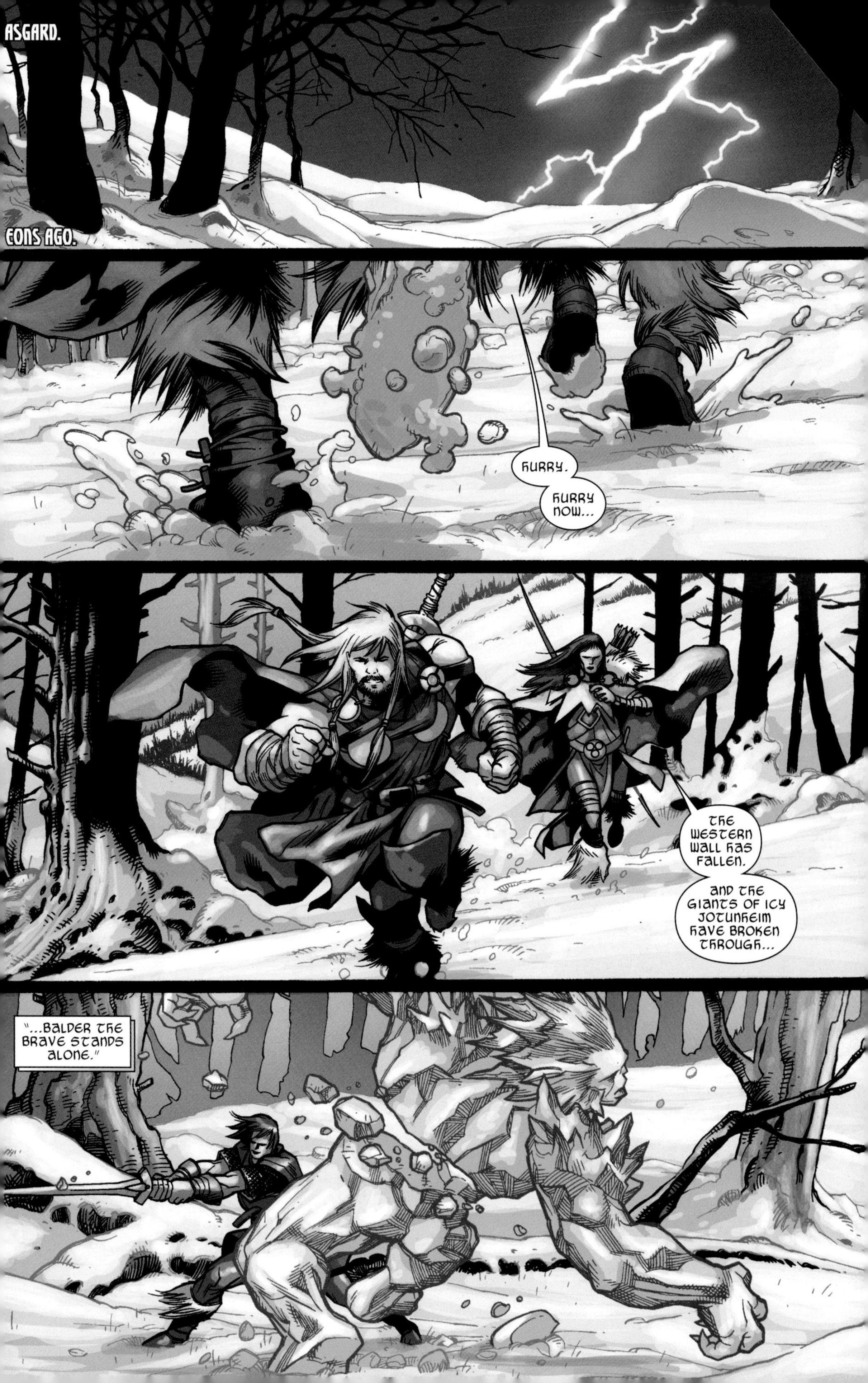
ASGARD.
EONS AGO.
HURRY.
HURRY NOW...
THE WESTERN WALL HAS FALLEN.
AND THE GIANTS OF ICY JOTUNHEIM HAVE BROKEN THROUGH...
"...BALDER THE BRAVE STANDS ALONE."

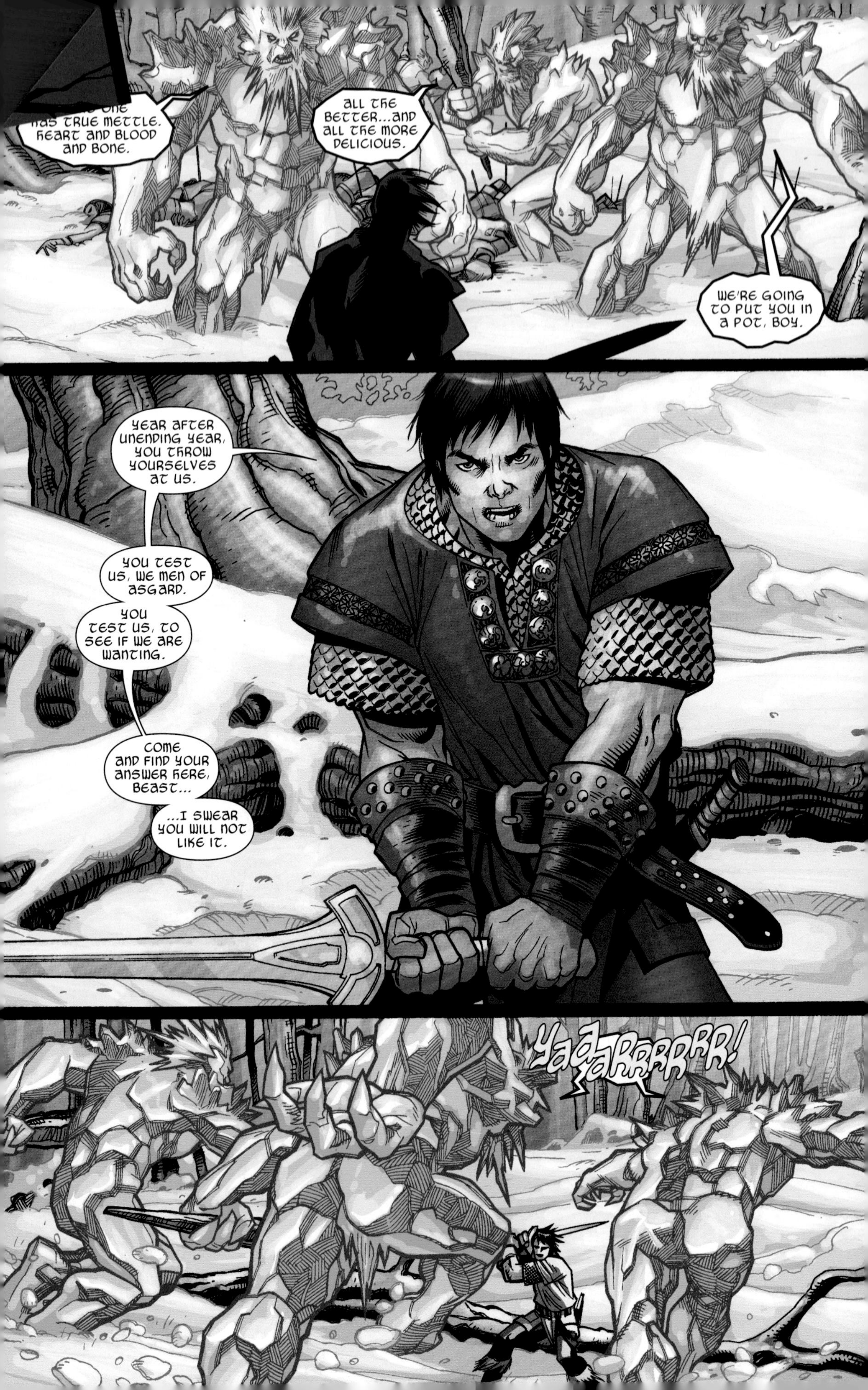

ONE HAS TRUE METTLE. HEART AND BLOOD AND BONE.
ALL THE BETTER...AND ALL THE MORE DELICIOUS.
WE'RE GOING TO PUT YOU IN A POT, BOY.
YEAR AFTER UNENDING YEAR, YOU THROW YOURSELVES AT US.
YOU TEST US, WE MEN OF ASGARD.
YOU TEST US, TO SEE IF WE ARE WANTING.
COME AND FIND YOUR ANSWER HERE, BEAST...
...I SWEAR YOU WILL NOT LIKE IT.
YAAARRRRRR!

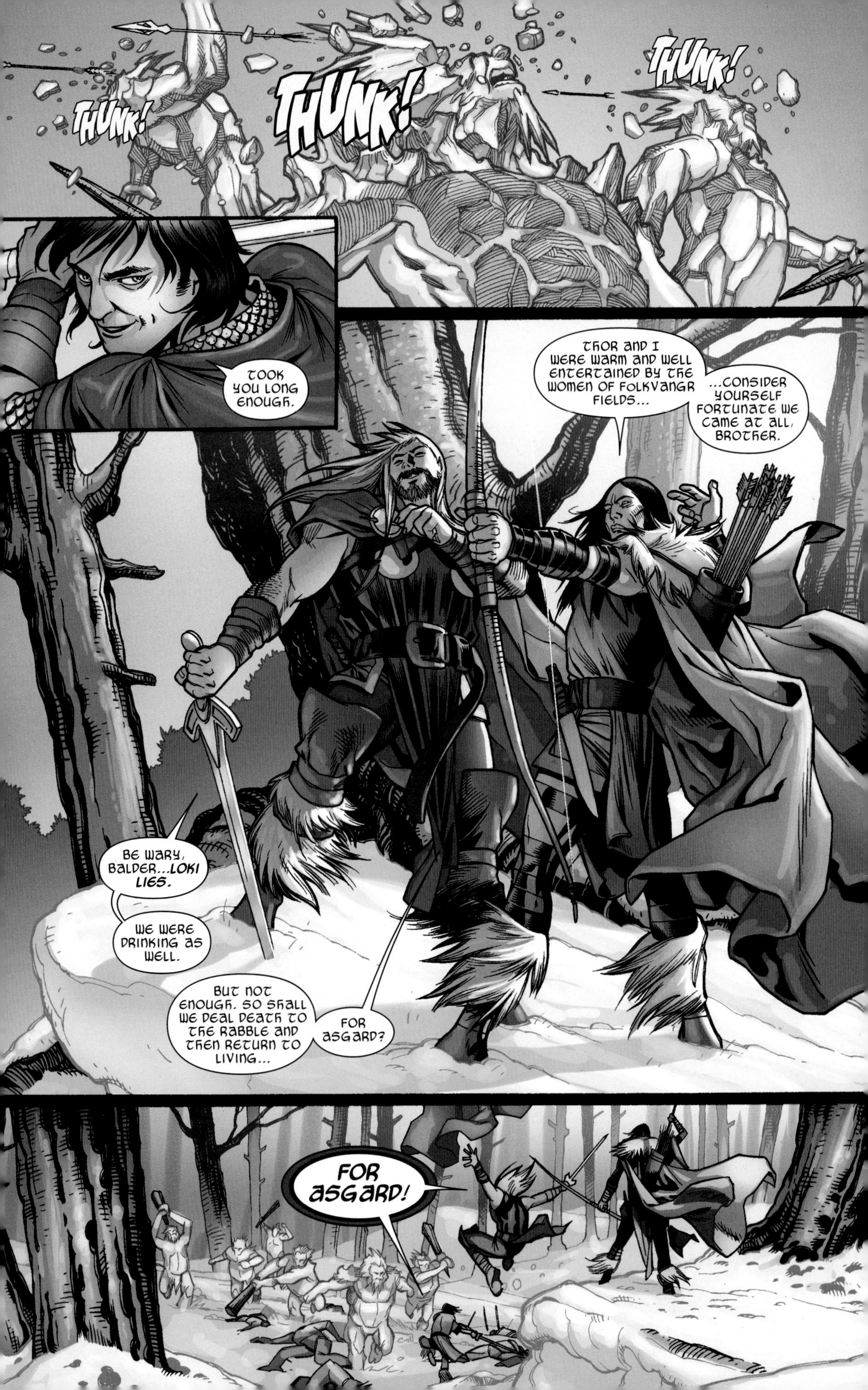
THUNK!
THUNK!
THUNK!
TOOK YOU LONG ENOUGH.
THOR AND I WERE WARM AND WELL ENTERTAINED BY THE WOMEN OF FOLKVANGR FIELDS...
...CONSIDER YOURSELF FORTUNATE WE CAME AT ALL, BROTHER.
BE WARY, BALDER...LOKI LIES.
WE WERE DRINKING AS WELL.
BUT NOT ENOUGH. SO SHALL WE DEAL DEATH TO THE RABBLE AND THEN RETURN TO LIVING...
FOR ASGARD?
FOR ASGARD!

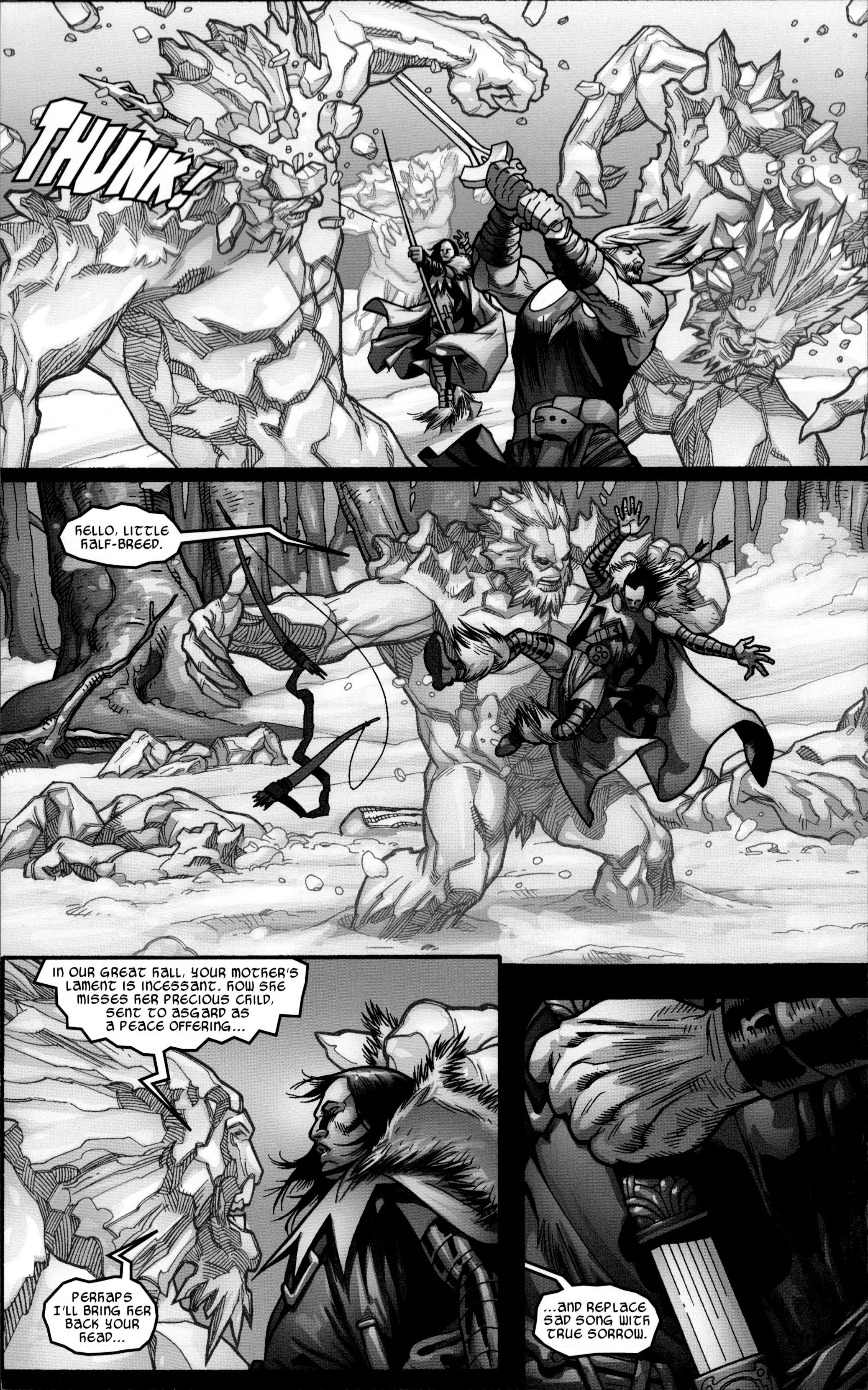
THUNK!
HELLO, LITTLE HALF-BREED.
IN OUR GREAT HALL, YOUR MOTHER'S LAMENT IS INCESSANT. HOW SHE MISSES HER PRECIOUS CHILD, SENT TO ASGARD AS A PEACE OFFERING...
PERHAPS I'LL BRING HER BACK YOUR HEAD...
...AND REPLACE SAD SONG WITH TRUE SORROW.

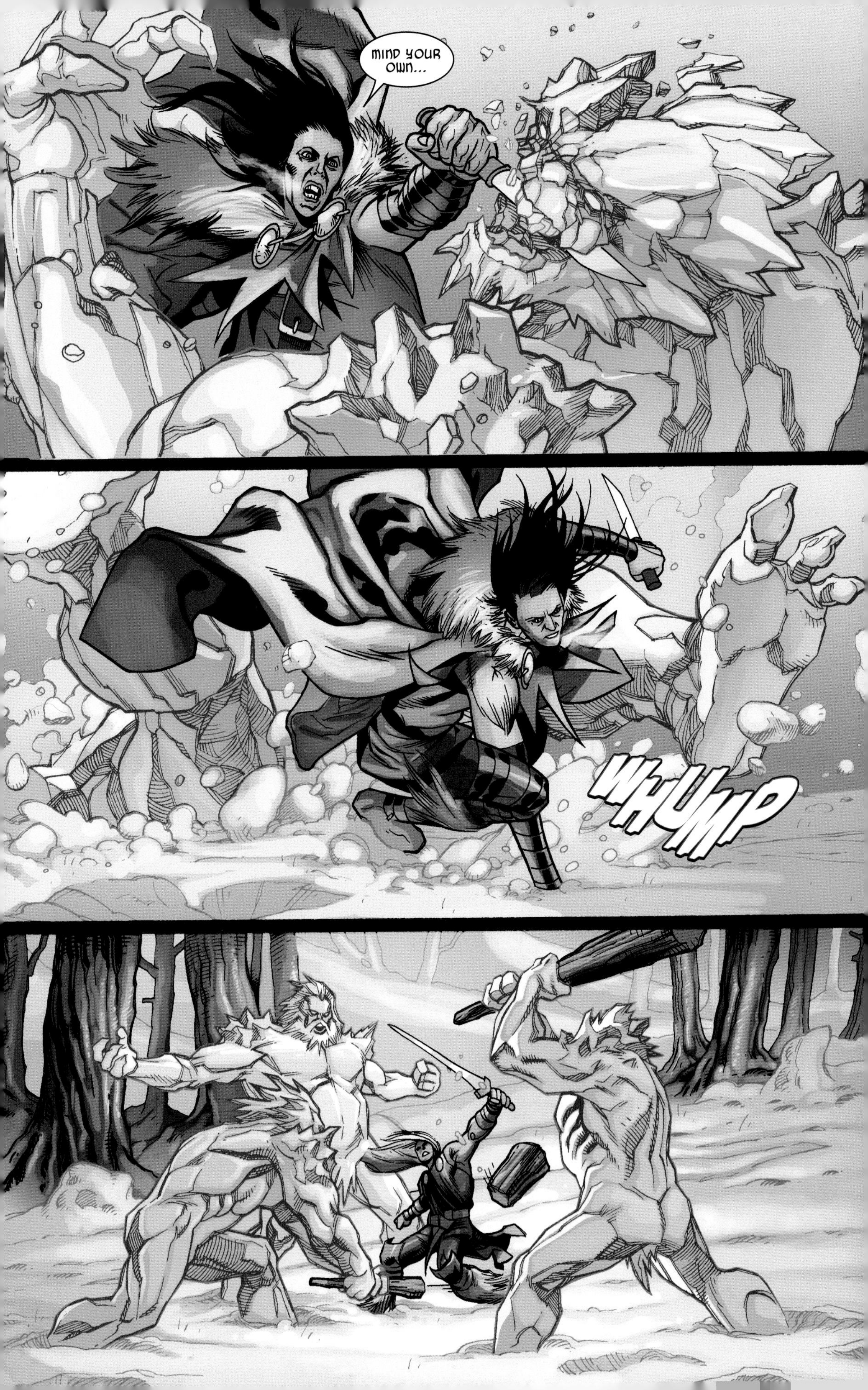
MIND YOUR OWN...
WHUMP

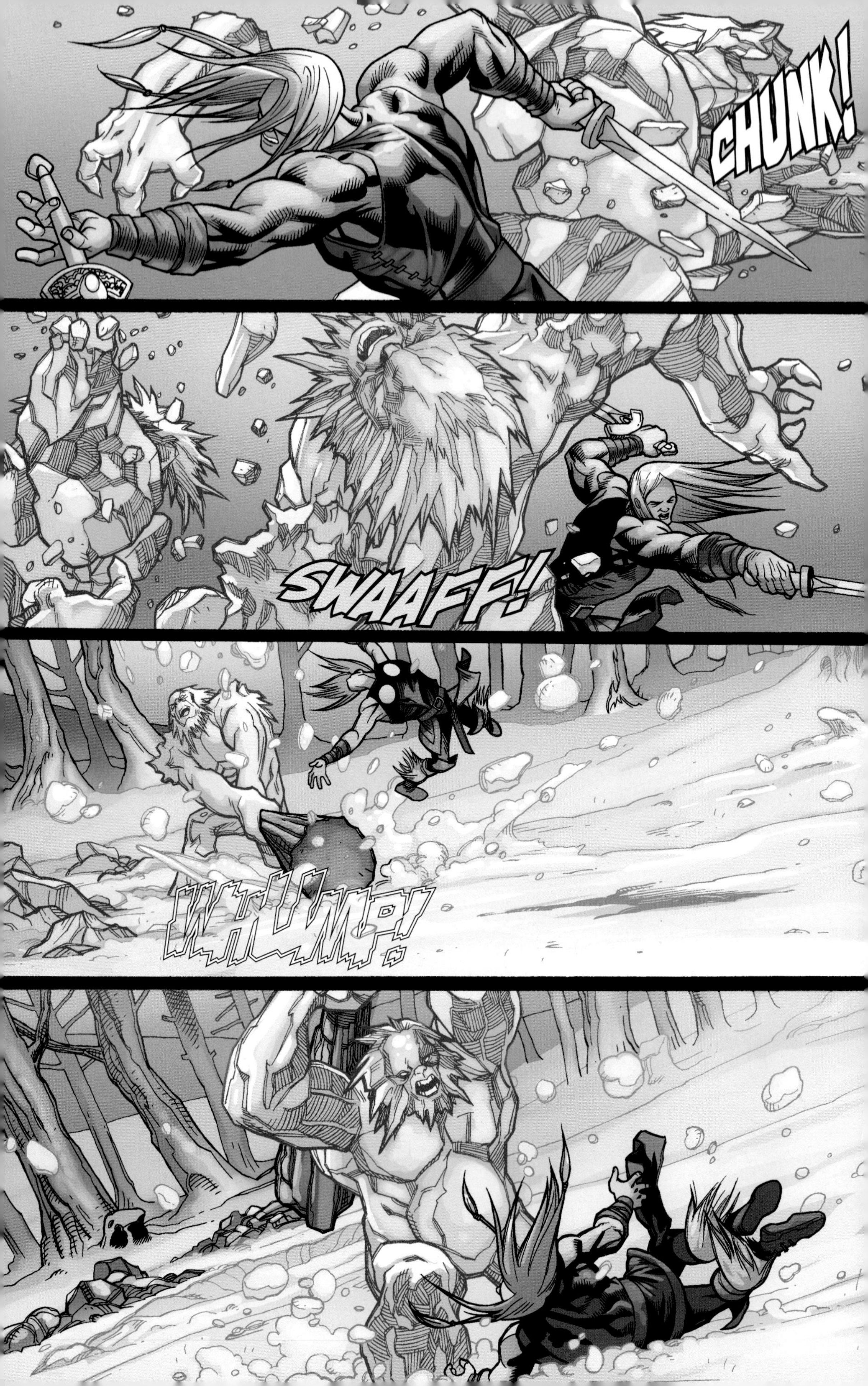
CHUNK!
SWAAFF!
WHUMP!

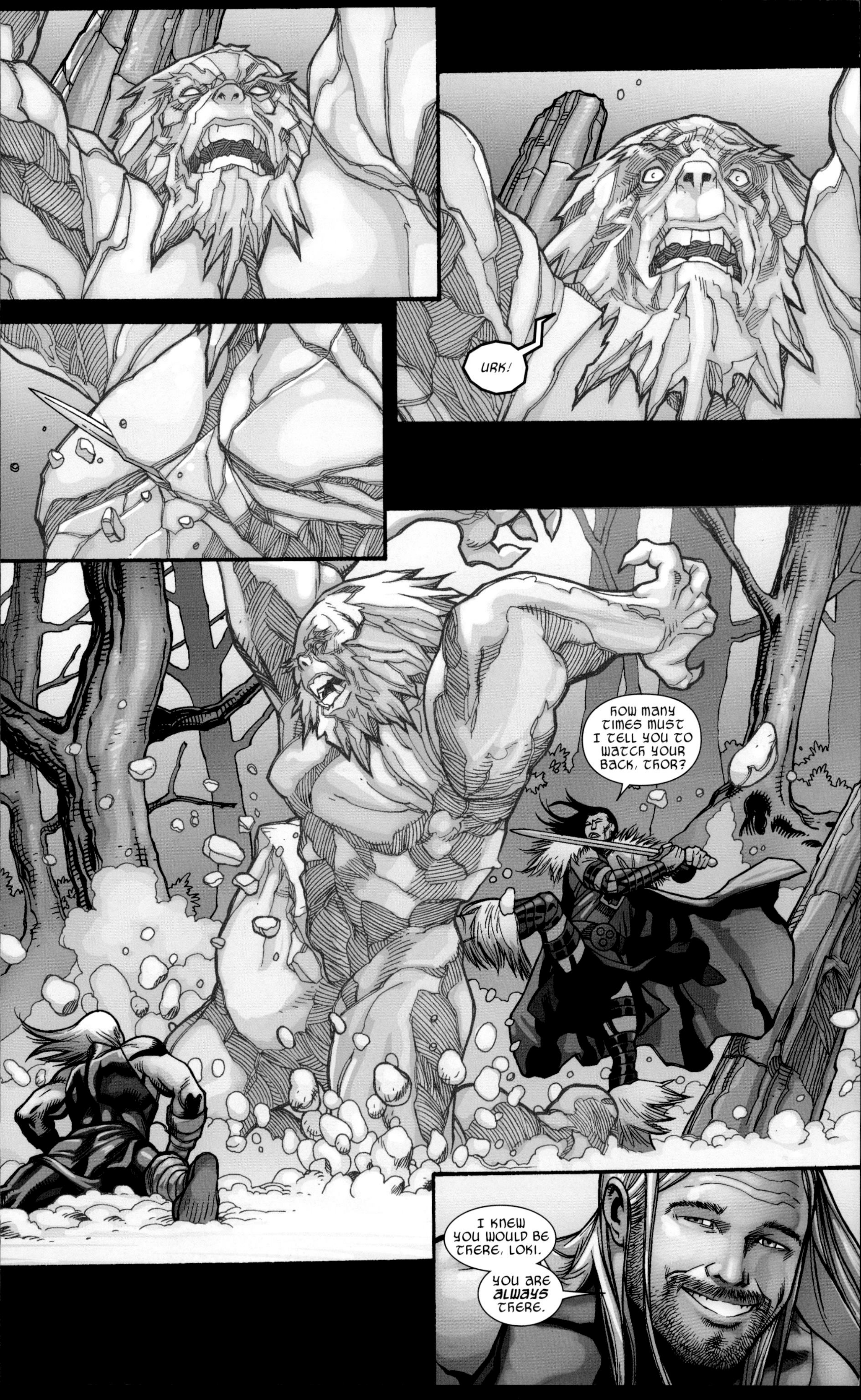
URK!
HOW MANY TIMES MUST I TELL YOU TO WATCH YOUR BACK, THOR?
I KNEW YOU WOULD BE THERE, LOKI.
YOU ARE ALWAYS THERE.

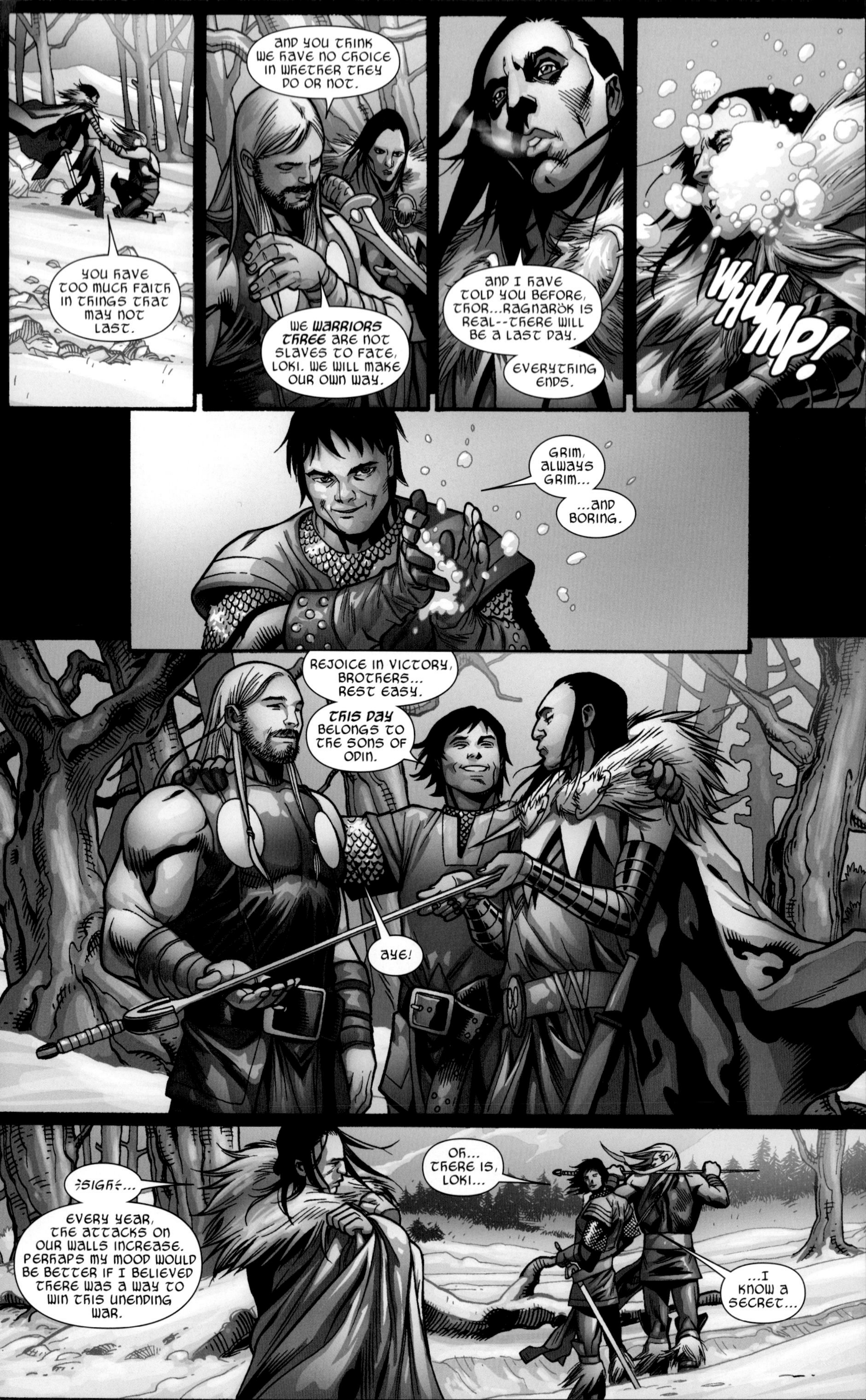
YOU HAVE TOO MUCH FAITH IN THINGS THAT MAY NOT LAST.
AND YOU THINK WE HAVE NO CHOICE IN WHETHER THEY DO OR NOT.
WE WARRIORS THREE ARE NOT SLAVES TO FATE, LOKI. WE WILL MAKE OUR OWN WAY.
AND I HAVE TOLD YOU BEFORE, THOR...RAGNARÖK IS REAL--THERE WILL BE A LAST DAY.
EVERYTHING ENDS.
WHUMP!
GRIM, ALWAYS GRIM...
...AND BORING.
REJOICE IN VICTORY, BROTHERS... REST EASY.
THIS DAY BELONGS TO THE SONS OF ODIN.
AYE!
-SIGH-...
EVERY YEAR, THE ATTACKS ON OUR WALLS INCREASE. PERHAPS MY MOOD WOULD BE BETTER IF I BELIEVED THERE WAS A WAY TO WIN THIS UNENDING WAR.
OH... THERE IS, LOKI...
...I KNOW A SECRET...

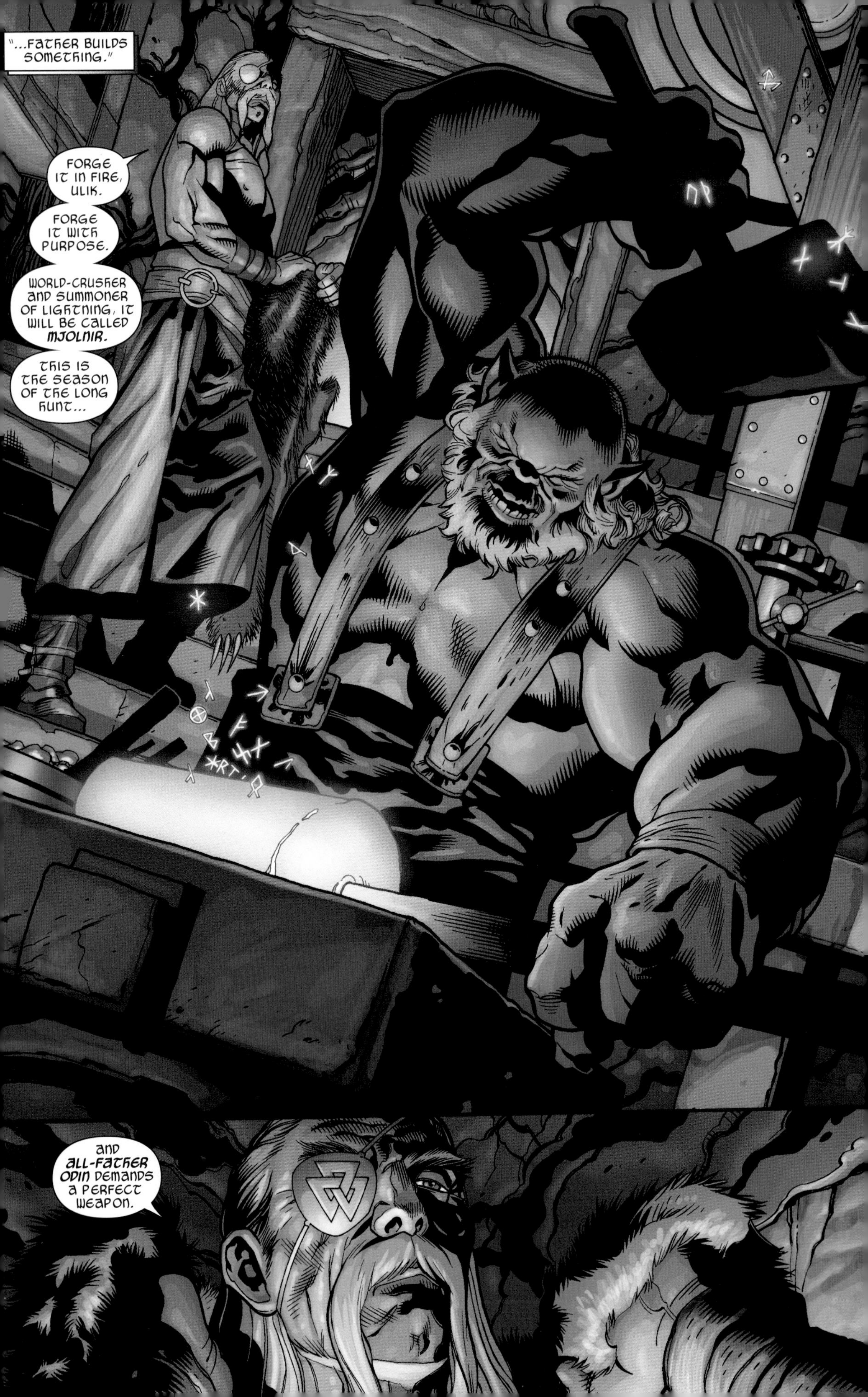
"...FATHER BUILDS SOMETHING."
FORGE IT IN FIRE, ULIK.
FORGE IT WITH PURPOSE.
WORLD-CRUSHER AND SUMMONER OF LIGHTNING, IT WILL BE CALLED MJOLNIR.
THIS IS THE SEASON OF THE LONG HUNT...
AND ALL-FATHER ODIN DEMANDS A PERFECT WEAPON.

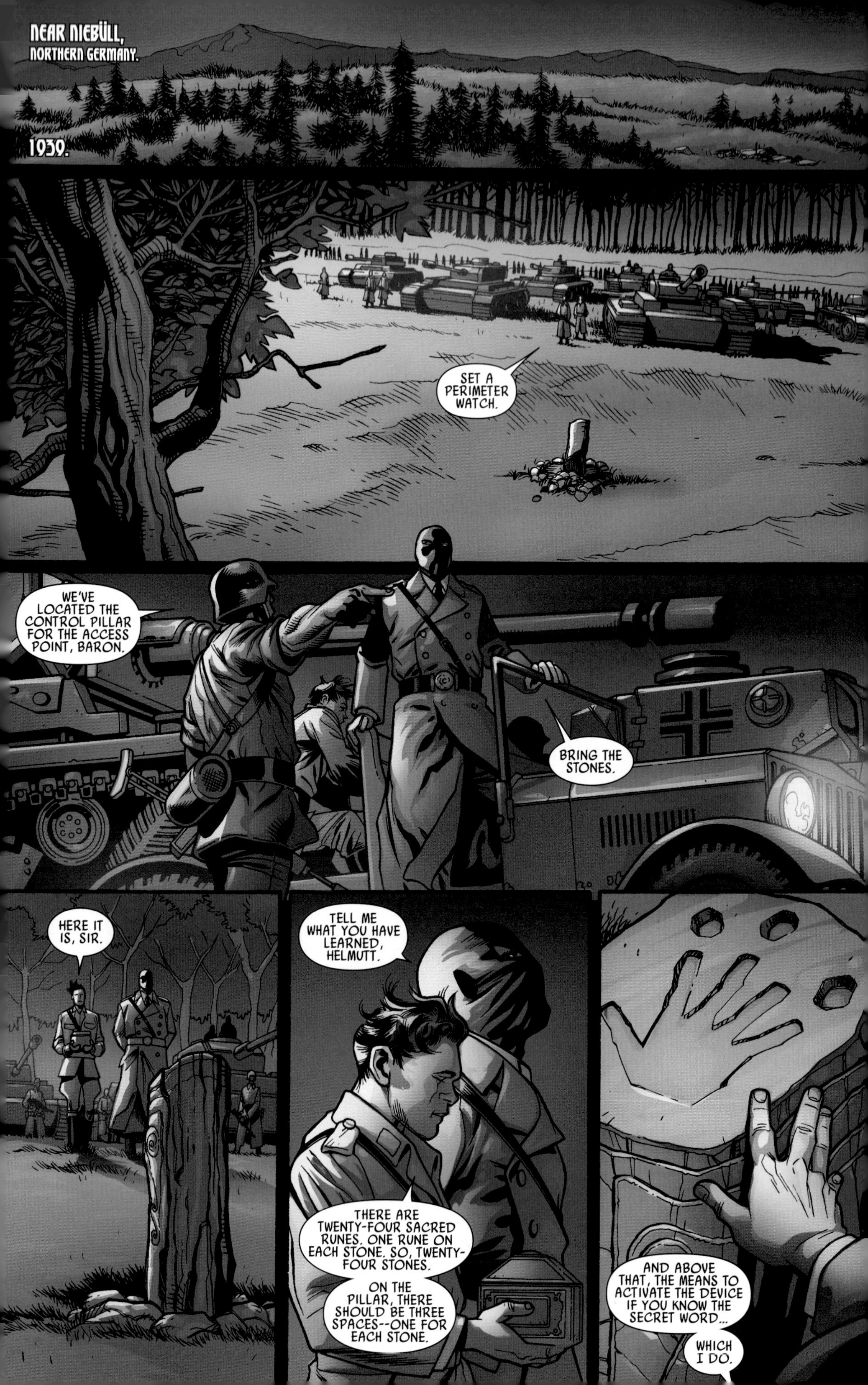
NEAR NIEBÜLL,
NORTHERN GERMANY.
1939.
SET A PERIMETER WATCH.
WE'VE LOCATED THE CONTROL PILLAR FOR THE ACCESS POINT, BARON.
BRING THE STONES.
HERE IT IS, SIR.
TELL ME WHAT YOU HAVE LEARNED, HELMUTT.
THERE ARE TWENTY-FOUR SACRED RUNES. ONE RUNE ON EACH STONE. SO, TWENTY-FOUR STONES.
ON THE PILLAR, THERE SHOULD BE THREE SPACES--ONE FOR EACH STONE.
AND ABOVE THAT, THE MEANS TO ACTIVATE THE DEVICE IF YOU KNOW THE SECRET WORD...
WHICH I DO.

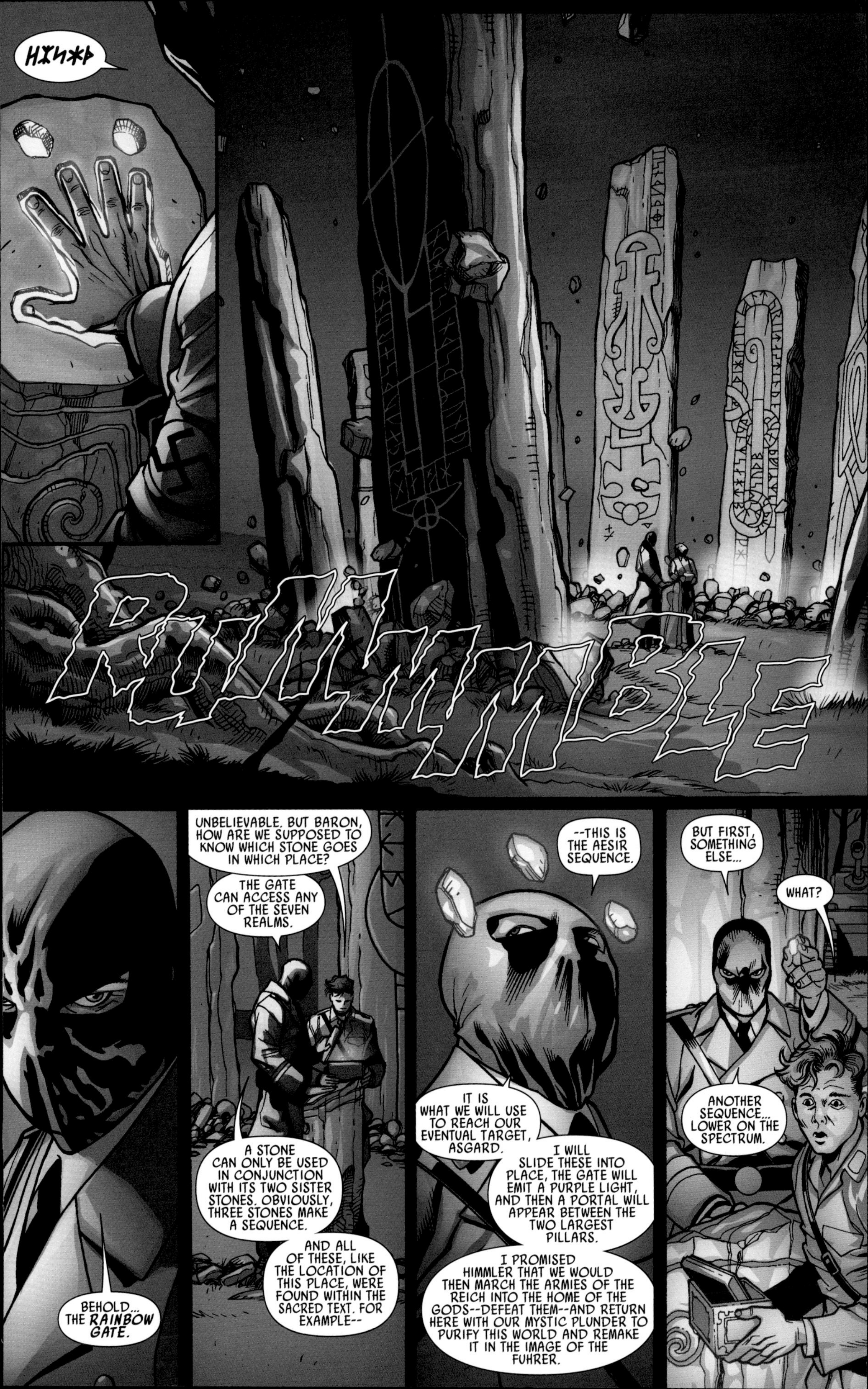

UNBELIEVABLE. BUT BARON, HOW ARE WE SUPPOSED TO KNOW WHICH STONE GOES IN WHICH PLACE?
THE GATE CAN ACCESS ANY OF THE SEVEN REALMS.
A STONE CAN ONLY BE USED IN CONJUNCTION WITH ITS TWO SISTER STONES. OBVIOUSLY, THREE STONES MAKE A SEQUENCE.
AND ALL OF THESE, LIKE THE LOCATION OF THIS PLACE, WERE FOUND WITHIN THE SACRED TEXT. FOR EXAMPLE--
BEHOLD... THE RAINBOW GATE.
--THIS IS THE AESIR SEQUENCE.
IT IS WHAT WE WILL USE TO REACH OUR EVENTUAL TARGET, ASGARD.
I WILL SLIDE THESE INTO PLACE, THE GATE WILL EMIT A PURPLE LIGHT, AND THEN A PORTAL WILL APPEAR BETWEEN THE TWO LARGEST PILLARS.
I PROMISED HIMMLER THAT WE WOULD THEN MARCH THE ARMIES OF THE REICH INTO THE HOME OF THE GODS--DEFEAT THEM--AND RETURN HERE WITH OUR MYSTIC PLUNDER TO PURIFY THIS WORLD AND REMAKE IT IN THE IMAGE OF THE FUHRER.
BUT FIRST, SOMETHING ELSE...
WHAT?
ANOTHER SEQUENCE... LOWER ON THE SPECTRUM.

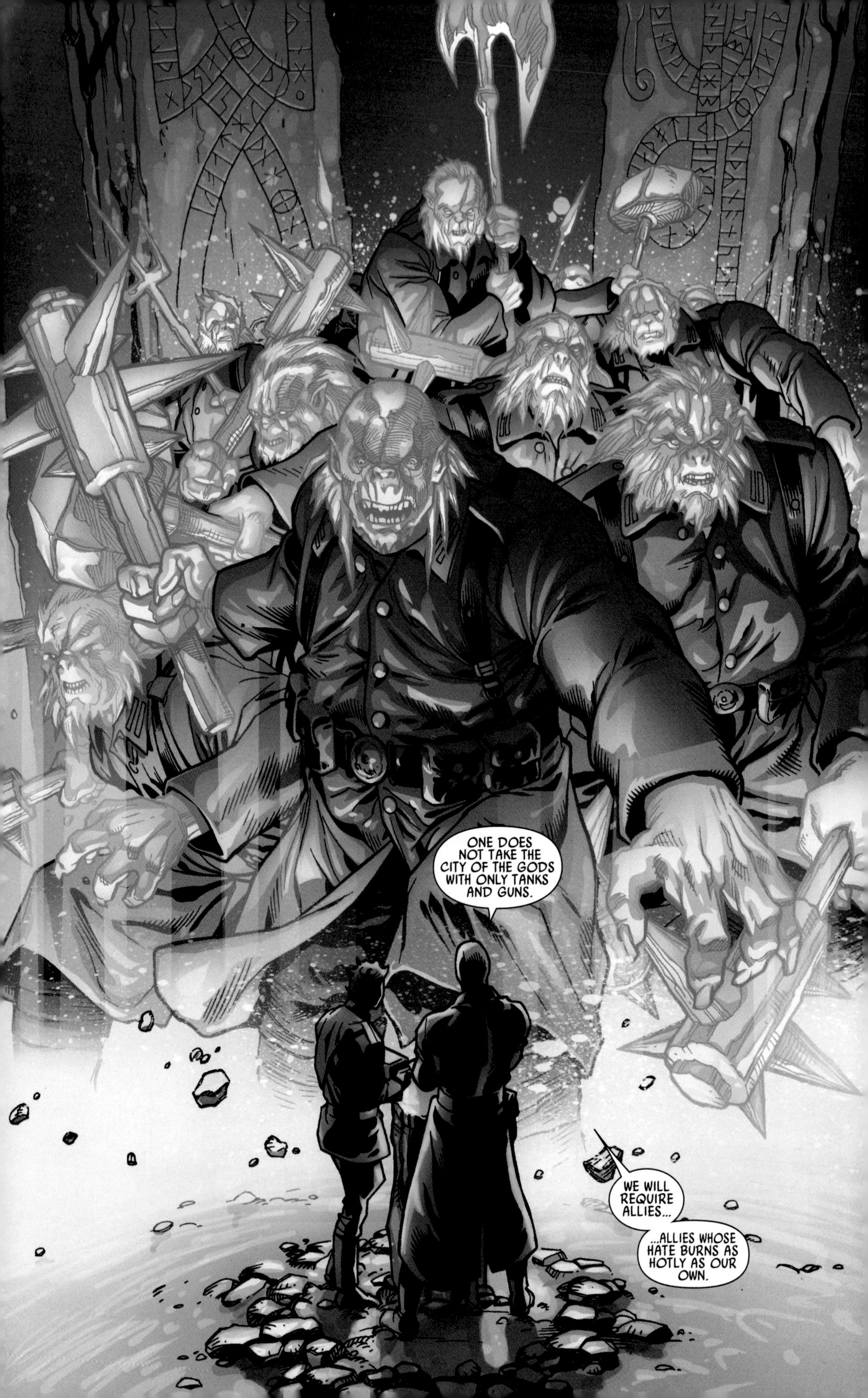
ONE DOES NOT TAKE THE CITY OF THE GODS WITH ONLY TANKS AND GUNS.
WE WILL REQUIRE ALLIES...
...ALLIES WHOSE HATE BURNS AS HOTLY AS OUR OWN.

2

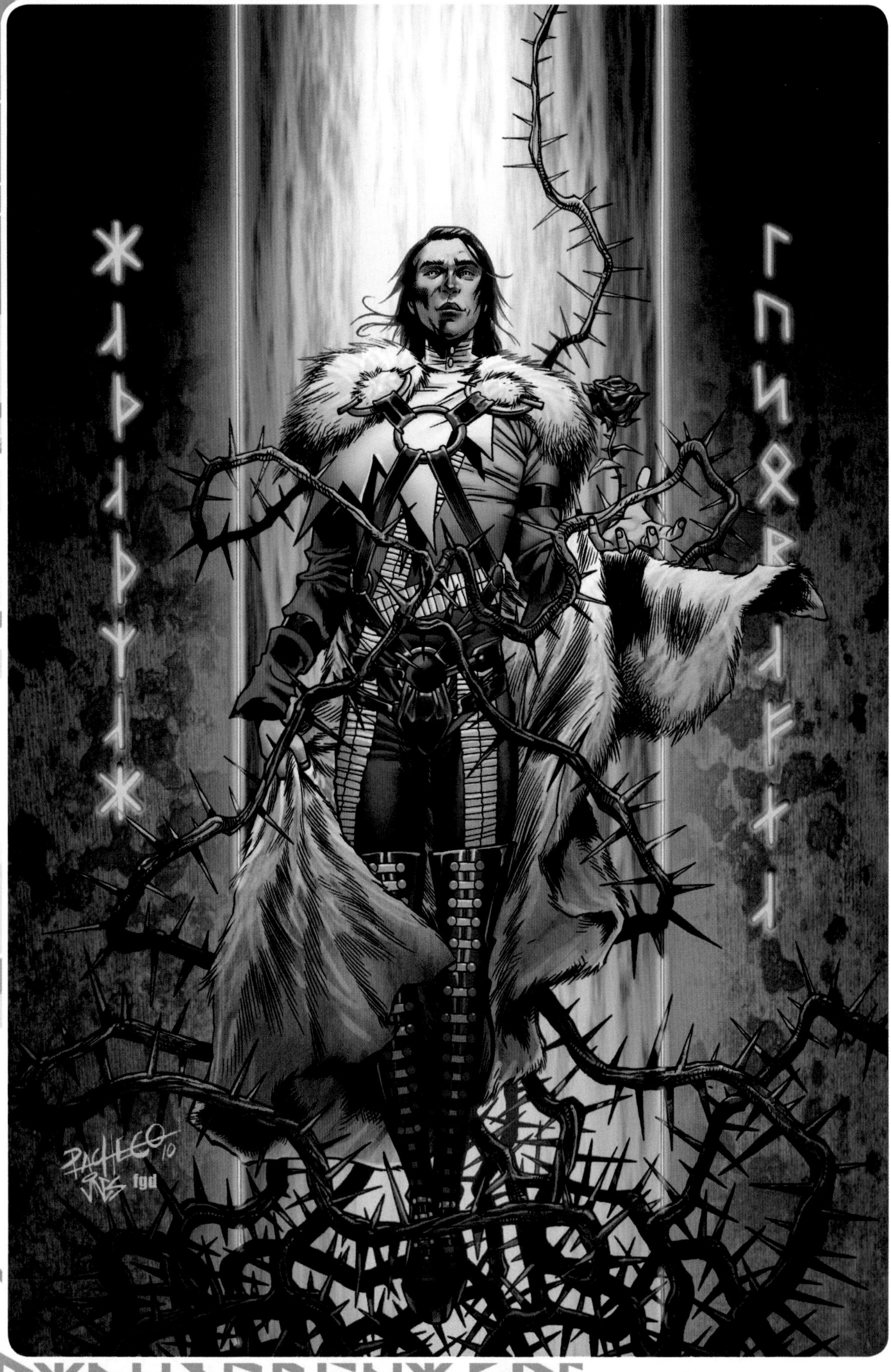

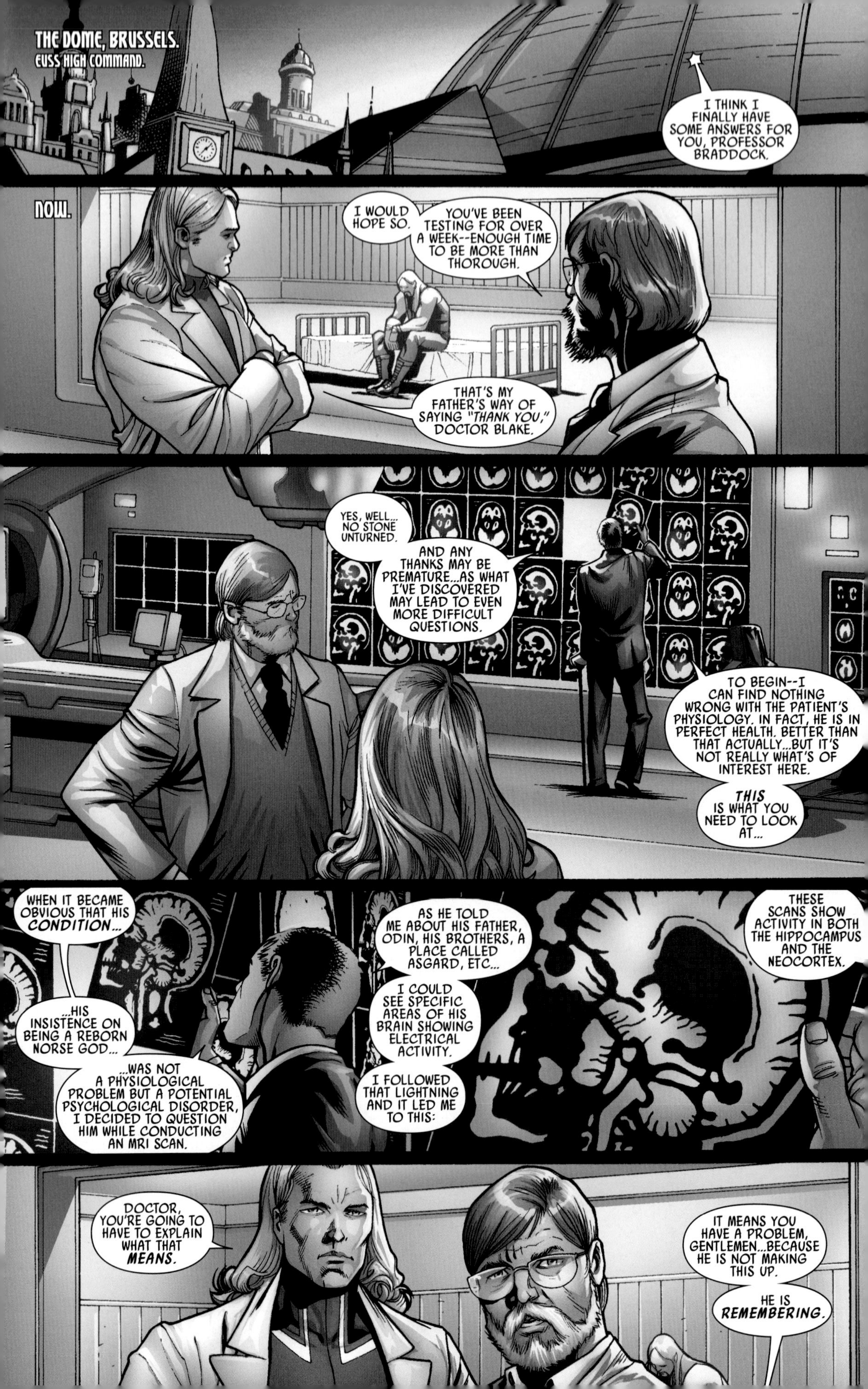
THE DOME, BRUSSELS.
EUSS HIGH COMMAND.
I THINK I FINALLY HAVE SOME ANSWERS FOR YOU, PROFESSOR BRADDOCK.
NOW.
I WOULD HOPE SO.
YOU'VE BEEN TESTING FOR OVER A WEEK--ENOUGH TIME TO BE MORE THAN THOROUGH.
THAT'S MY FATHER'S WAY OF SAYING "THANK YOU," DOCTOR BLAKE.
YES, WELL... NO STONE UNTURNED.
AND ANY THANKS MAY BE PREMATURE...AS WHAT I'VE DISCOVERED MAY LEAD TO EVEN MORE DIFFICULT QUESTIONS.
TO BEGIN--I CAN FIND NOTHING WRONG WITH THE PATIENT'S PHYSIOLOGY. IN FACT, HE IS IN PERFECT HEALTH. BETTER THAN THAT ACTUALLY...BUT IT'S NOT REALLY WHAT'S OF INTEREST HERE.
THIS IS WHAT YOU NEED TO LOOK AT...
WHEN IT BECAME OBVIOUS THAT HIS CONDITION...
...HIS INSISTENCE ON BEING A REBORN NORSE GOD...
...WAS NOT A PHYSIOLOGICAL PROBLEM BUT A POTENTIAL PSYCHOLOGICAL DISORDER, I DECIDED TO QUESTION HIM WHILE CONDUCTING AN MRI SCAN.
AS HE TOLD ME ABOUT HIS FATHER, ODIN, HIS BROTHERS, A PLACE CALLED ASGARD, ETC...
I COULD SEE SPECIFIC AREAS OF HIS BRAIN SHOWING ELECTRICAL ACTIVITY.
I FOLLOWED THAT LIGHTNING AND IT LED ME TO THIS:
THESE SCANS SHOW ACTIVITY IN BOTH THE HIPPOCAMPUS AND THE NEOCORTEX.
DOCTOR, YOU'RE GOING TO HAVE TO EXPLAIN WHAT THAT MEANS.
IT MEANS YOU HAVE A PROBLEM, GENTLEMEN...BECAUSE HE IS NOT MAKING THIS UP.
HE IS REMEMBERING.

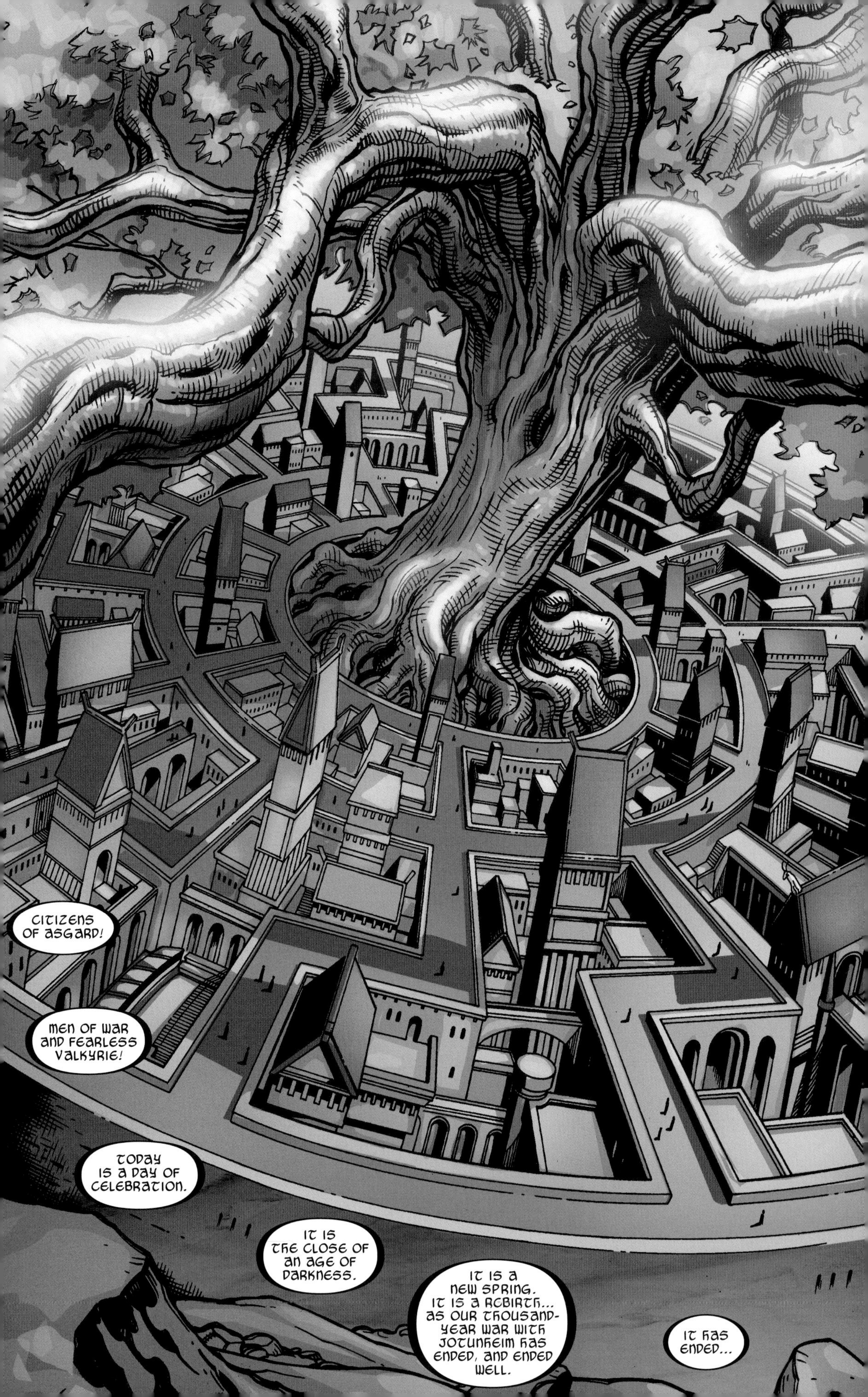
CITIZENS OF ASGARD!
MEN OF WAR AND FEARLESS VALKYRIE!
TODAY IS A DAY OF CELEBRATION.
IT IS THE CLOSE OF AN AGE OF DARKNESS.
IT IS A NEW SPRING. IT IS A REBIRTH... AS OUR THOUSAND-YEAR WAR WITH JOTUNHEIM HAS ENDED, AND ENDED WELL.
IT HAS ENDED...

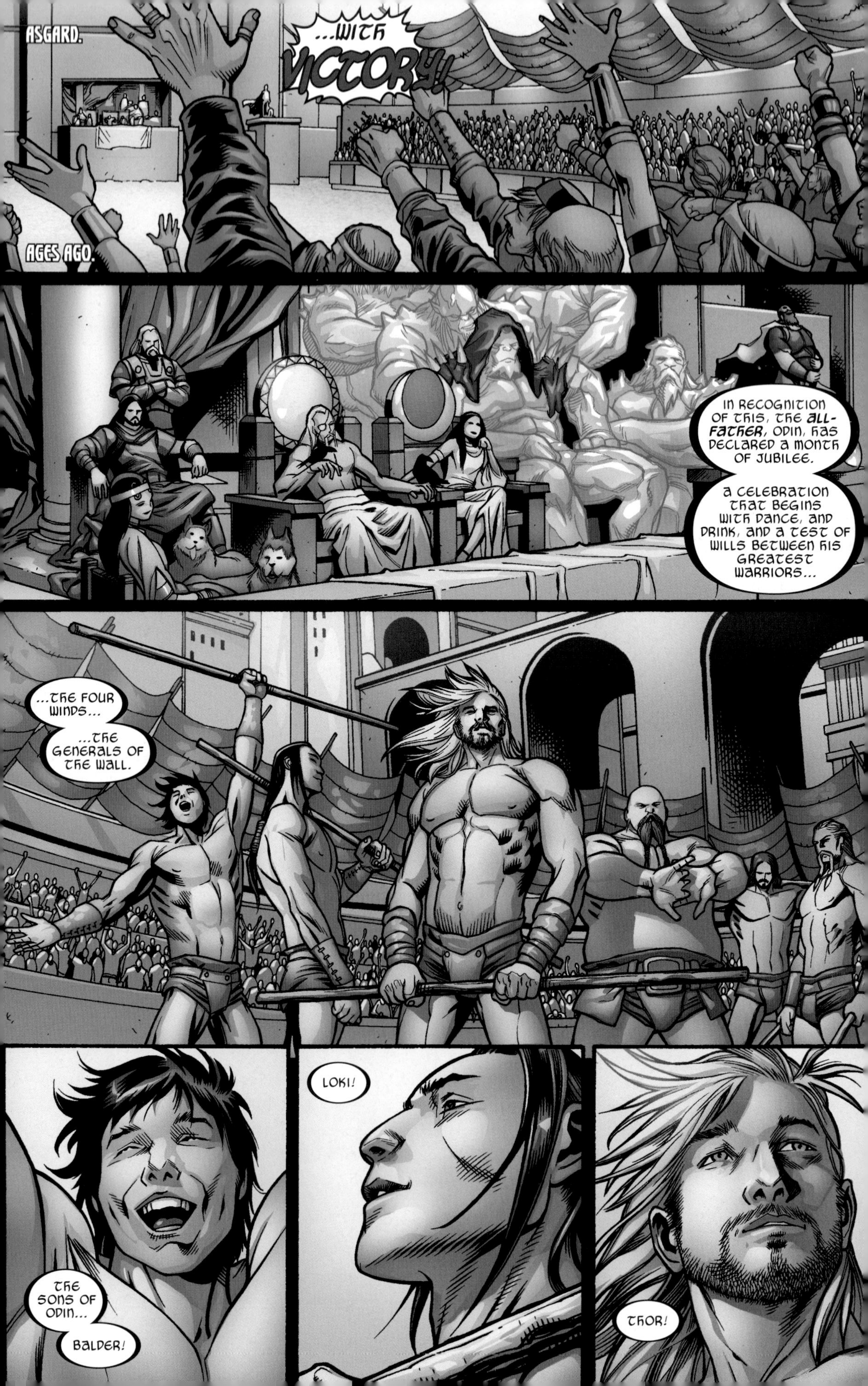
ASGARD.
...WITH VICTORY!
AGES AGO.
IN RECOGNITION OF THIS, THE ALL-FATHER, ODIN, HAS DECLARED A MONTH OF JUBILEE.
A CELEBRATION THAT BEGINS WITH DANCE, AND DRINK, AND A TEST OF WILLS BETWEEN HIS GREATEST WARRIORS...
...THE FOUR WINDS...
...THE GENERALS OF THE WALL.
THE SONS OF ODIN...
BALDER!
LOKI!
THOR!

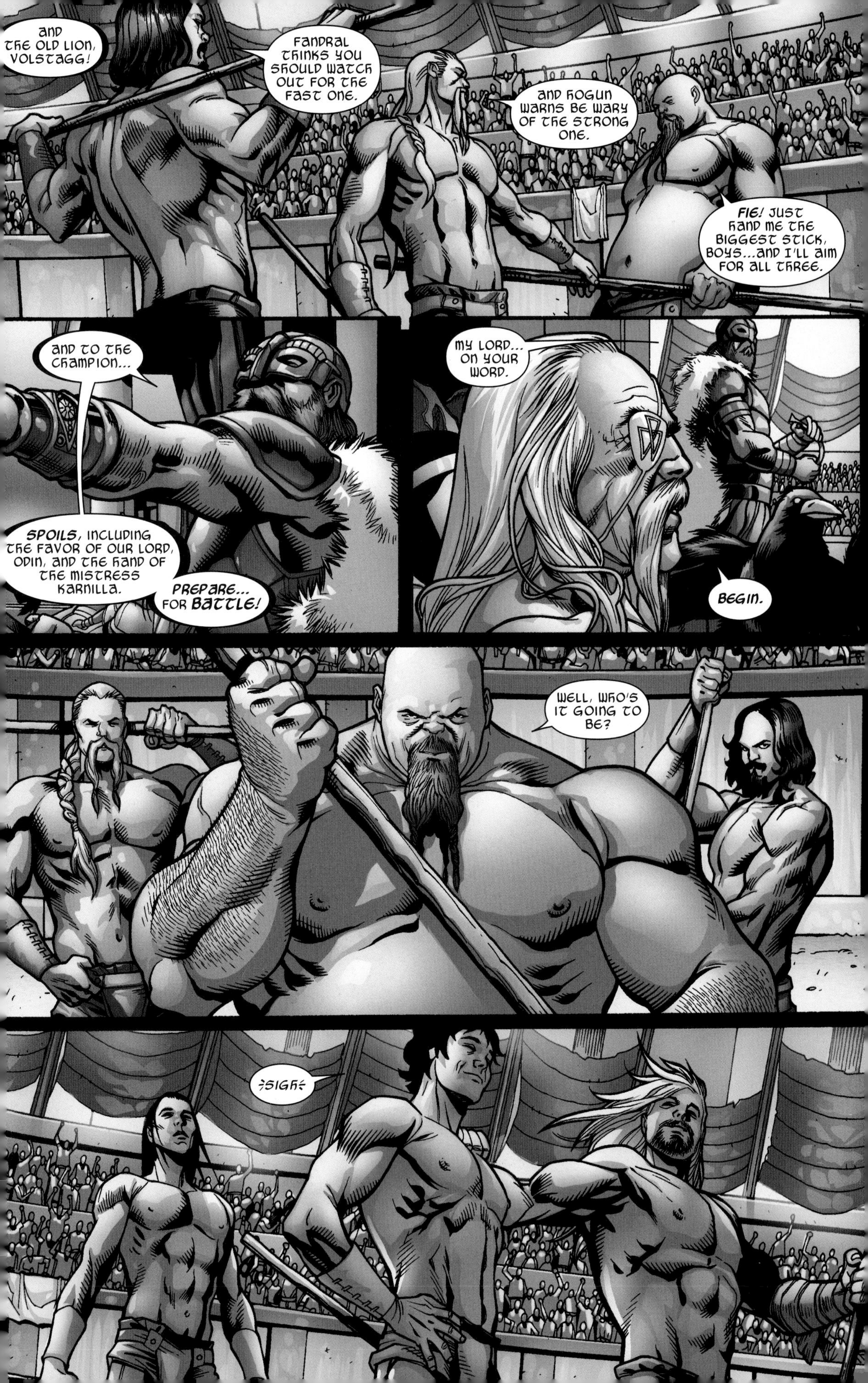
AND THE OLD LION, VOLSTAGG!
FANDRAL THINKS YOU SHOULD WATCH OUT FOR THE FAST ONE.
AND HOGUN WARNS BE WARY OF THE STRONG ONE.
FIE! JUST HAND ME THE BIGGEST STICK, BOYS...AND I'LL AIM FOR ALL THREE.
AND TO THE CHAMPION...
SPOILS, INCLUDING THE FAVOR OF OUR LORD, ODIN, AND THE HAND OF THE MISTRESS KARNILLA.
PREPARE... FOR BATTLE!
MY LORD... ON YOUR WORD.
BEGIN.
WELL, WHO'S IT GOING TO BE?
SIGH

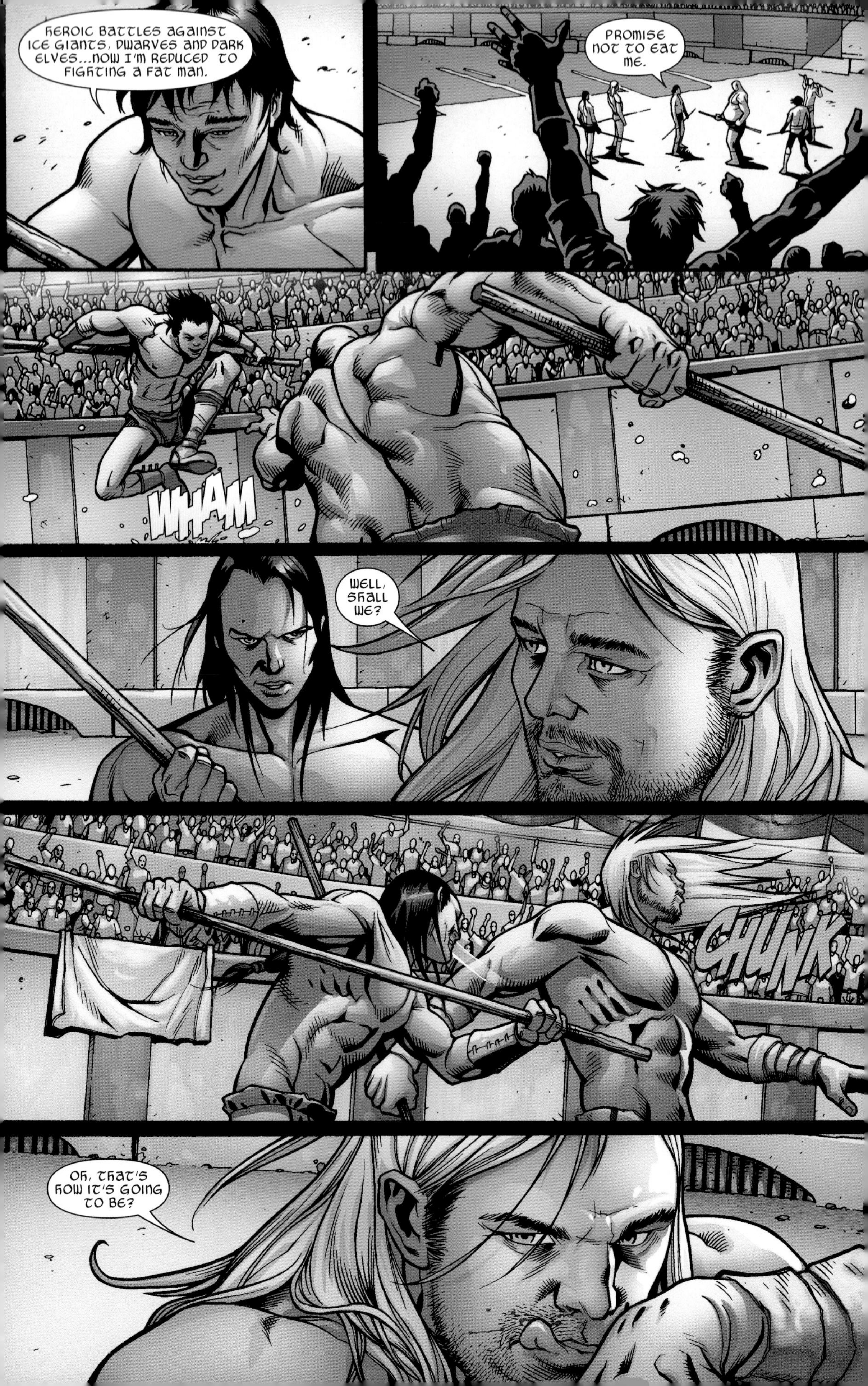
HEROIC BATTLES AGAINST ICE GIANTS, DWARVES AND DARK ELVES...NOW I'M REDUCED TO FIGHTING A FAT MAN.
PROMISE NOT TO EAT ME.
WHAM
WELL, SHALL WE?
CHUNK
OH, THAT'S HOW IT'S GOING TO BE?

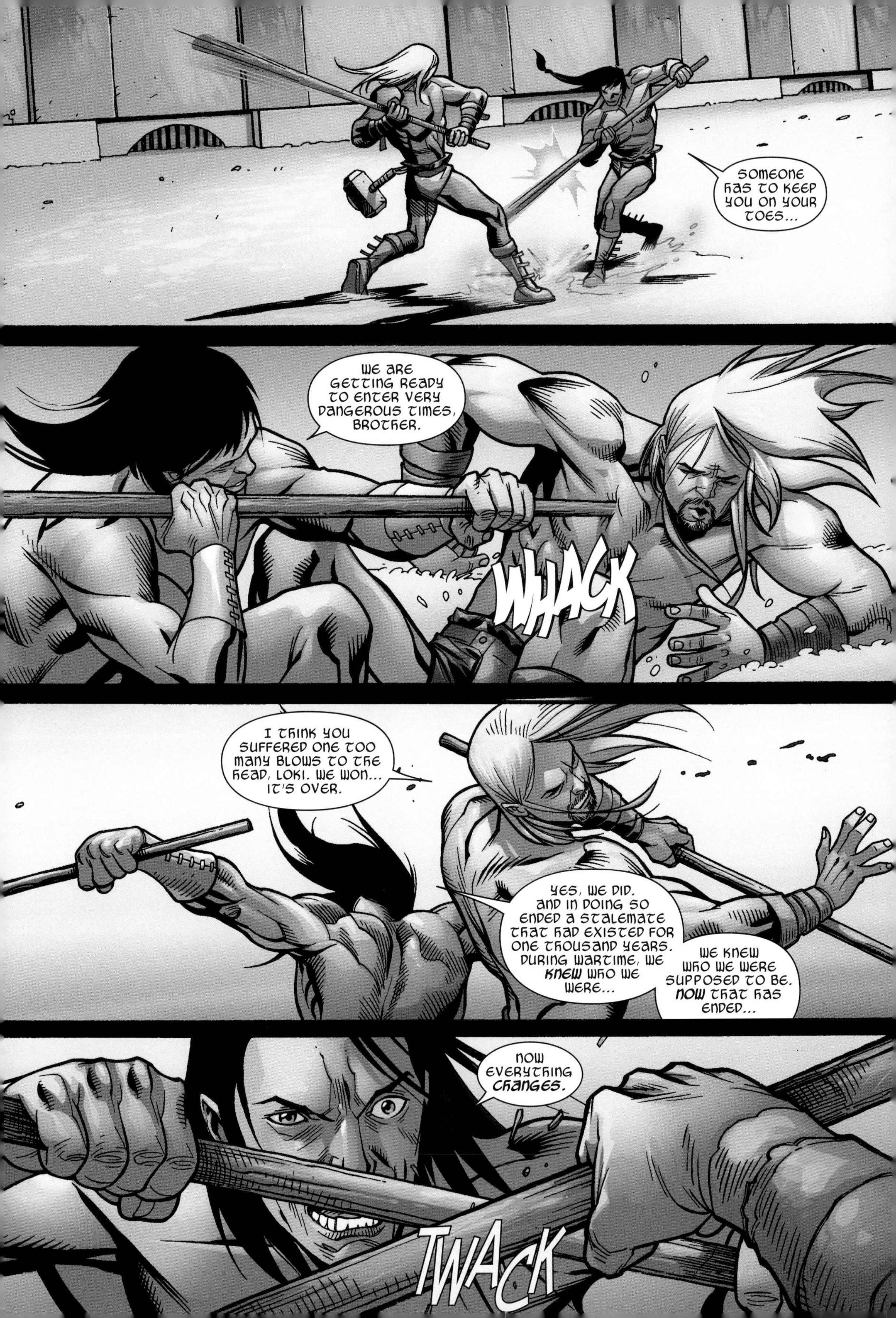
SOMEONE HAS TO KEEP YOU ON YOUR TOES...
WE ARE GETTING READY TO ENTER VERY DANGEROUS TIMES, BROTHER.
WHACK
I THINK YOU SUFFERED ONE TOO MANY BLOWS TO THE HEAD, LOKI. WE WON... IT'S OVER.
YES, WE DID. AND IN DOING SO ENDED A STALEMATE THAT HAD EXISTED FOR ONE THOUSAND YEARS. DURING WARTIME, WE KNEW WHO WE WERE...
WE KNEW WHO WE WERE SUPPOSED TO BE. NOW THAT HAS ENDED...
NOW EVERYTHING CHANGES.
TWACK

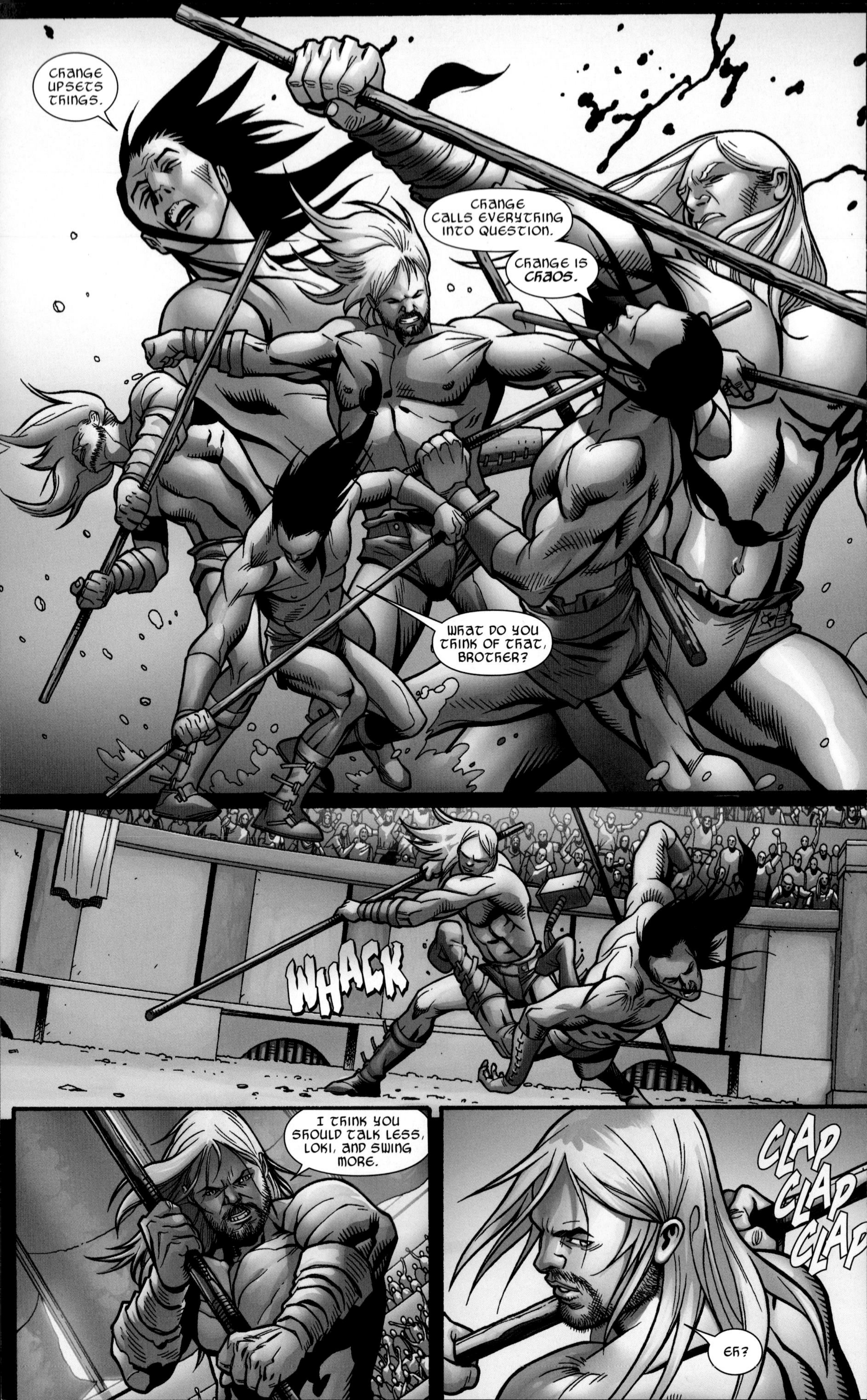
CHANGE UPSETS THINGS.
CHANGE CALLS EVERYTHING INTO QUESTION.
CHANGE IS CHAOS.
WHAT DO YOU THINK OF THAT, BROTHER?
WHACK
I THINK YOU SHOULD TALK LESS, LOKI, AND SWING MORE.
CLAP CLAP CLAP
EH?

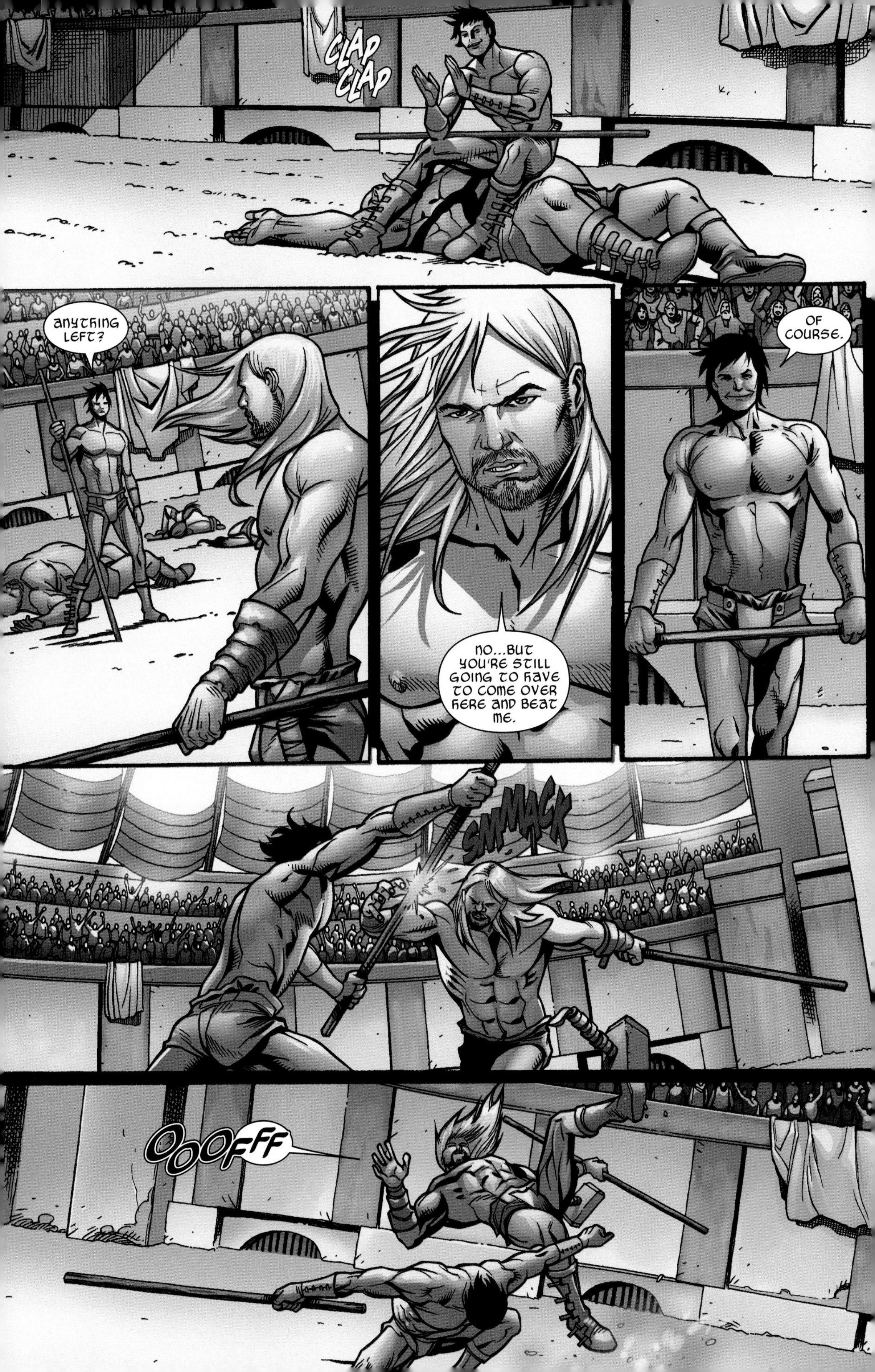
CLAP CLAP
ANYTHING LEFT?
NO...BUT YOU'RE STILL GOING TO HAVE TO COME OVER HERE AND BEAT ME.
OF COURSE.
SMMACK
OOOFFF

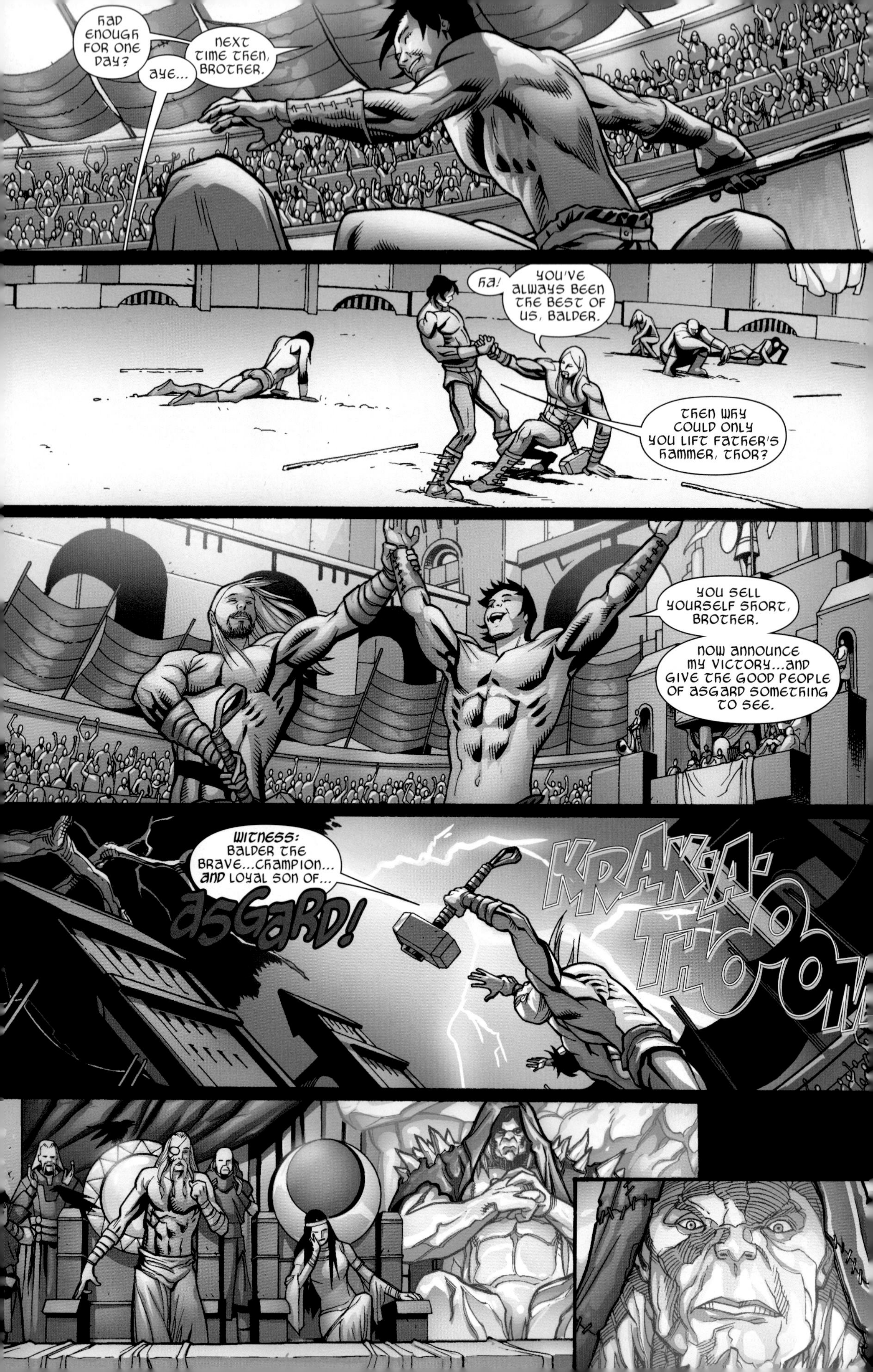

HAD ENOUGH FOR ONE DAY?
NEXT TIME THEN, BROTHER.
AYE...
HA!
YOU'VE ALWAYS BEEN THE BEST OF US, BALDER.
THEN WHY COULD ONLY YOU LIFT FATHER'S HAMMER, THOR?
YOU SELL YOURSELF SHORT, BROTHER.
NOW ANNOUNCE MY VICTORY...AND GIVE THE GOOD PEOPLE OF ASGARD SOMETHING TO SEE.
WITNESS: BALDER THE BRAVE...CHAMPION... AND LOYAL SON OF...
ASGARD!
KRAK-A-THOOOM

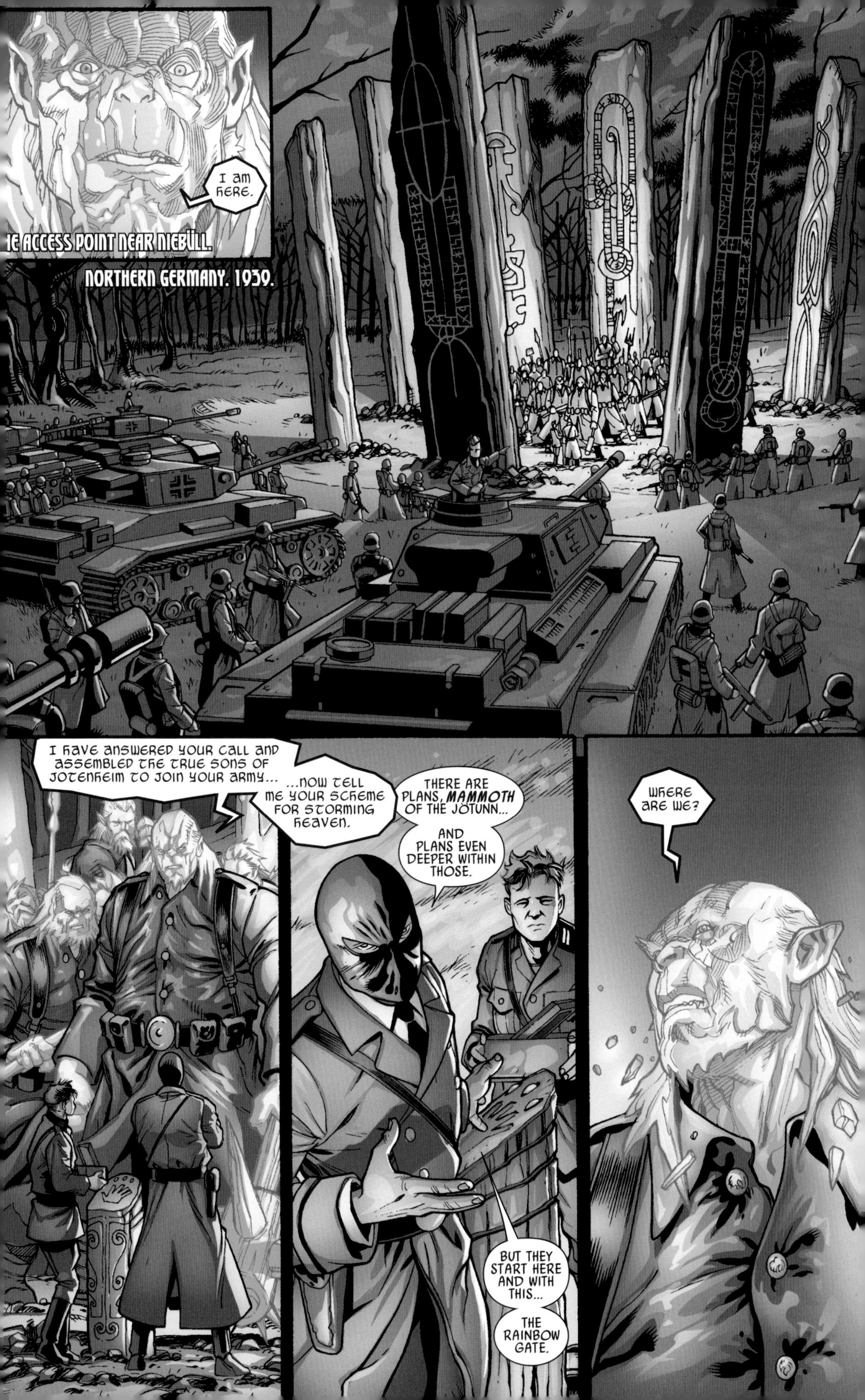
I am here.
IE ACCESS POINT NEAR NIEBÜLL.
NORTHERN GERMANY. 1939.
I have answered your call and assembled the true sons of Jotenheim to join your army...
...now tell me your scheme for storming heaven.
THERE ARE PLANS, MAMMOTH OF THE JÖTUNN...
AND PLANS EVEN DEEPER WITHIN THOSE.
BUT THEY START HERE AND WITH THIS...
THE RAINBOW GATE.
Where are we?

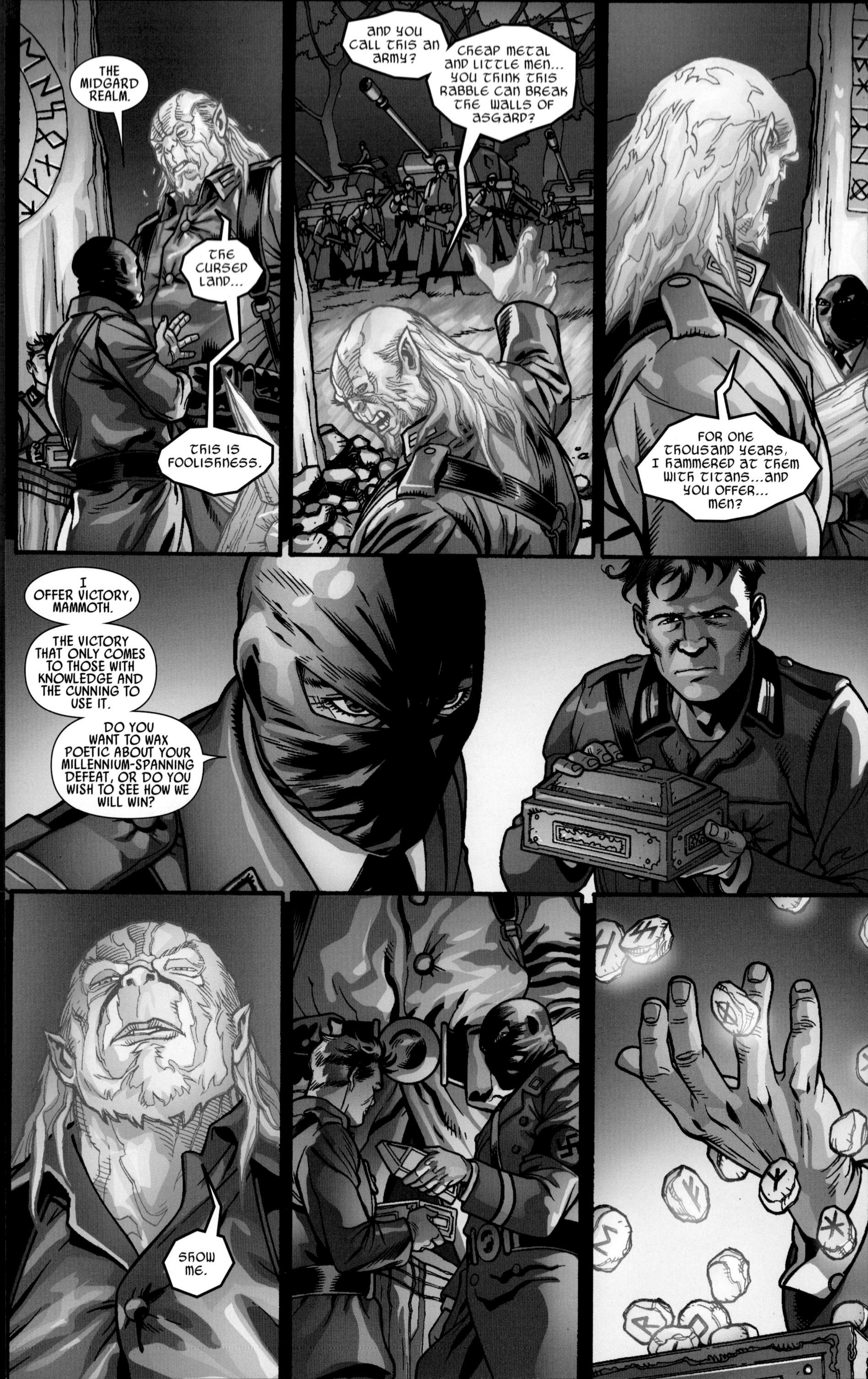
THE MIDGARD REALM.
THE CURSED LAND...
THIS IS FOOLISHNESS.
AND YOU CALL THIS AN ARMY?
CHEAP METAL AND LITTLE MEN... YOU THINK THIS RABBLE CAN BREAK THE WALLS OF ASGARD?
FOR ONE THOUSAND YEARS, I HAMMERED AT THEM WITH TITANS...AND YOU OFFER... MEN?
I OFFER VICTORY, MAMMOTH.
THE VICTORY THAT ONLY COMES TO THOSE WITH KNOWLEDGE AND THE CUNNING TO USE IT.
DO YOU WANT TO WAX POETIC ABOUT YOUR MILLENNIUM-SPANNING DEFEAT, OR DO YOU WISH TO SEE HOW WE WILL WIN?
SHOW ME.

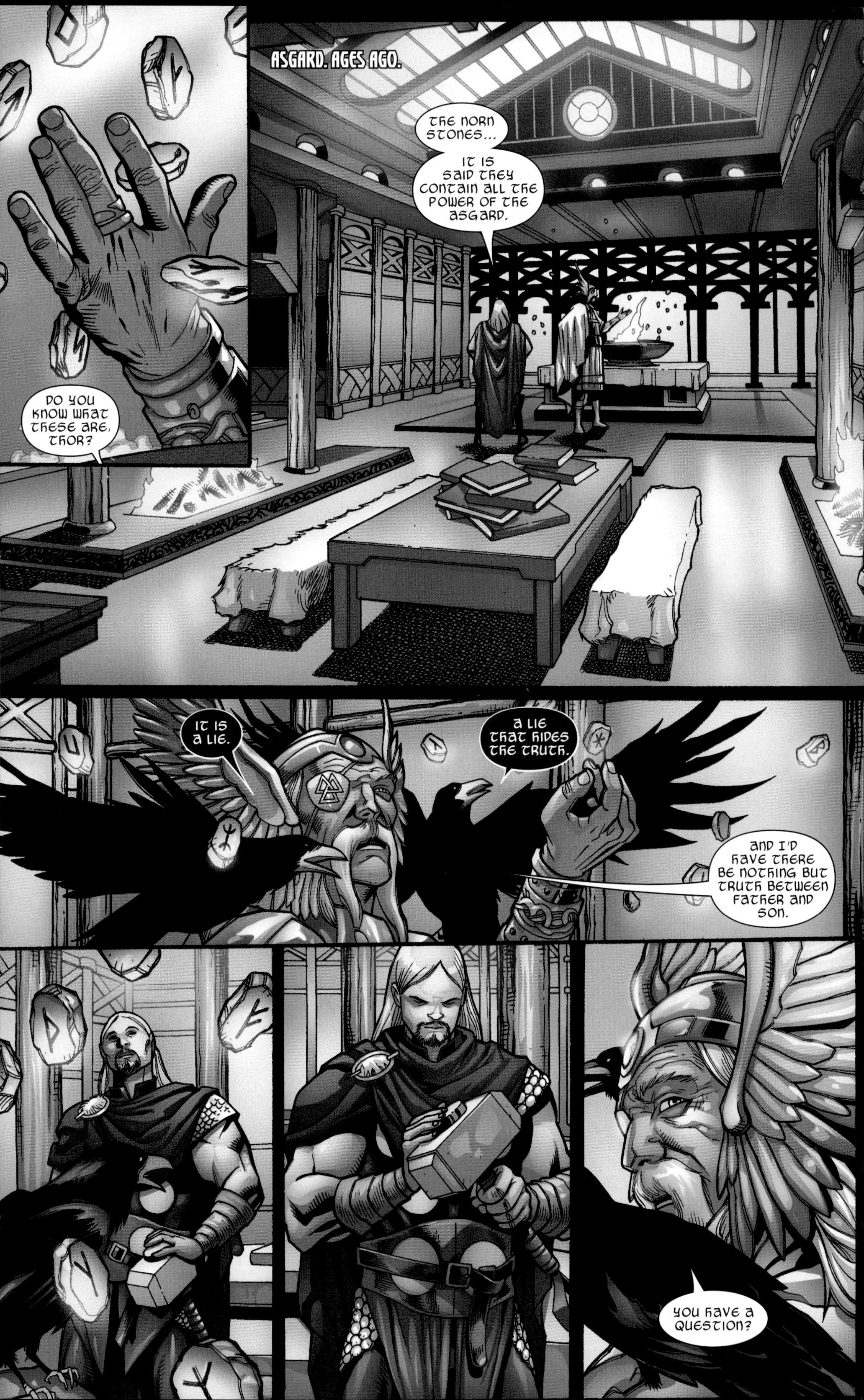
ASGARD. AGES AGO.
DO YOU KNOW WHAT THESE ARE, THOR?
THE NORN STONES...
IT IS SAID THEY CONTAIN ALL THE POWER OF THE ASGARD.
IT IS A LIE.
A LIE THAT HIDES THE TRUTH.
AND I'D HAVE THERE BE NOTHING BUT TRUTH BETWEEN FATHER AND SON.
YOU HAVE A QUESTION?

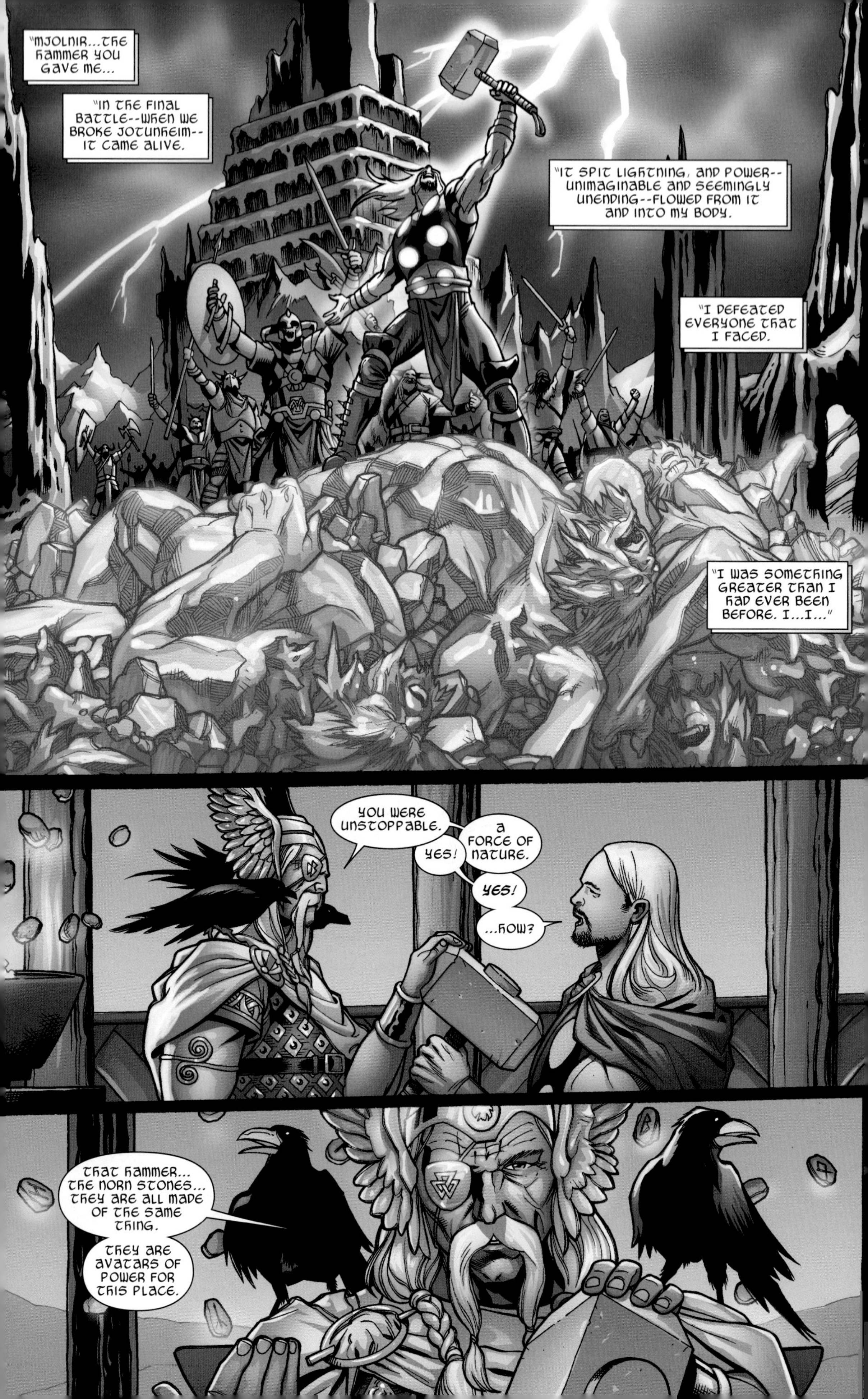
"MJOLNIR...THE HAMMER YOU GAVE ME...
"IN THE FINAL BATTLE--WHEN WE BROKE JOTUNHEIM--IT CAME ALIVE.
"IT SPIT LIGHTNING, AND POWER--UNIMAGINABLE AND SEEMINGLY UNENDING--FLOWED FROM IT AND INTO MY BODY.
"I DEFEATED EVERYONE THAT I FACED.
"I WAS SOMETHING GREATER THAN I HAD EVER BEEN BEFORE. I...I..."
YOU WERE UNSTOPPABLE.
A FORCE OF NATURE.
YES!
YES!
...HOW?
THAT HAMMER... THE NORN STONES... THEY ARE ALL MADE OF THE SAME THING.
THEY ARE AVATARS OF POWER FOR THIS PLACE.

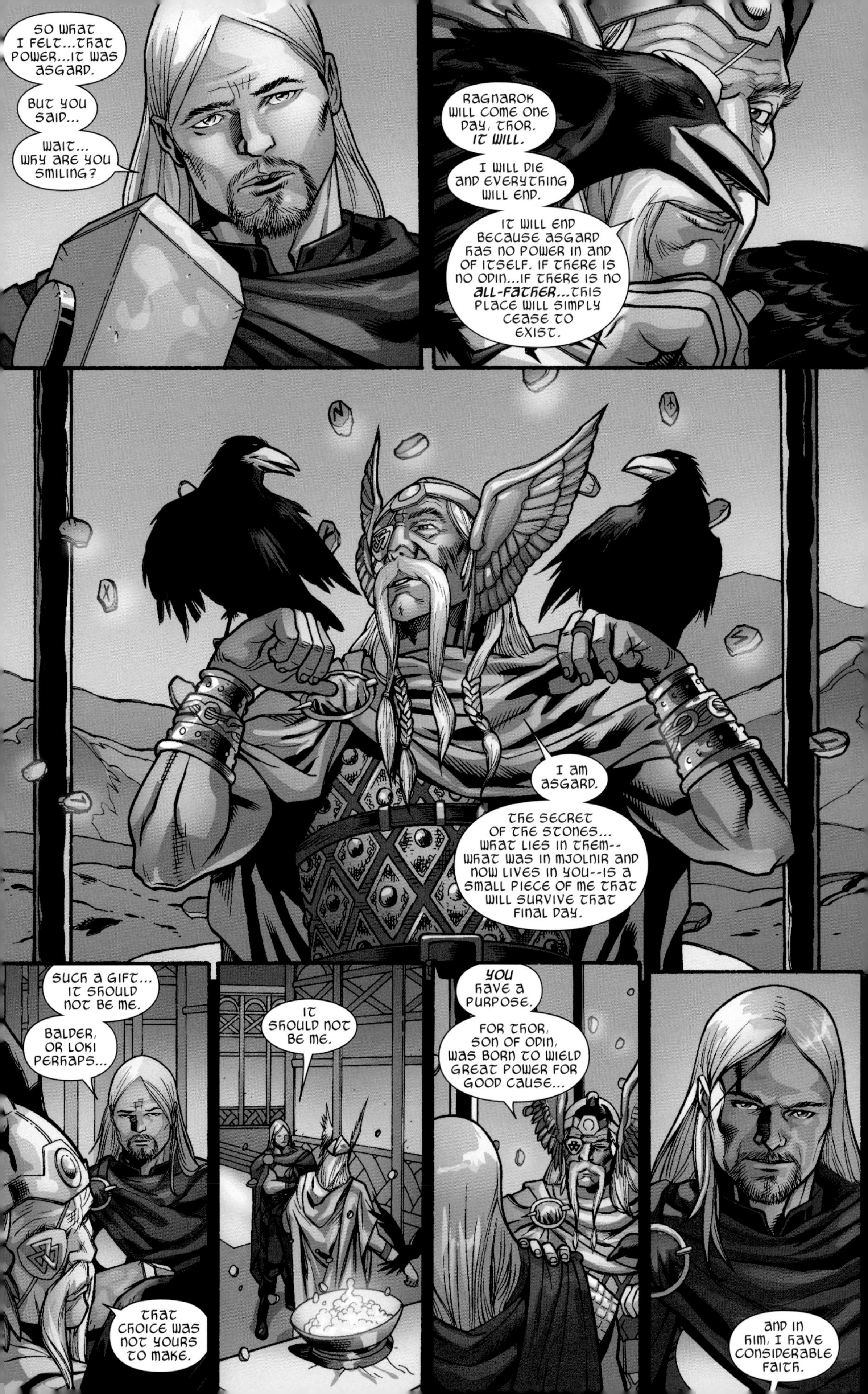
SO WHAT I FELT...THAT POWER...IT WAS ASGARD.
BUT YOU SAID...
WAIT... WHY ARE YOU SMILING?
RAGNAROK WILL COME ONE DAY, THOR. *IT WILL.*
I WILL DIE AND EVERYTHING WILL END.
IT WILL END BECAUSE ASGARD HAS NO POWER IN AND OF ITSELF. IF THERE IS NO ODIN...IF THERE IS NO **ALL-FATHER...** THIS PLACE WILL SIMPLY CEASE TO EXIST.
I AM ASGARD.
THE SECRET OF THE STONES... WHAT LIES IN THEM-- WHAT WAS IN MJOLNIR AND NOW LIVES IN YOU--IS A SMALL PIECE OF ME THAT WILL SURVIVE THAT FINAL DAY.
SUCH A GIFT... IT SHOULD NOT BE ME.
BALDER, OR LOKI PERHAPS...
THAT CHOICE WAS NOT YOURS TO MAKE.
IT SHOULD NOT BE ME.
YOU HAVE A PURPOSE.
FOR THOR, SON OF ODIN, WAS BORN TO WIELD GREAT POWER FOR GOOD CAUSE...
AND IN HIM, I HAVE CONSIDERABLE FAITH.

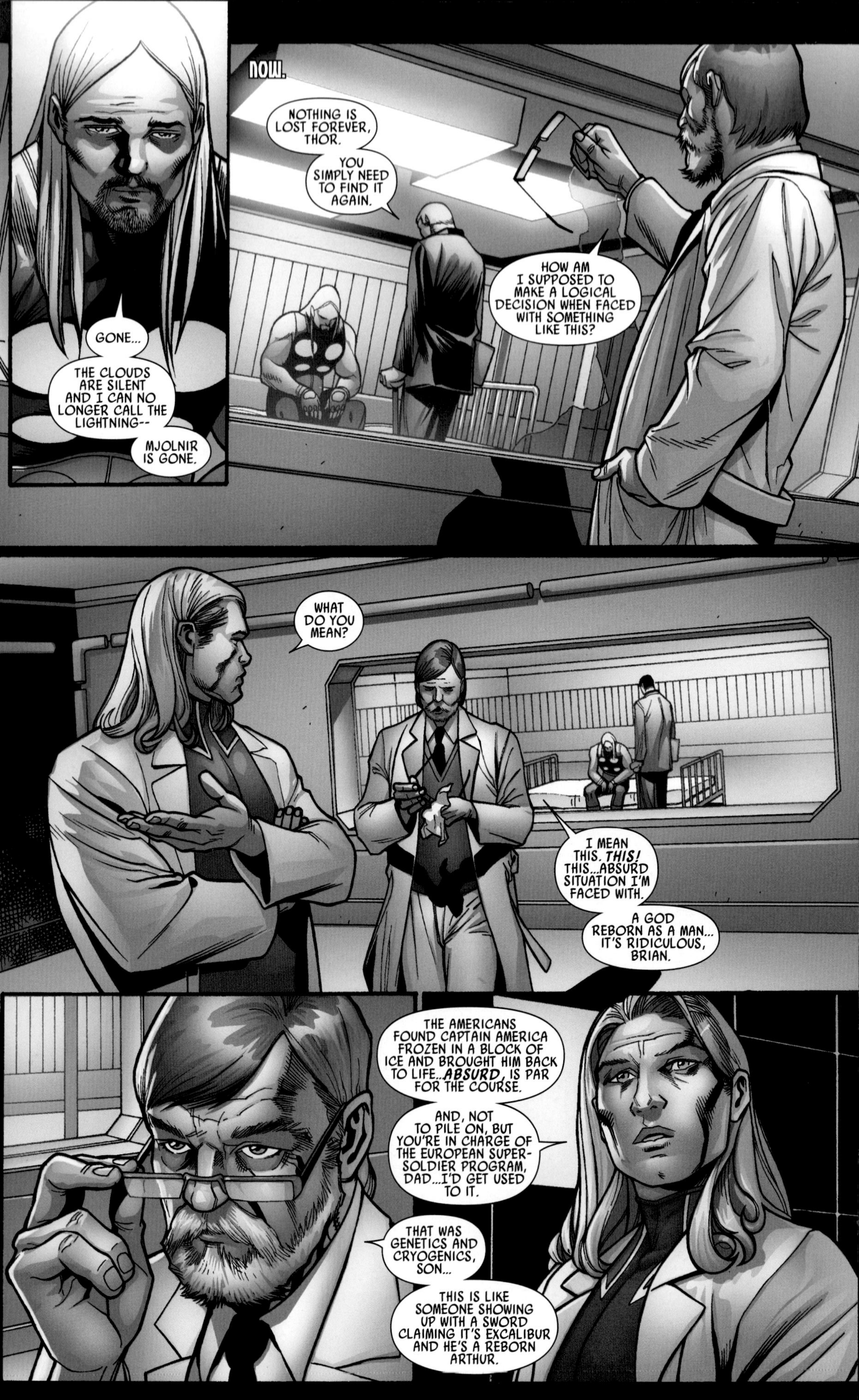
NOW.
GONE...
THE CLOUDS ARE SILENT AND I CAN NO LONGER CALL THE LIGHTNING--
MJOLNIR IS GONE.
NOTHING IS LOST FOREVER, THOR.
YOU SIMPLY NEED TO FIND IT AGAIN.
HOW AM I SUPPOSED TO MAKE A LOGICAL DECISION WHEN FACED WITH SOMETHING LIKE THIS?
WHAT DO YOU MEAN?
I MEAN THIS. THIS! THIS...ABSURD SITUATION I'M FACED WITH.
A GOD REBORN AS A MAN... IT'S RIDICULOUS, BRIAN.
THE AMERICANS FOUND CAPTAIN AMERICA FROZEN IN A BLOCK OF ICE AND BROUGHT HIM BACK TO LIFE...ABSURD, IS PAR FOR THE COURSE.
AND, NOT TO PILE ON, BUT YOU'RE IN CHARGE OF THE EUROPEAN SUPER-SOLDIER PROGRAM, DAD...I'D GET USED TO IT.
THAT WAS GENETICS AND CRYOGENICS, SON...
THIS IS LIKE SOMEONE SHOWING UP WITH A SWORD CLAIMING IT'S EXCALIBUR AND HE'S A REBORN ARTHUR.

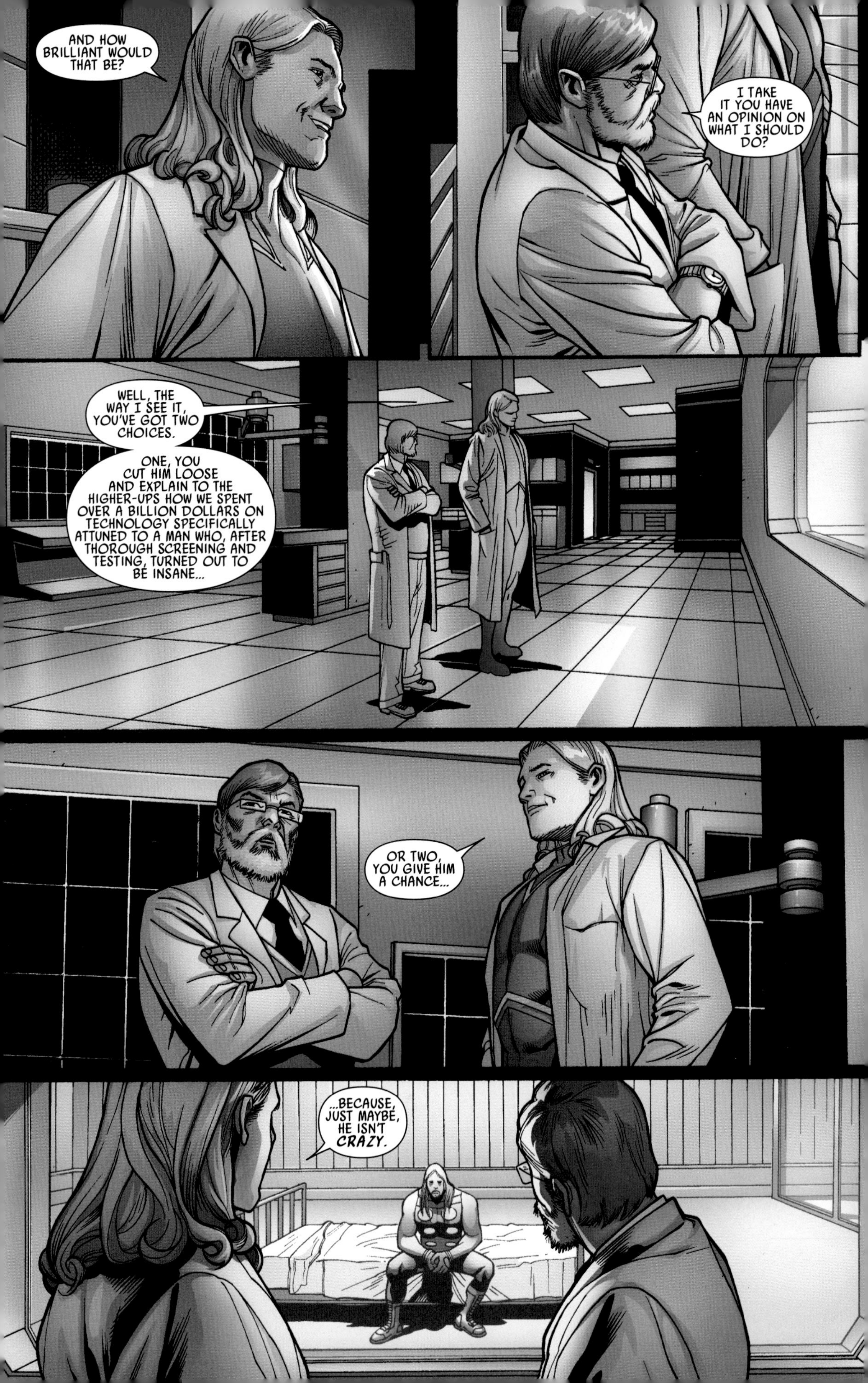
AND HOW BRILLIANT WOULD THAT BE?
I TAKE IT YOU HAVE AN OPINION ON WHAT I SHOULD DO?
WELL, THE WAY I SEE IT, YOU'VE GOT TWO CHOICES.
ONE, YOU CUT HIM LOOSE AND EXPLAIN TO THE HIGHER-UPS HOW WE SPENT OVER A BILLION DOLLARS ON TECHNOLOGY SPECIFICALLY ATTUNED TO A MAN WHO, AFTER THOROUGH SCREENING AND TESTING, TURNED OUT TO BE INSANE...
OR TWO, YOU GIVE HIM A CHANCE...
...BECAUSE, JUST MAYBE, HE ISN'T *CRAZY*.

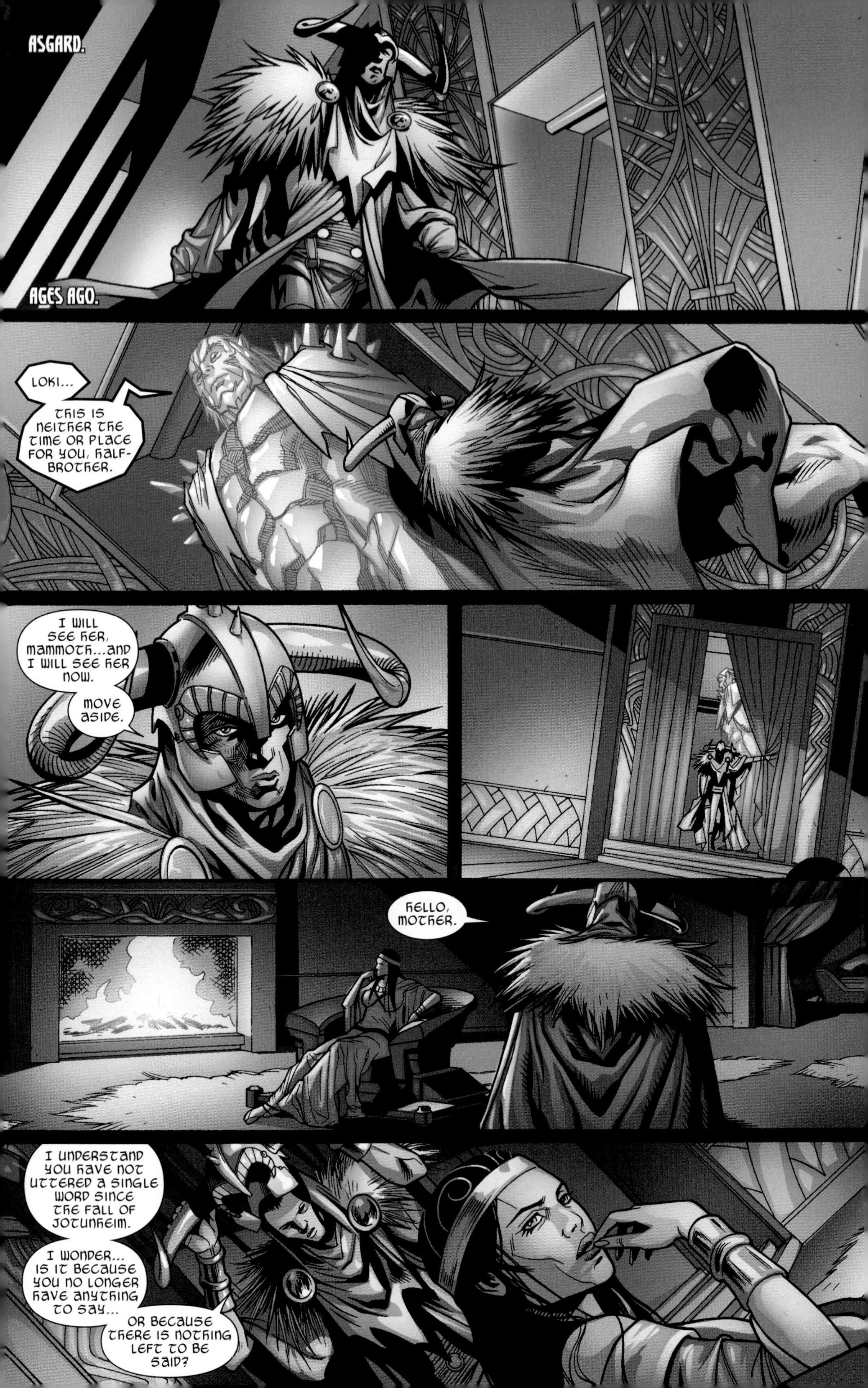
ASGARD.
AGES AGO.
LOKI...
THIS IS NEITHER THE TIME OR PLACE FOR YOU, HALF-BROTHER.
I WILL SEE HER, MAMMOTH...AND I WILL SEE HER NOW.
MOVE ASIDE.
HELLO, MOTHER.
I UNDERSTAND YOU HAVE NOT UTTERED A SINGLE WORD SINCE THE FALL OF JOTUNHEIM.
I WONDER... IS IT BECAUSE YOU NO LONGER HAVE ANYTHING TO SAY...
OR BECAUSE THERE IS NOTHING LEFT TO BE SAID?

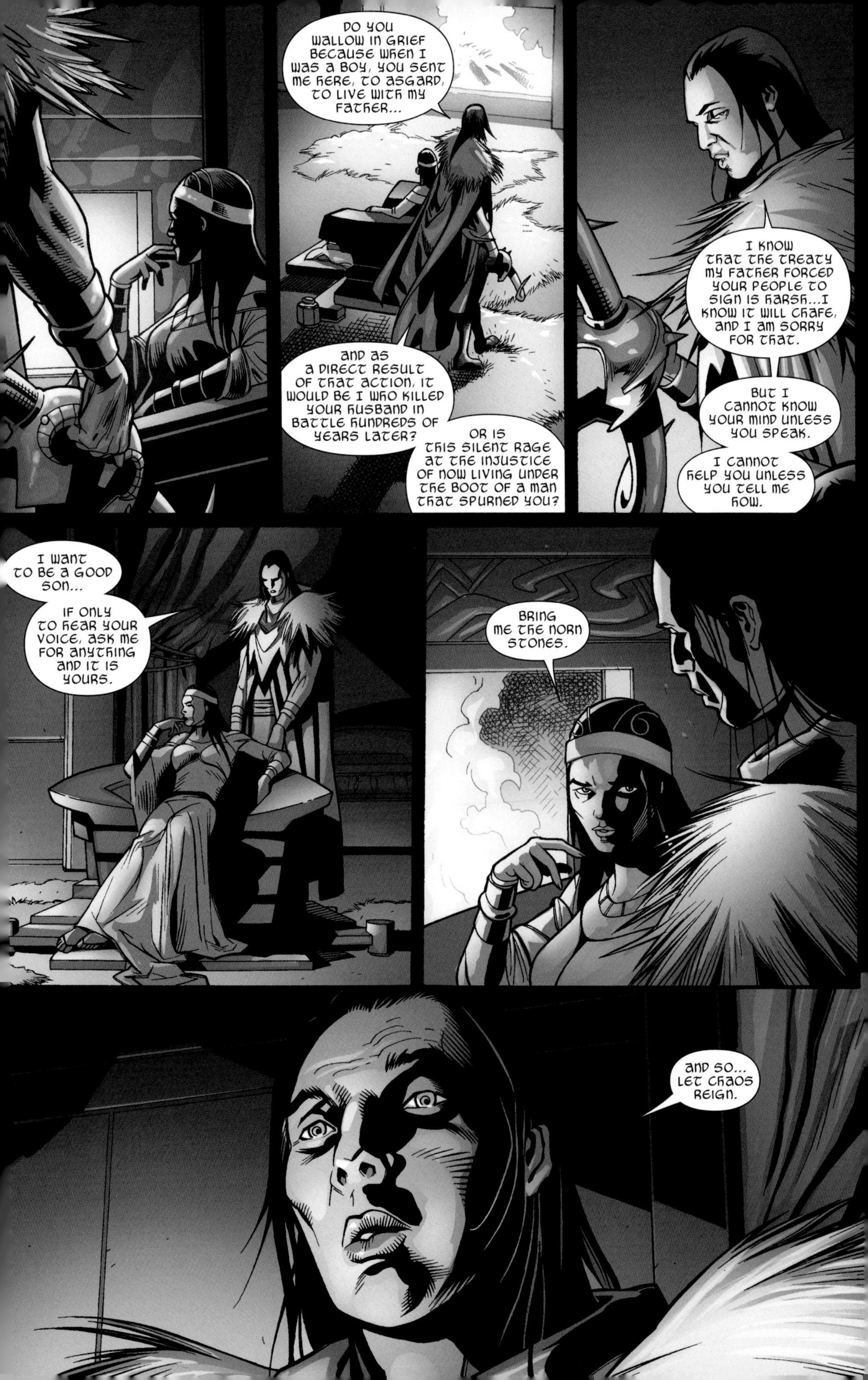
DO YOU WALLOW IN GRIEF BECAUSE WHEN I WAS A BOY, YOU SENT ME HERE, TO ASGARD, TO LIVE WITH MY FATHER...
AND AS A DIRECT RESULT OF THAT ACTION, IT WOULD BE I WHO KILLED YOUR HUSBAND IN BATTLE HUNDREDS OF YEARS LATER?
OR IS THIS SILENT RAGE AT THE INJUSTICE OF NOW LIVING UNDER THE BOOT OF A MAN THAT SPURNED YOU?
I KNOW THAT THE TREATY MY FATHER FORCED YOUR PEOPLE TO SIGN IS HARSH...I KNOW IT WILL CHAFE, AND I AM SORRY FOR THAT.
BUT I CANNOT KNOW YOUR MIND UNLESS YOU SPEAK.
I CANNOT HELP YOU UNLESS YOU TELL ME HOW.
I WANT TO BE A GOOD SON...
IF ONLY TO HEAR YOUR VOICE, ASK ME FOR ANYTHING AND IT IS YOURS.
BRING ME THE NORN STONES.
AND SO... LET CHAOS REIGN.

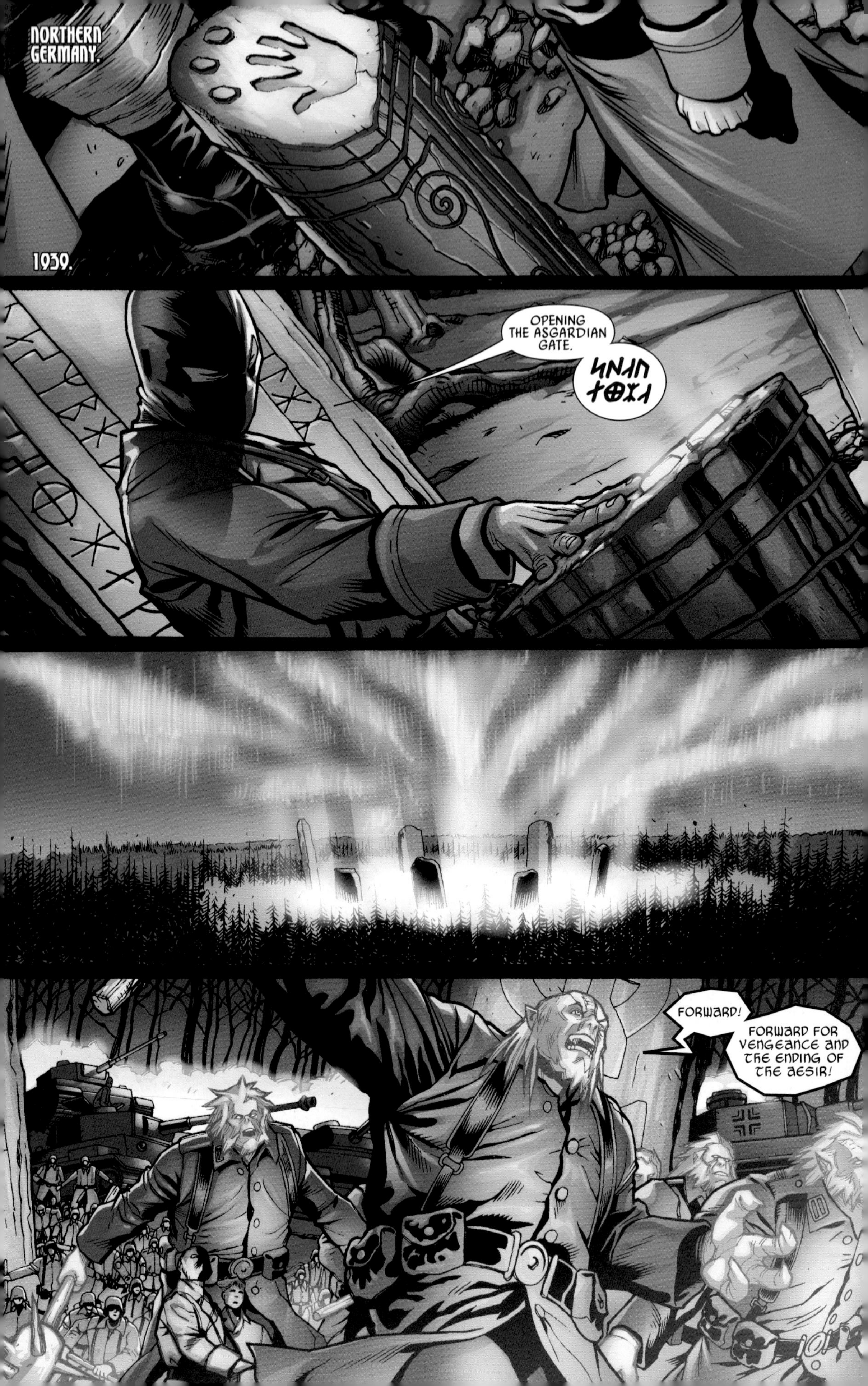
NORTHERN GERMANY.
1939.
OPENING THE ASGARDIAN GATE.
FORWARD!
FORWARD FOR VENGEANCE AND THE ENDING OF THE AESIR!

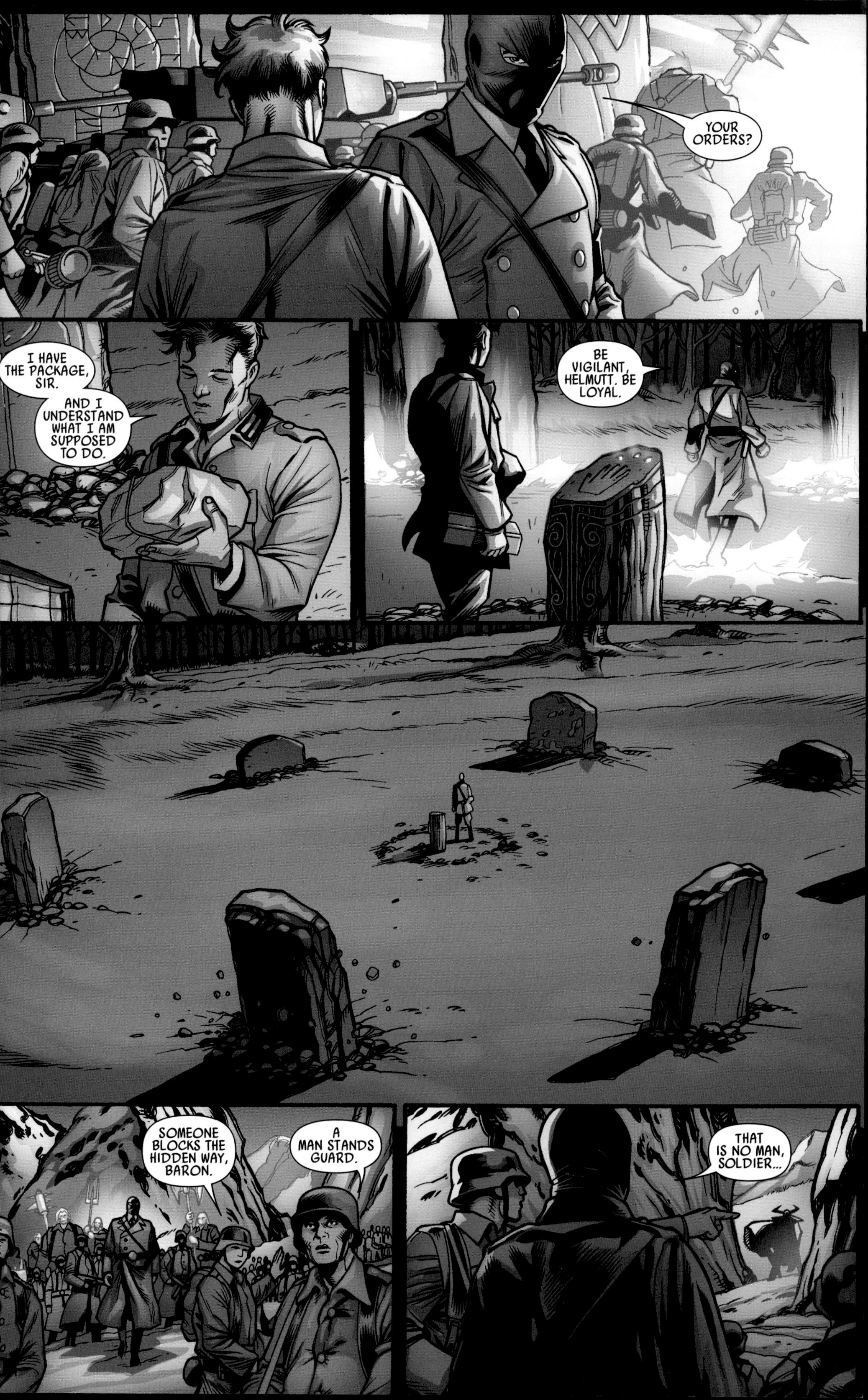
YOUR ORDERS?
I HAVE THE PACKAGE, SIR.
AND I UNDERSTAND WHAT I AM SUPPOSED TO DO.
BE VIGILANT, HELMUTT. BE LOYAL.
SOMEONE BLOCKS THE HIDDEN WAY, BARON.
A MAN STANDS GUARD.
THAT IS NO MAN, SOLDIER...

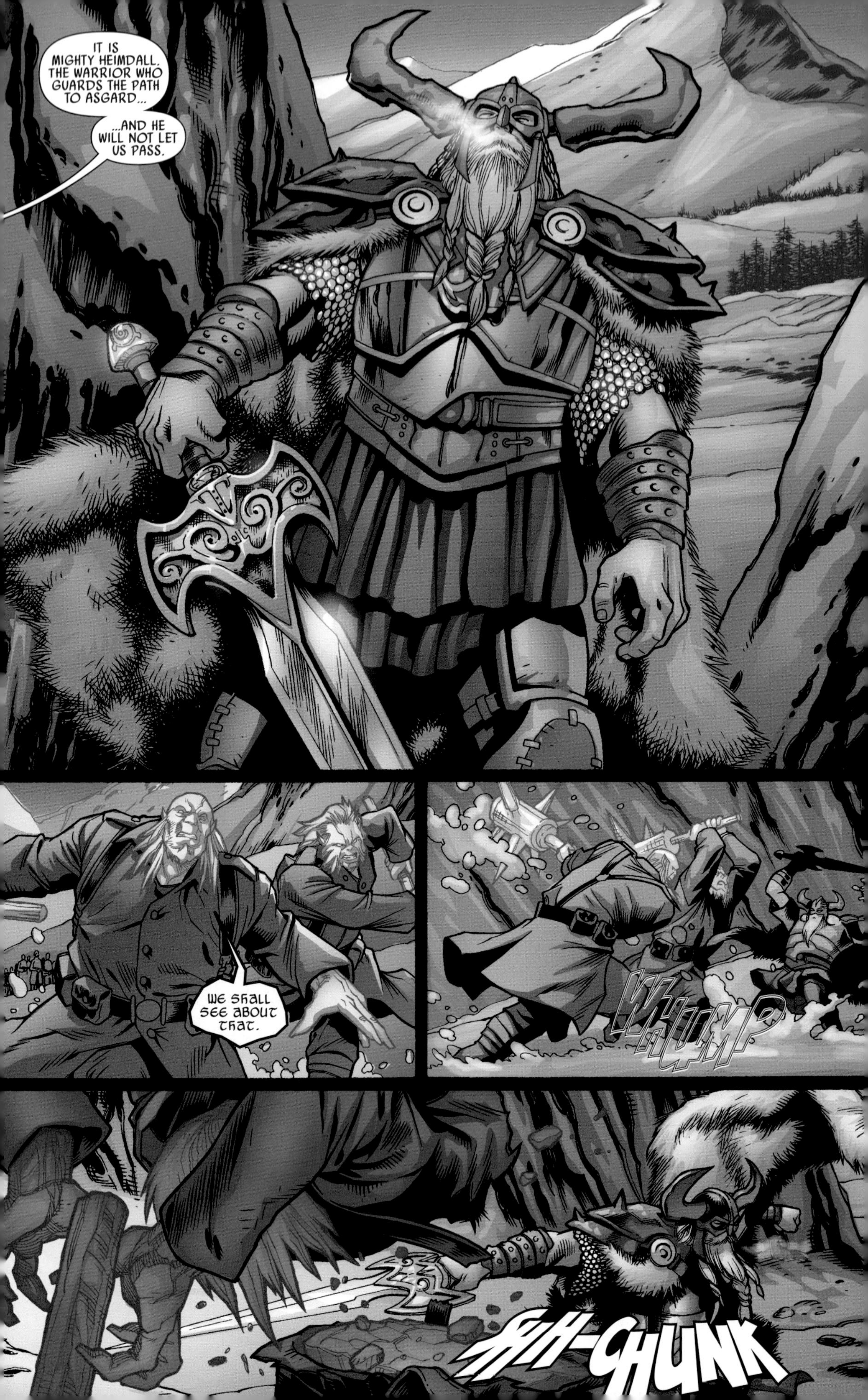
IT IS MIGHTY HEIMDALL, THE WARRIOR WHO GUARDS THE PATH TO ASGARD...
...AND HE WILL NOT LET US PASS.
WE SHALL SEE ABOUT THAT.
WHUMP
SHH-CHUNK

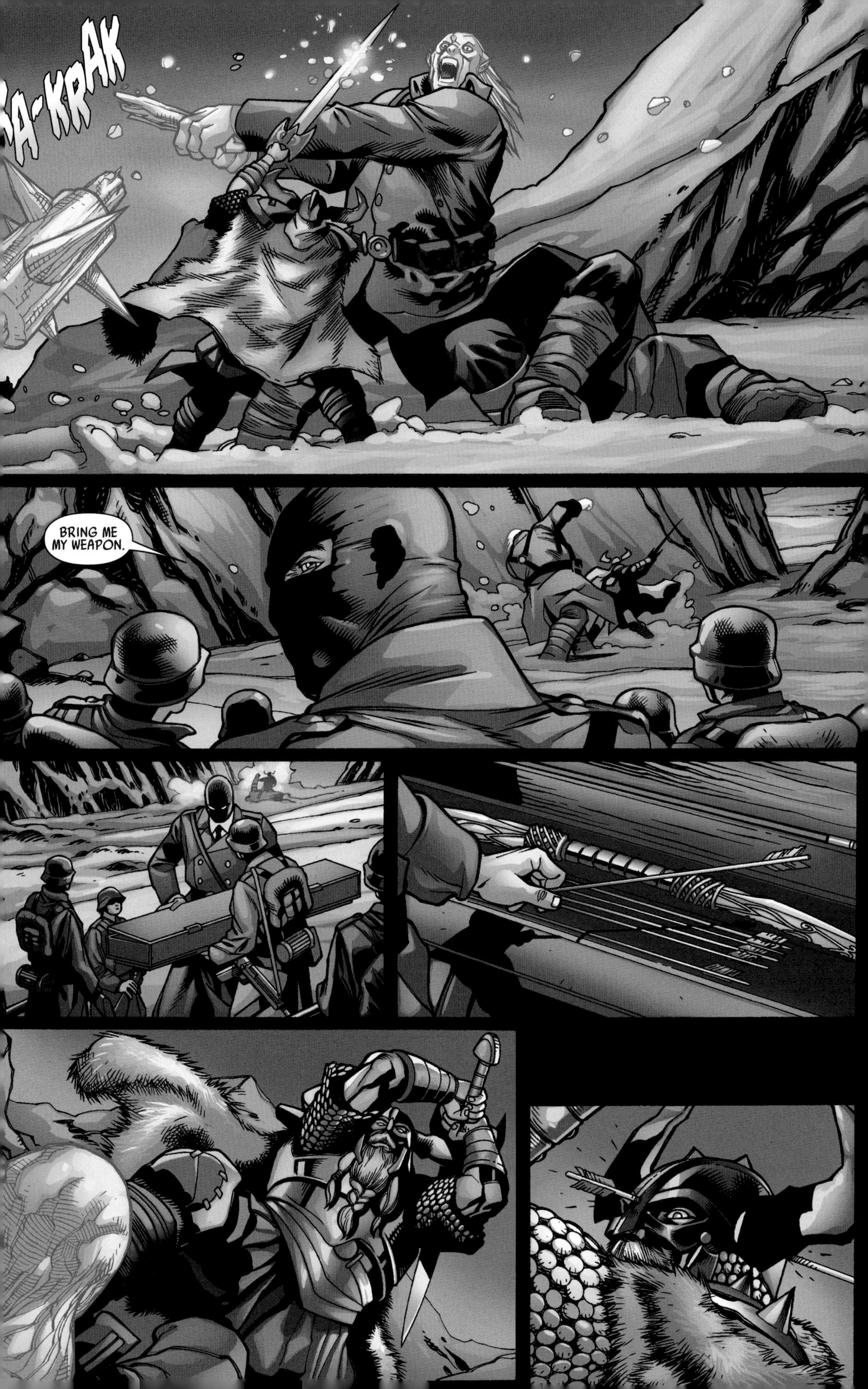

KA-KRAK
BRING ME MY WEAPON.

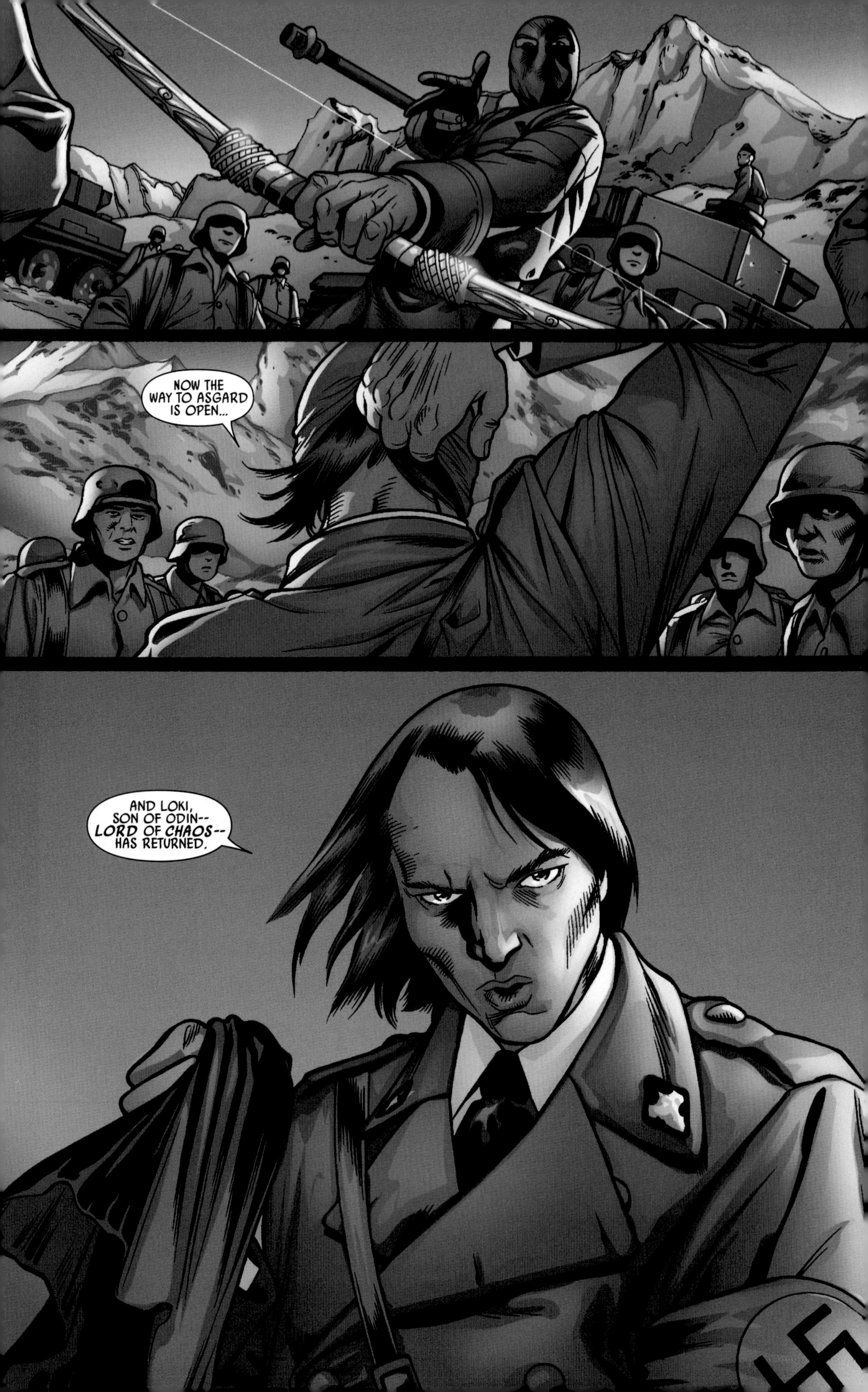
NOW THE WAY TO ASGARD IS OPEN...
AND LOKI, SON OF ODIN-- LORD OF CHAOS-- HAS RETURNED.

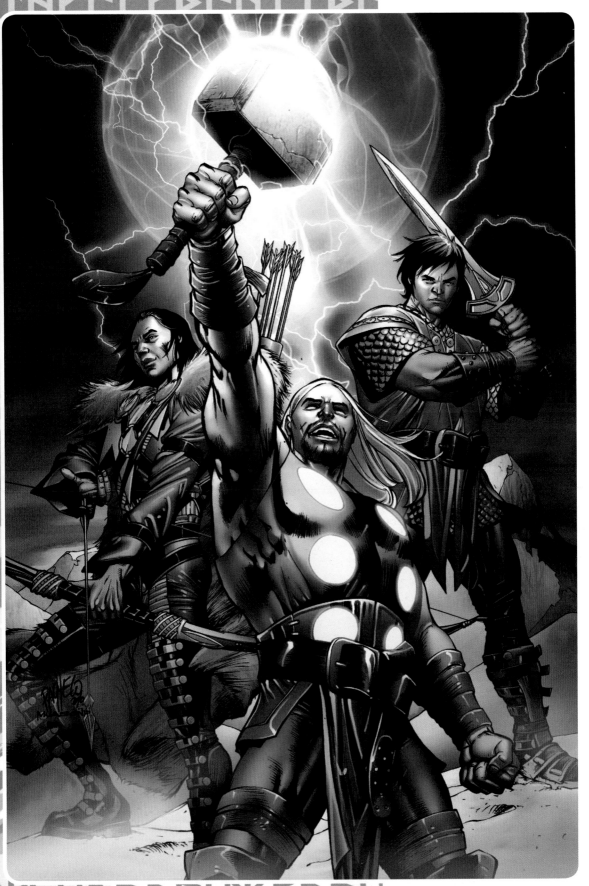

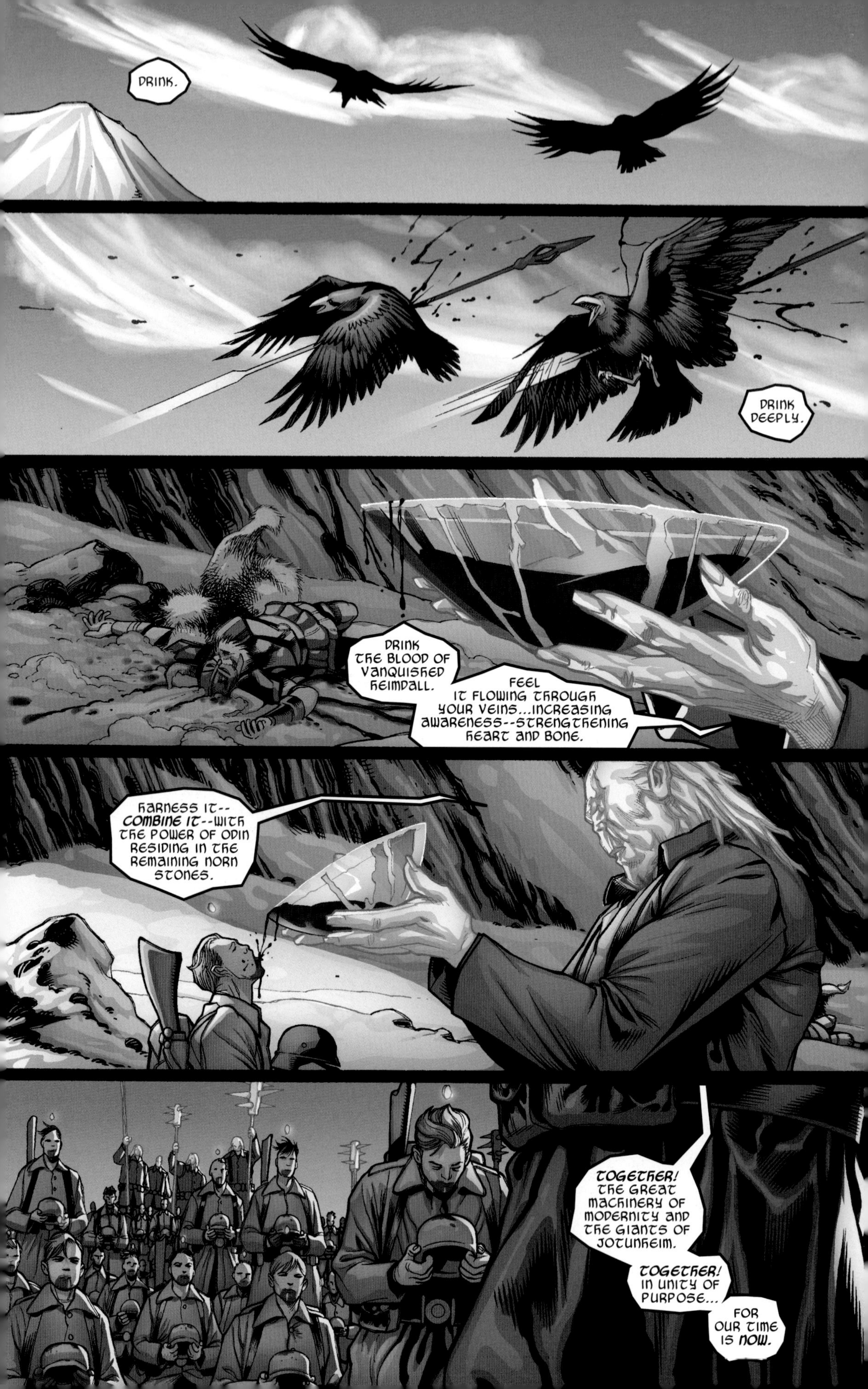
DRINK.
DRINK DEEPLY.
DRINK THE BLOOD OF VANQUISHED HEIMDALL.
FEEL IT FLOWING THROUGH YOUR VEINS...INCREASING AWARENESS--STRENGTHENING HEART AND BONE.
HARNESS IT--*COMBINE IT*--WITH THE POWER OF ODIN RESIDING IN THE REMAINING NORN STONES.
TOGETHER! THE GREAT MACHINERY OF MODERNITY AND THE GIANTS OF JOTUNHEIM.
TOGETHER! IN UNITY OF PURPOSE...
FOR OUR TIME IS *NOW.*

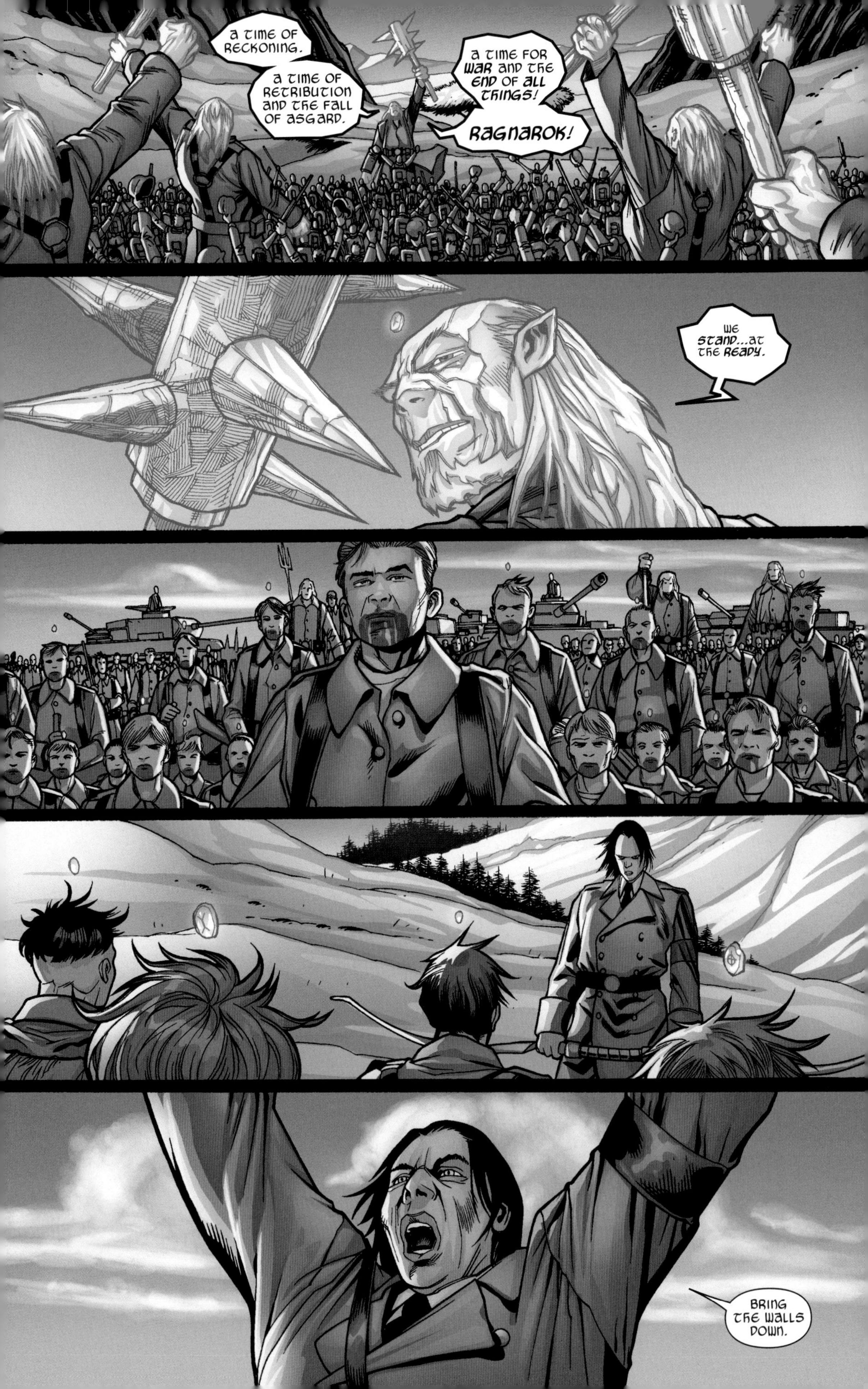
A TIME OF RECKONING.
A TIME OF RETRIBUTION AND THE FALL OF ASGARD.
A TIME FOR WAR AND THE END OF ALL THINGS!
RAGNAROK!
WE STAND...AT THE READY.
BRING THE WALLS DOWN.

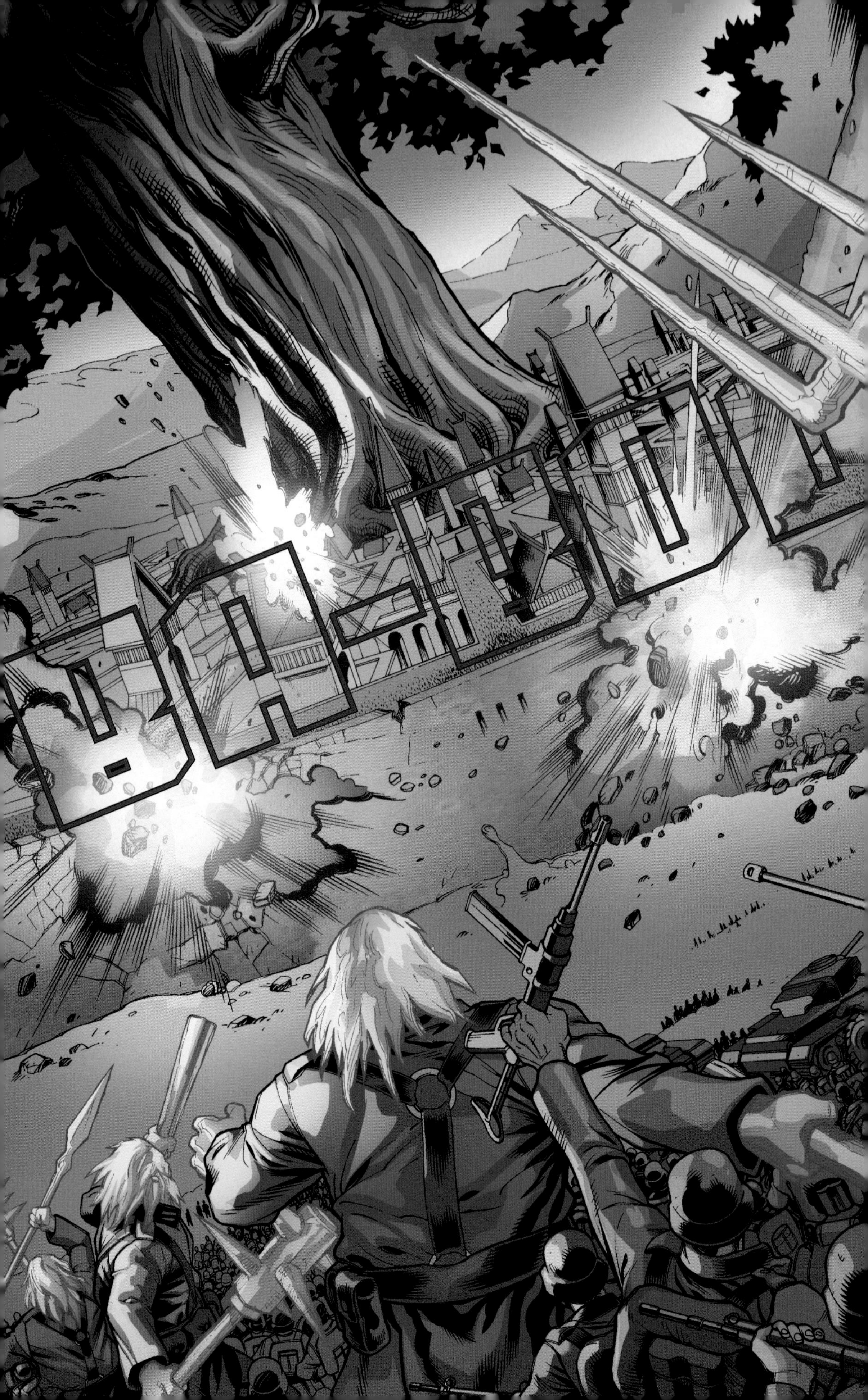

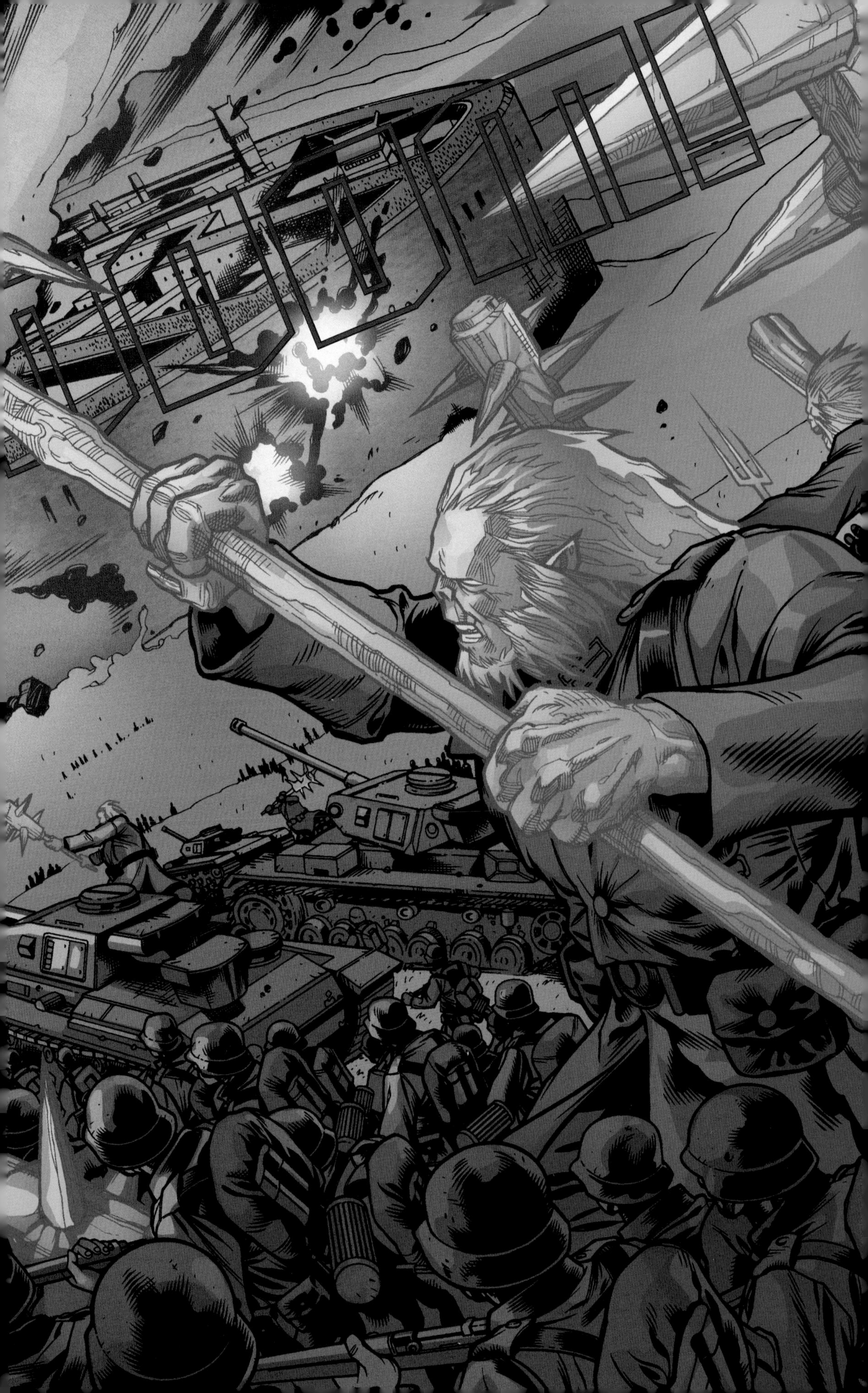

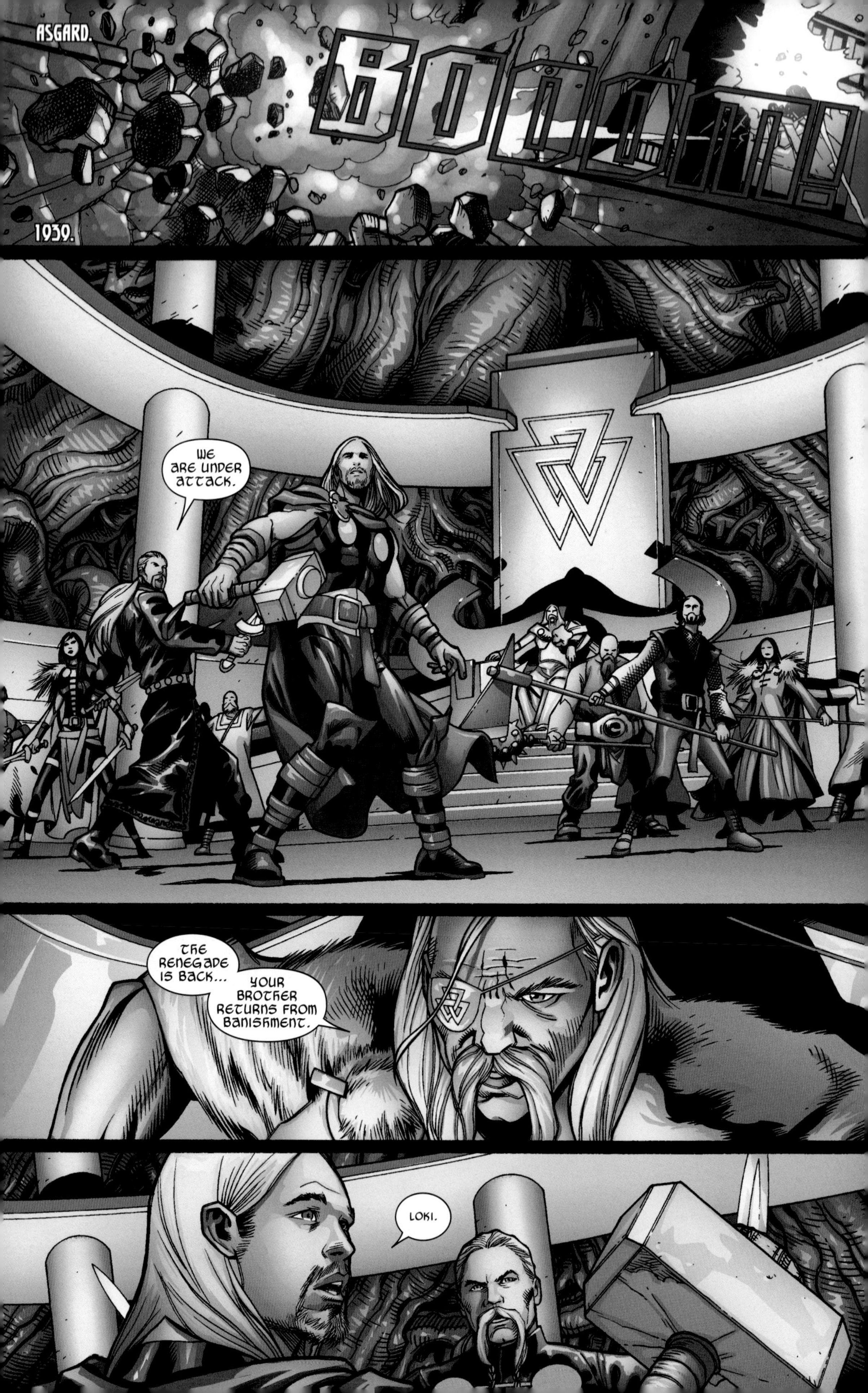
ASGARD.
BOOOOM!
1939.
WE ARE UNDER ATTACK.
THE RENEGADE IS BACK...
YOUR BROTHER RETURNS FROM BANISHMENT.
LOKI.

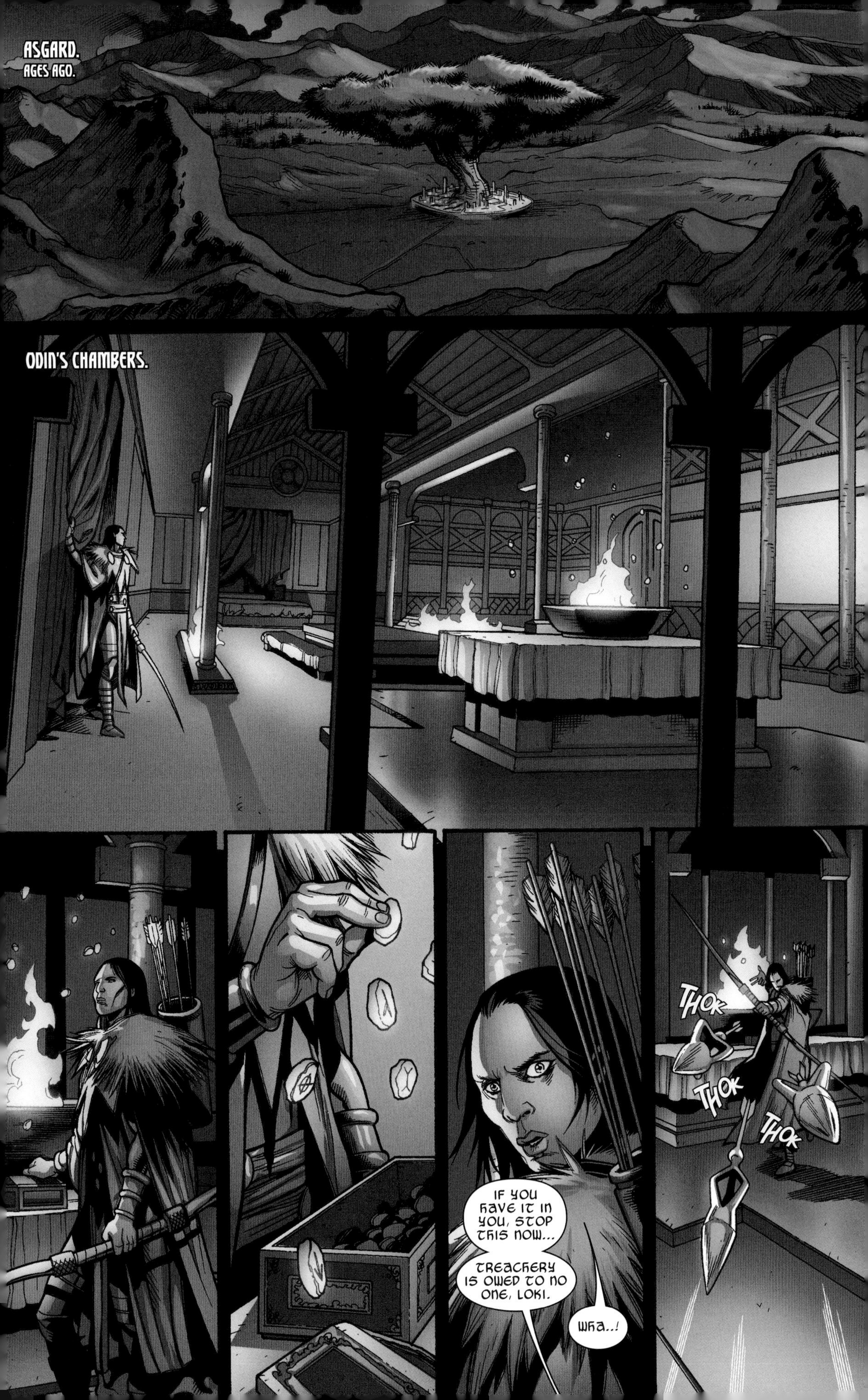
ASGARD.
AGES AGO.
ODIN'S CHAMBERS.
IF YOU HAVE IT IN YOU, STOP THIS NOW...
TREACHERY IS OWED TO NO ONE, LOKI.
WHA..!
THOK
THOK
THOK

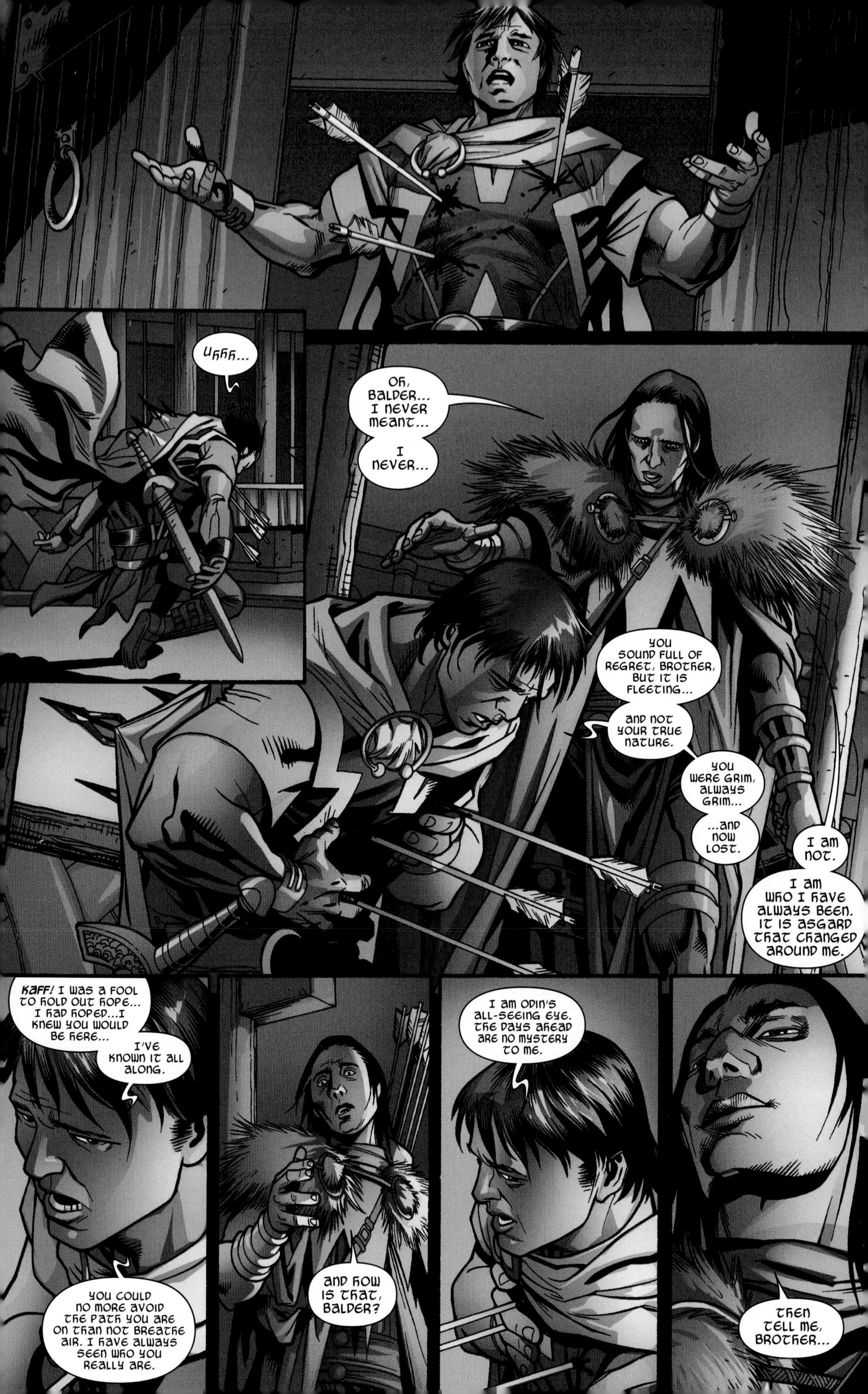
UHHH...
OH, BALDER... I NEVER MEANT...
I NEVER...
YOU SOUND FULL OF REGRET, BROTHER, BUT IT IS FLEETING...
AND NOT YOUR TRUE NATURE.
YOU WERE GRIM, ALWAYS GRIM...
...AND NOW LOST.
I AM NOT.
I AM WHO I HAVE ALWAYS BEEN. IT IS ASGARD THAT CHANGED AROUND ME.
KAFF! I WAS A FOOL TO HOLD OUT HOPE... I HAD HOPED...I KNEW YOU WOULD BE HERE...
I'VE KNOWN IT ALL ALONG.
YOU COULD NO MORE AVOID THE PATH YOU ARE ON THAN NOT BREATHE AIR. I HAVE ALWAYS SEEN WHO YOU REALLY ARE.
AND HOW IS THAT, BALDER?
I AM ODIN'S ALL-SEEING EYE. THE DAYS AHEAD ARE NO MYSTERY TO ME.
THEN TELL ME, BROTHER...

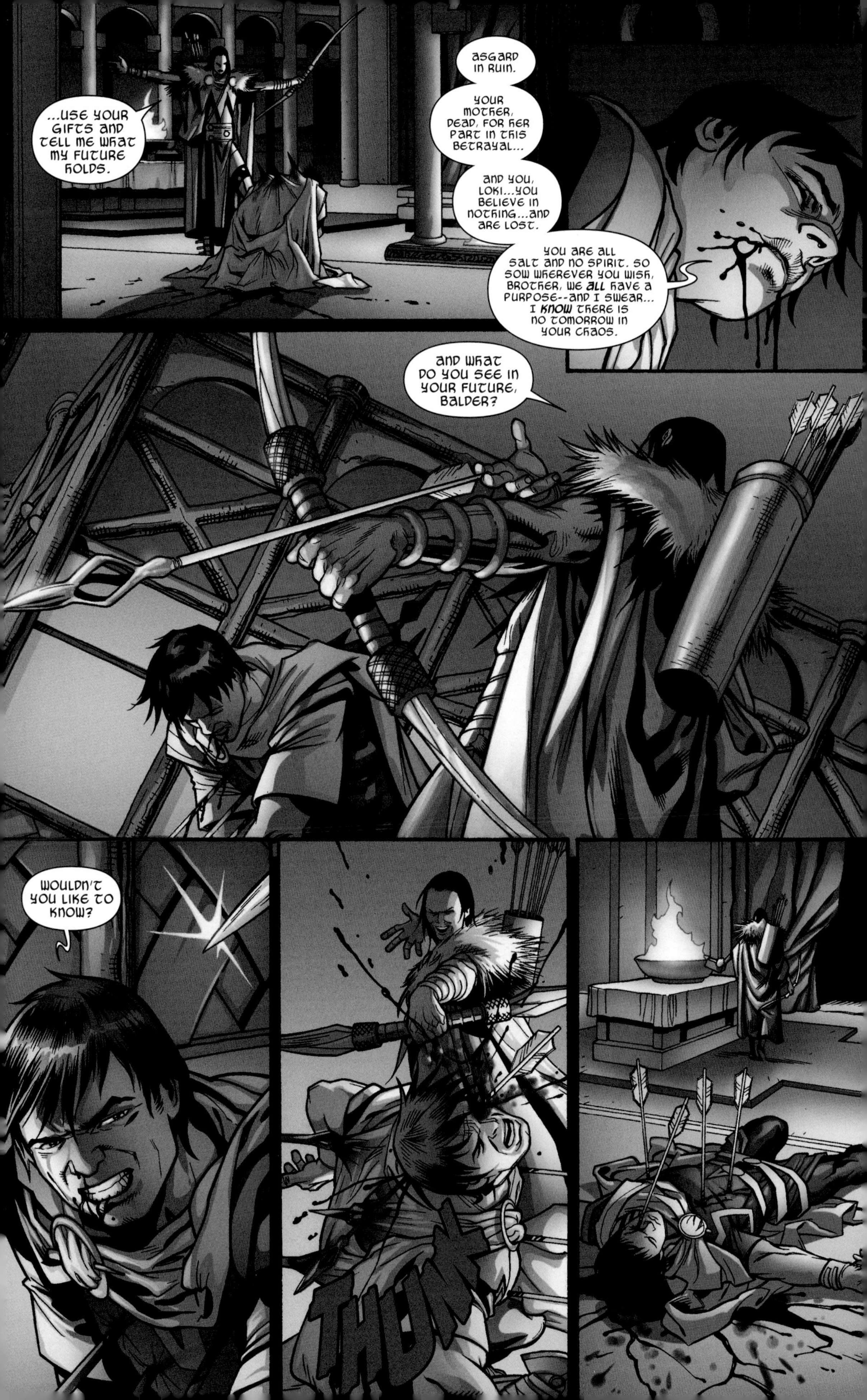
...USE YOUR GIFTS AND TELL ME WHAT MY FUTURE HOLDS.
ASGARD IN RUIN.
YOUR MOTHER, DEAD, FOR HER PART IN THIS BETRAYAL...
AND YOU, LOKI...YOU BELIEVE IN NOTHING...AND ARE LOST.
YOU ARE ALL SALT AND NO SPIRIT. SO SOW WHEREVER YOU WISH, BROTHER, WE **ALL** HAVE A PURPOSE--AND I SWEAR... I **KNOW** THERE IS NO TOMORROW IN YOUR CHAOS.
AND WHAT DO YOU SEE IN YOUR FUTURE, BALDER?
WOULDN'T YOU LIKE TO KNOW?
THU

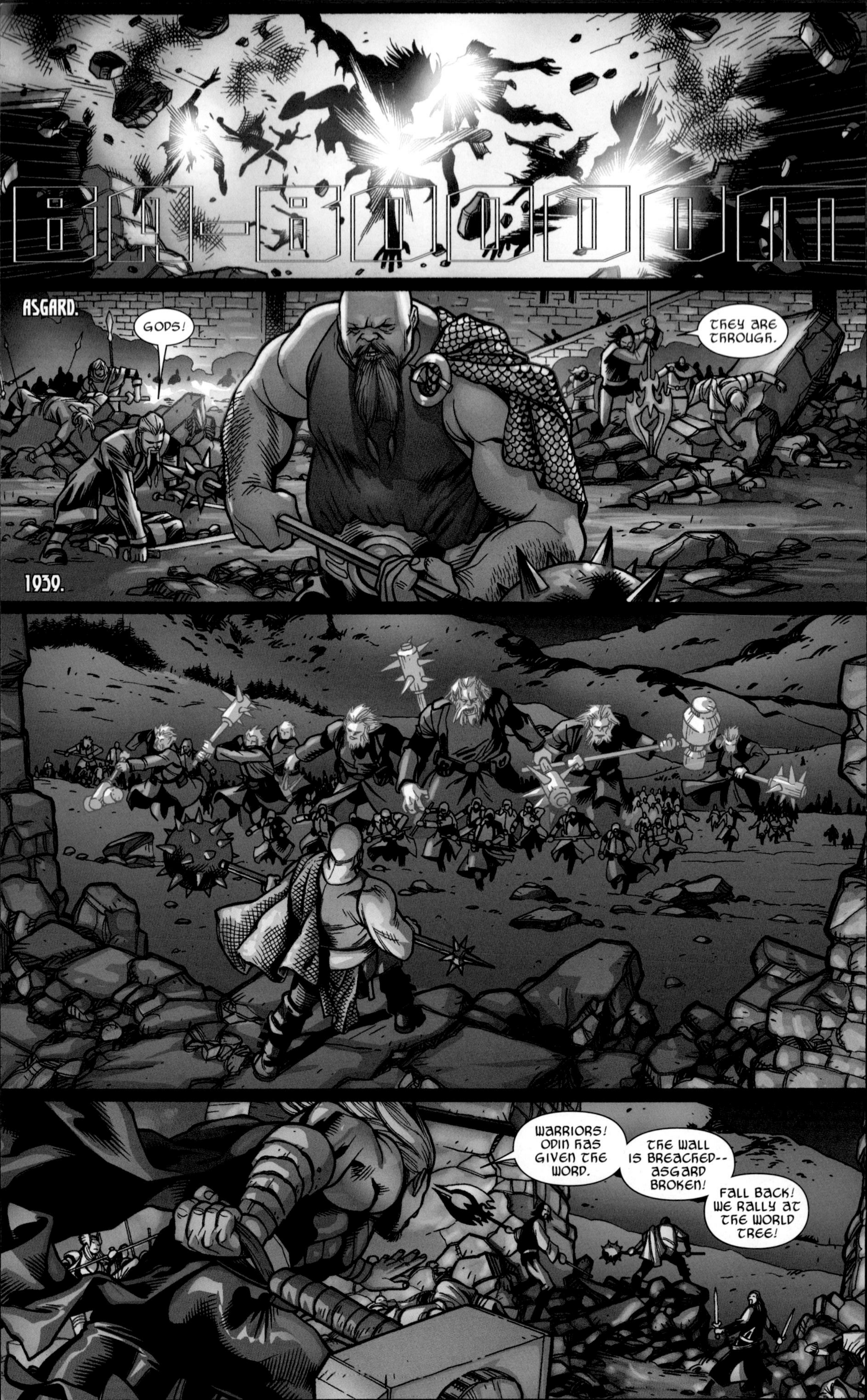
ASGARD.
GODS!
THEY ARE THROUGH.
1939.
WARRIORS! ODIN HAS GIVEN THE WORD.
THE WALL IS BREACHED-- ASGARD BROKEN!
FALL BACK! WE RALLY AT THE WORLD TREE!

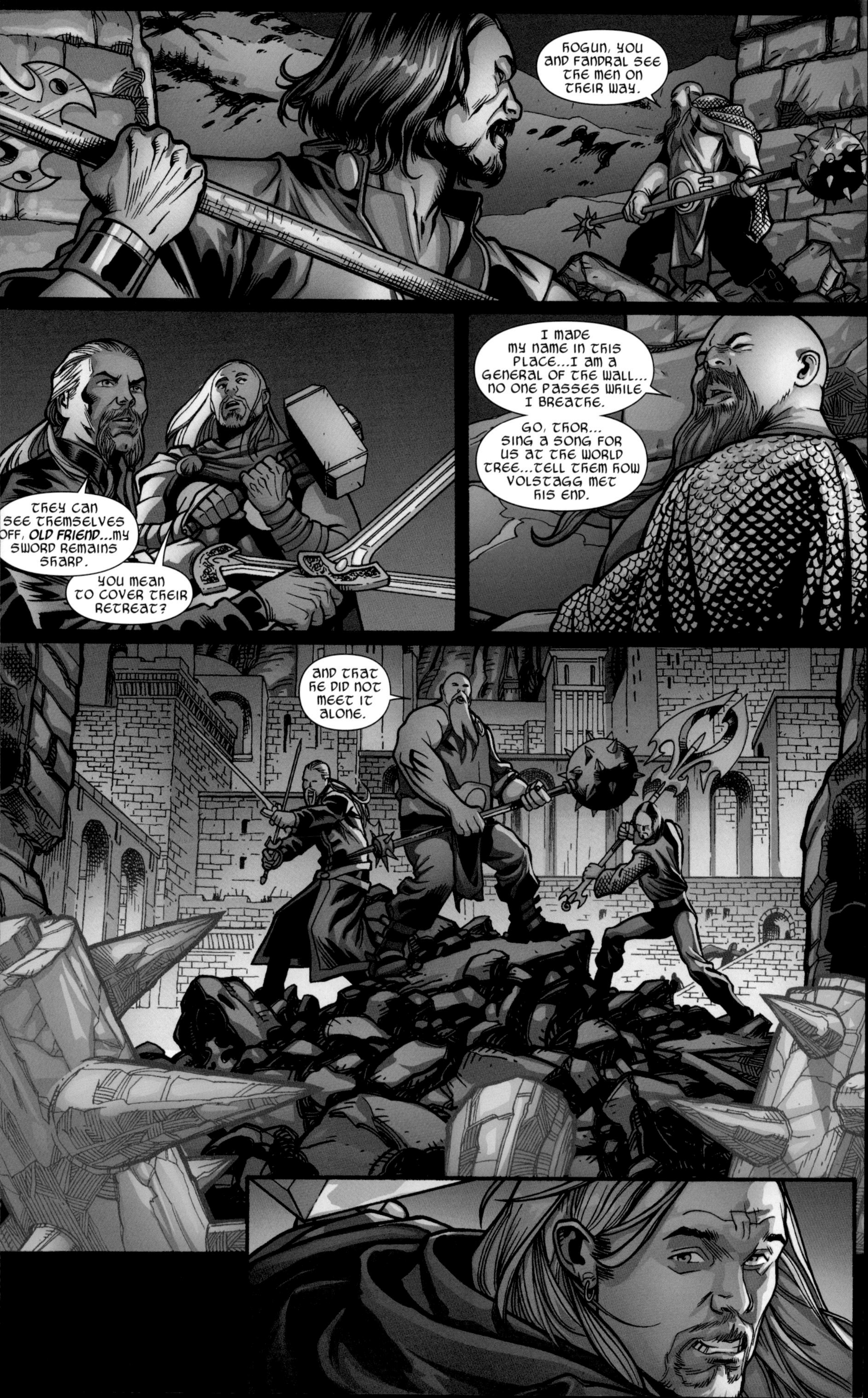
HOGUN, YOU AND FANDRAL SEE THE MEN ON THEIR WAY.
YOU MEAN TO COVER THEIR RETREAT?
THEY CAN SEE THEMSELVES OFF, OLD FRIEND...MY SWORD REMAINS SHARP.
I MADE MY NAME IN THIS PLACE...I AM A GENERAL OF THE WALL... NO ONE PASSES WHILE I BREATHE.
GO, THOR... SING A SONG FOR US AT THE WORLD TREE...TELL THEM HOW VOLSTAGG MET HIS END.
AND THAT HE DID NOT MEET IT ALONE.

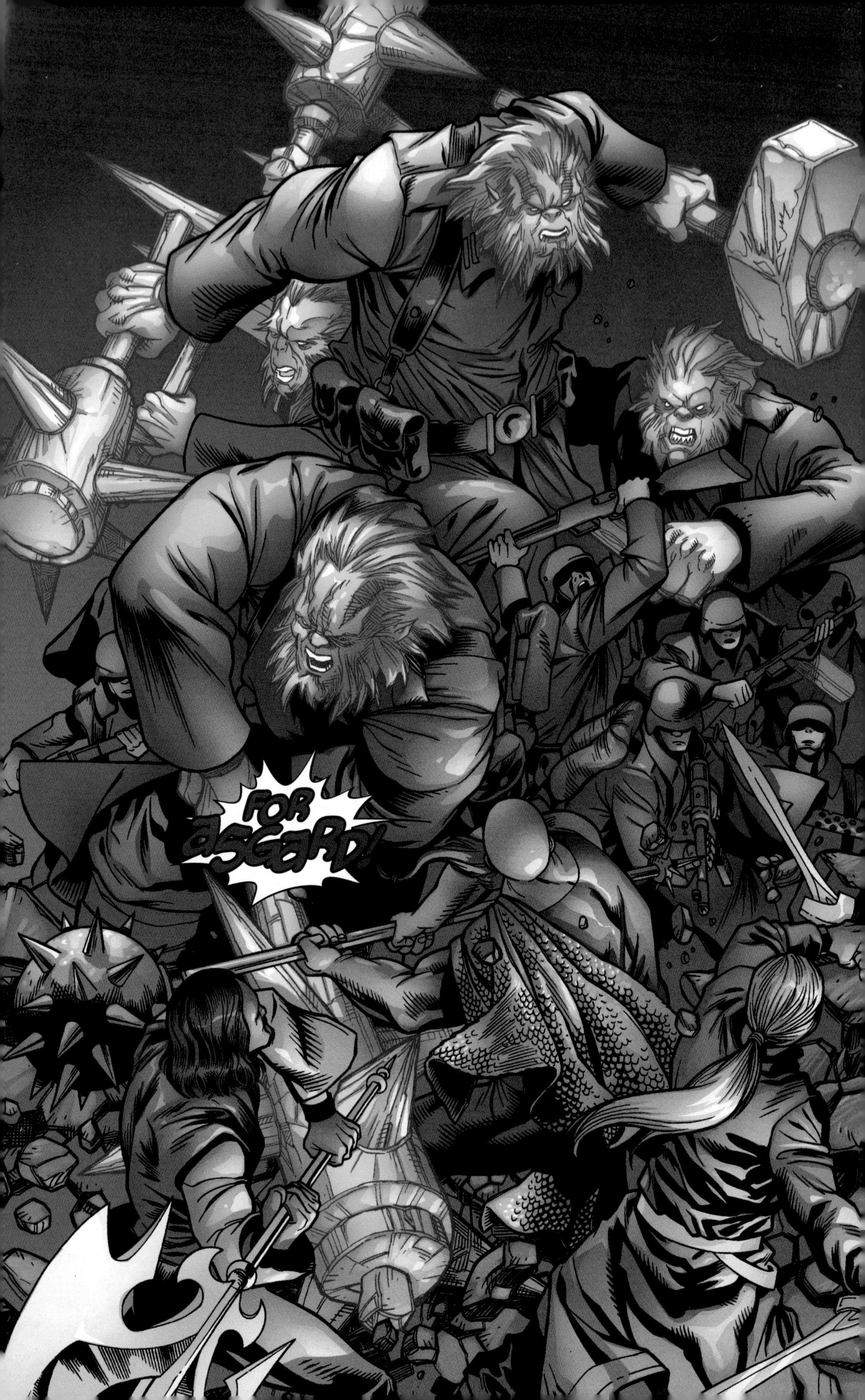
FOR ASGARD!

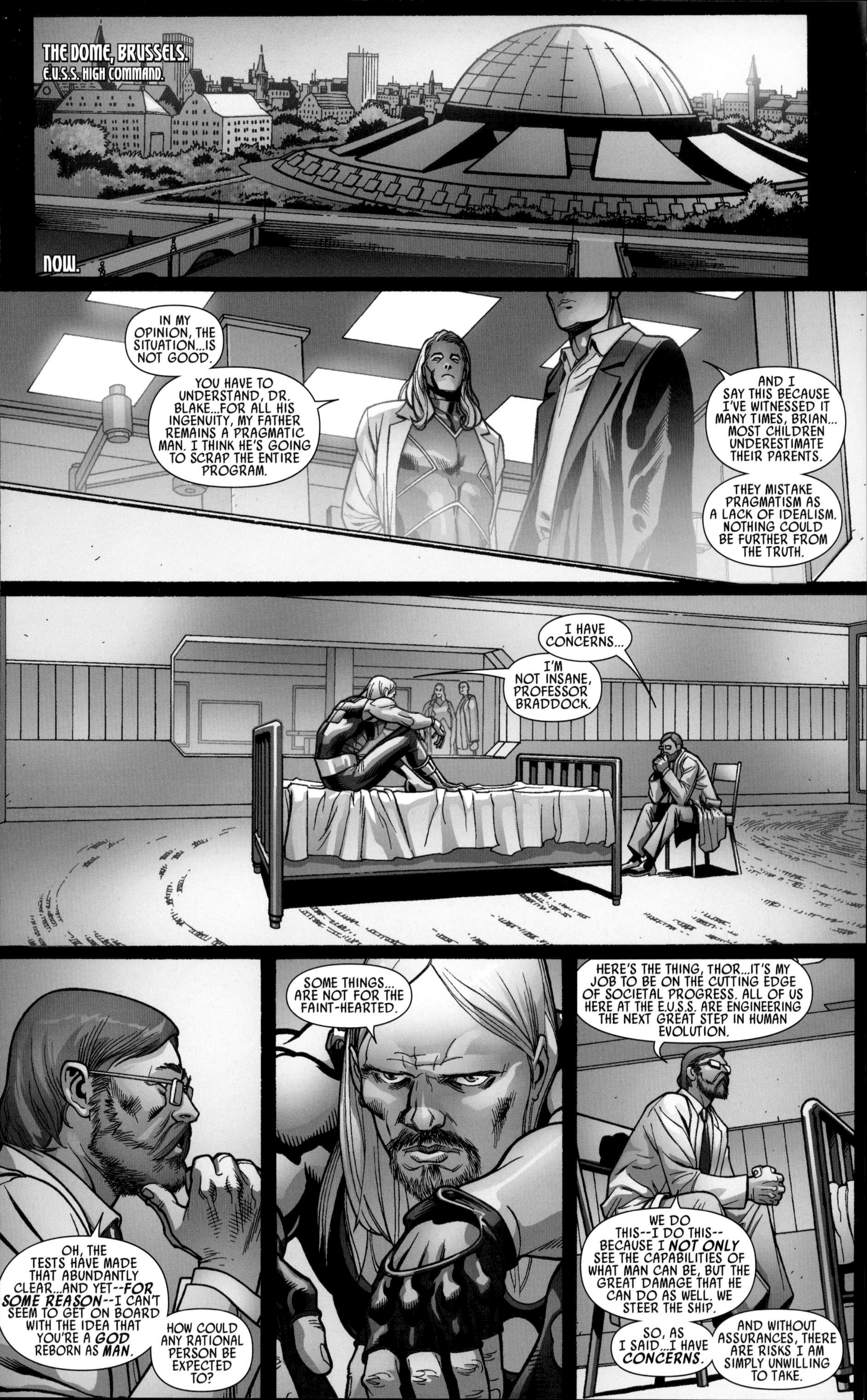
THE DOME, BRUSSELS.
E.U.S.S. HIGH COMMAND.
NOW.
IN MY OPINION, THE SITUATION...IS NOT GOOD.
YOU HAVE TO UNDERSTAND, DR. BLAKE...FOR ALL HIS INGENUITY, MY FATHER REMAINS A PRAGMATIC MAN. I THINK HE'S GOING TO SCRAP THE ENTIRE PROGRAM.
AND I SAY THIS BECAUSE I'VE WITNESSED IT MANY TIMES, BRIAN... MOST CHILDREN UNDERESTIMATE THEIR PARENTS.
THEY MISTAKE PRAGMATISM AS A LACK OF IDEALISM. NOTHING COULD BE FURTHER FROM THE TRUTH.
I HAVE CONCERNS...
I'M NOT INSANE, PROFESSOR BRADDOCK.
OH, THE TESTS HAVE MADE THAT ABUNDANTLY CLEAR...AND YET--FOR SOME REASON--I CAN'T SEEM TO GET ON BOARD WITH THE IDEA THAT YOU'RE A GOD REBORN AS MAN.
HOW COULD ANY RATIONAL PERSON BE EXPECTED TO?
SOME THINGS... ARE NOT FOR THE FAINT-HEARTED.
HERE'S THE THING, THOR...IT'S MY JOB TO BE ON THE CUTTING EDGE OF SOCIETAL PROGRESS. ALL OF US HERE AT THE E.U.S.S. ARE ENGINEERING THE NEXT GREAT STEP IN HUMAN EVOLUTION.
WE DO THIS--I DO THIS--BECAUSE I NOT ONLY SEE THE CAPABILITIES OF WHAT MAN CAN BE, BUT THE GREAT DAMAGE THAT HE CAN DO AS WELL. WE STEER THE SHIP.
SO, AS I SAID...I HAVE CONCERNS.
AND WITHOUT ASSURANCES, THERE ARE RISKS I AM SIMPLY UNWILLING TO TAKE.

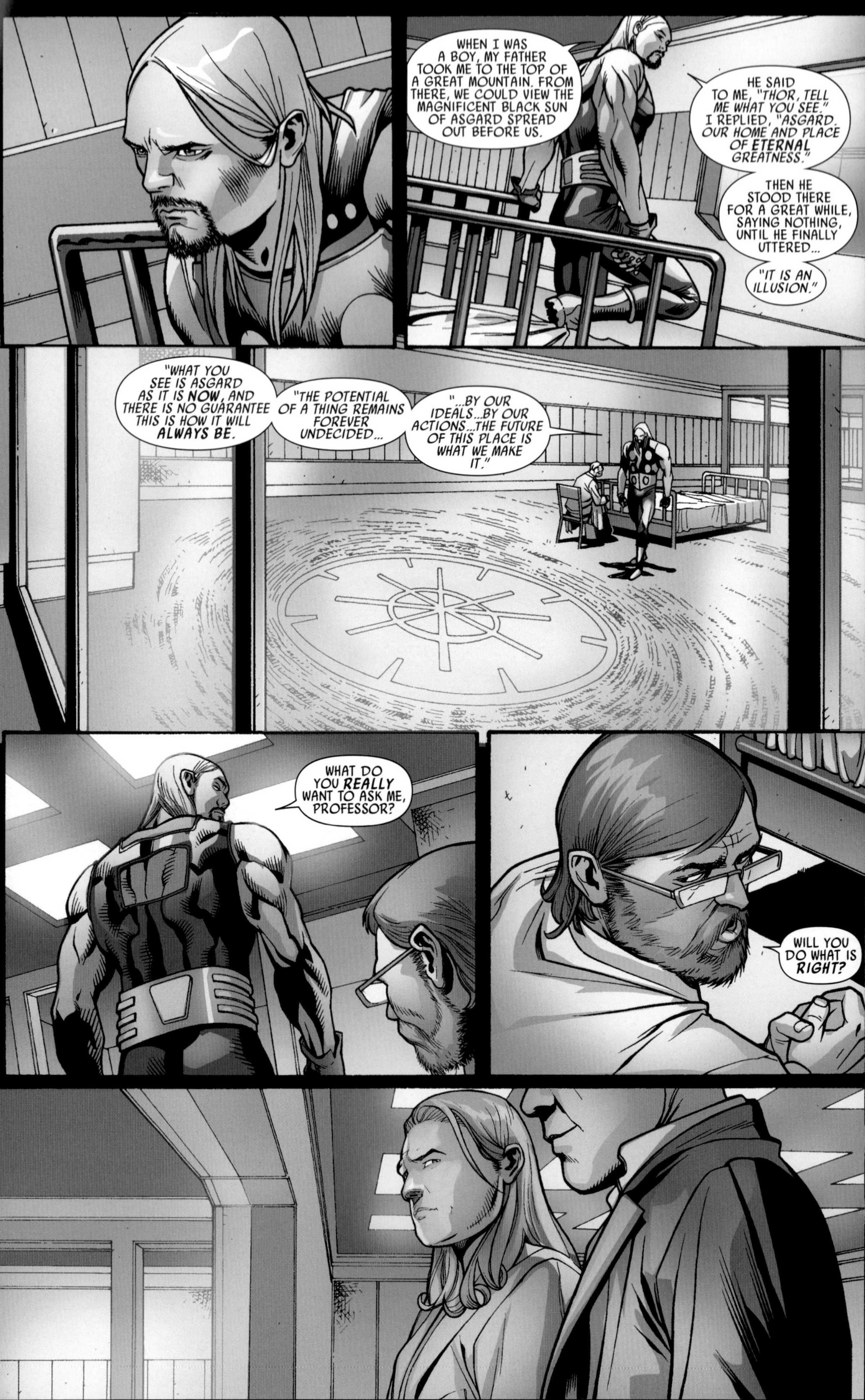
WHEN I WAS A BOY, MY FATHER TOOK ME TO THE TOP OF A GREAT MOUNTAIN. FROM THERE, WE COULD VIEW THE MAGNIFICENT BLACK SUN OF ASGARD SPREAD OUT BEFORE US.
HE SAID TO ME, "THOR, TELL ME WHAT YOU SEE." I REPLIED, "ASGARD. OUR HOME AND PLACE OF **ETERNAL** GREATNESS."
THEN HE STOOD THERE FOR A GREAT WHILE, SAYING NOTHING, UNTIL HE FINALLY UTTERED...
"IT IS AN ILLUSION."
"WHAT YOU SEE IS ASGARD AS IT IS **NOW**, AND THERE IS NO GUARANTEE THIS IS HOW IT WILL **ALWAYS BE**.
"THE POTENTIAL OF A THING REMAINS FOREVER UNDECIDED...
"...BY OUR IDEALS...BY OUR ACTIONS...THE FUTURE OF THIS PLACE IS WHAT WE MAKE IT."
WHAT DO YOU **REALLY** WANT TO ASK ME, PROFESSOR?
WILL YOU DO WHAT IS **RIGHT?**

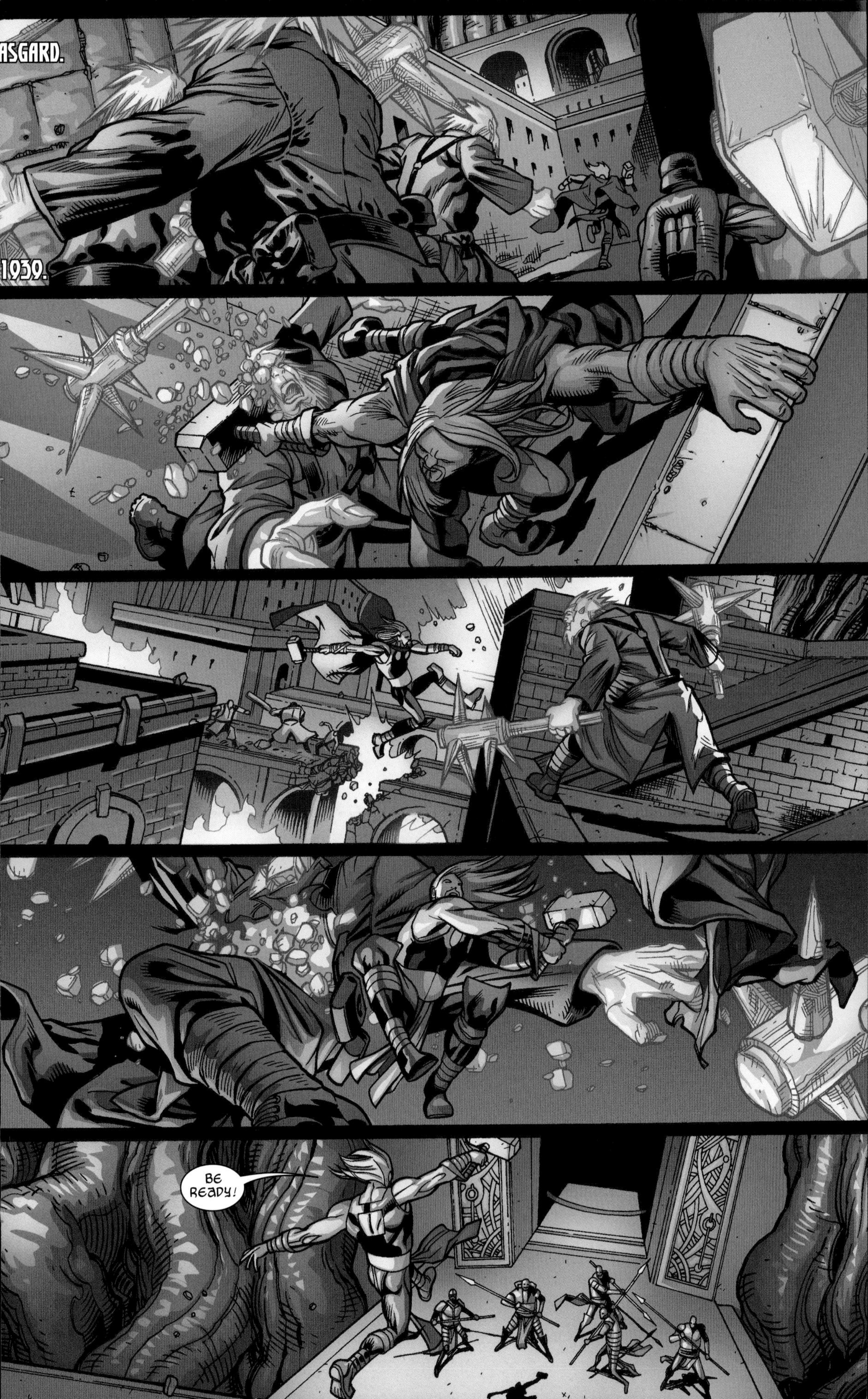
ASGARD.
1939.
BE READY!

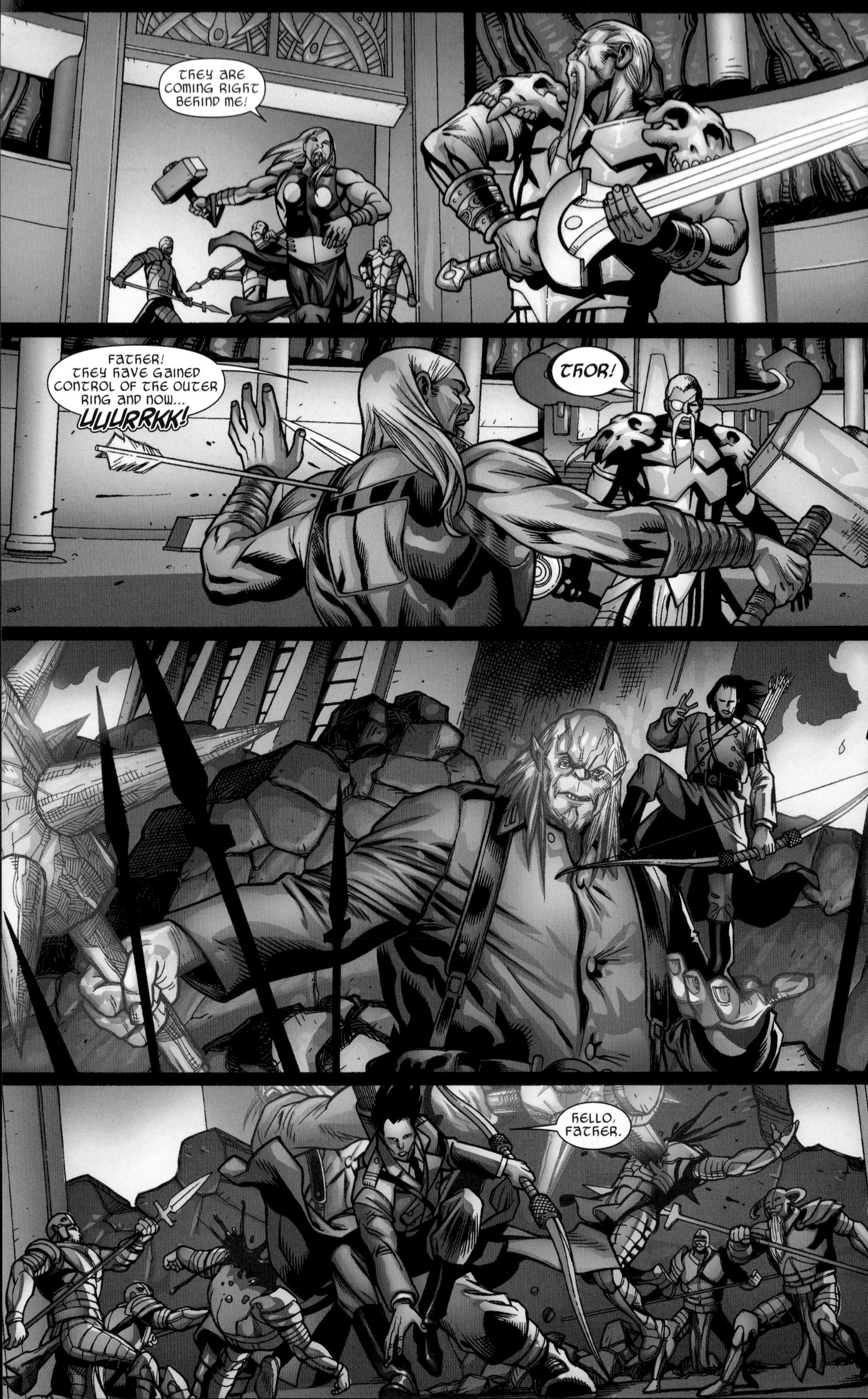
THEY ARE COMING RIGHT BEHIND ME!
FATHER! THEY HAVE GAINED CONTROL OF THE OUTER RING AND NOW... UUURRKK!
THOR!
HELLO, FATHER.

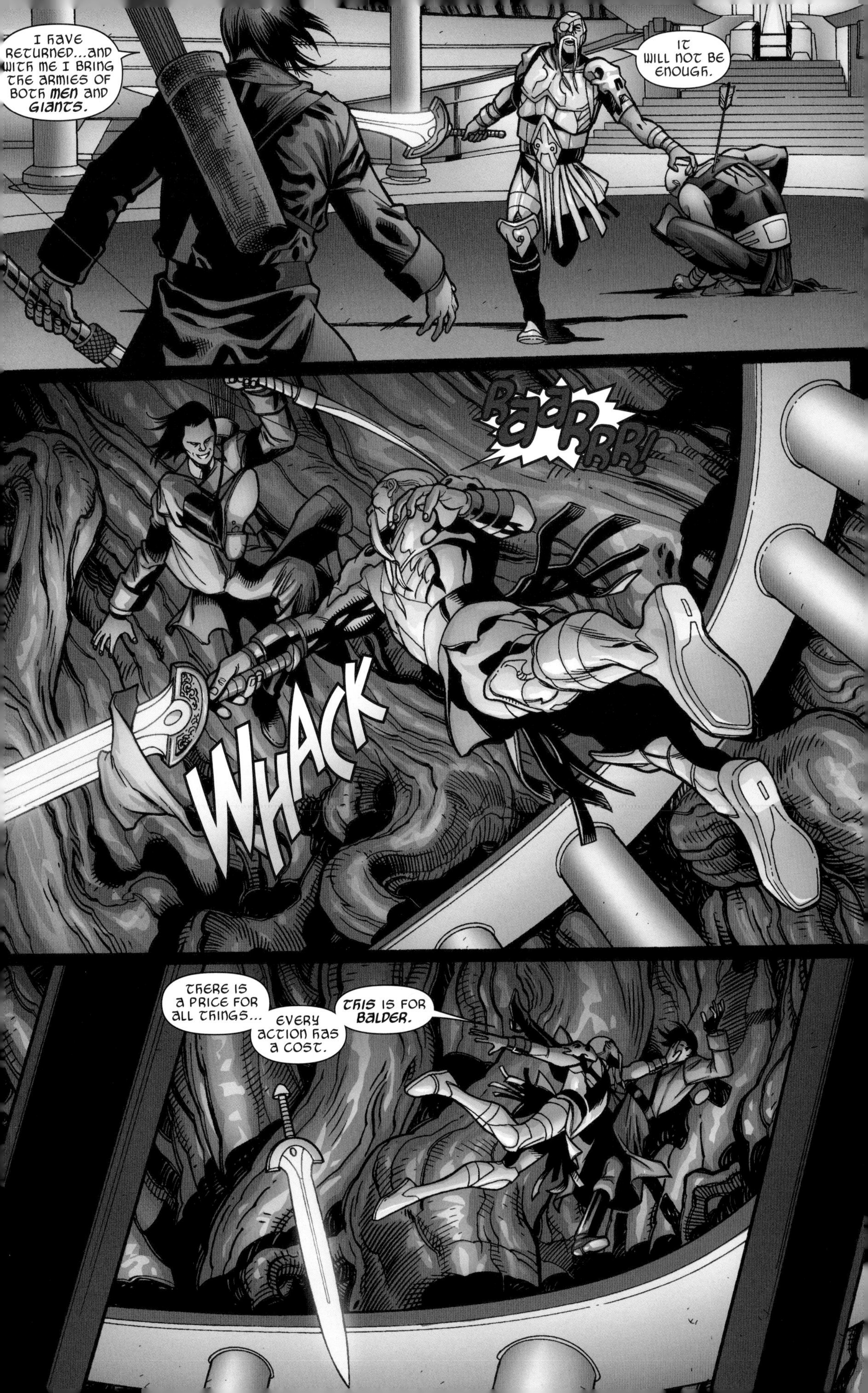
I HAVE RETURNED...AND WITH ME I BRING THE ARMIES OF BOTH MEN AND GIANTS.
IT WILL NOT BE ENOUGH.
RAAARRRR!
WHACK
THERE IS A PRICE FOR ALL THINGS...
EVERY ACTION HAS A COST.
THIS IS FOR BALDER.

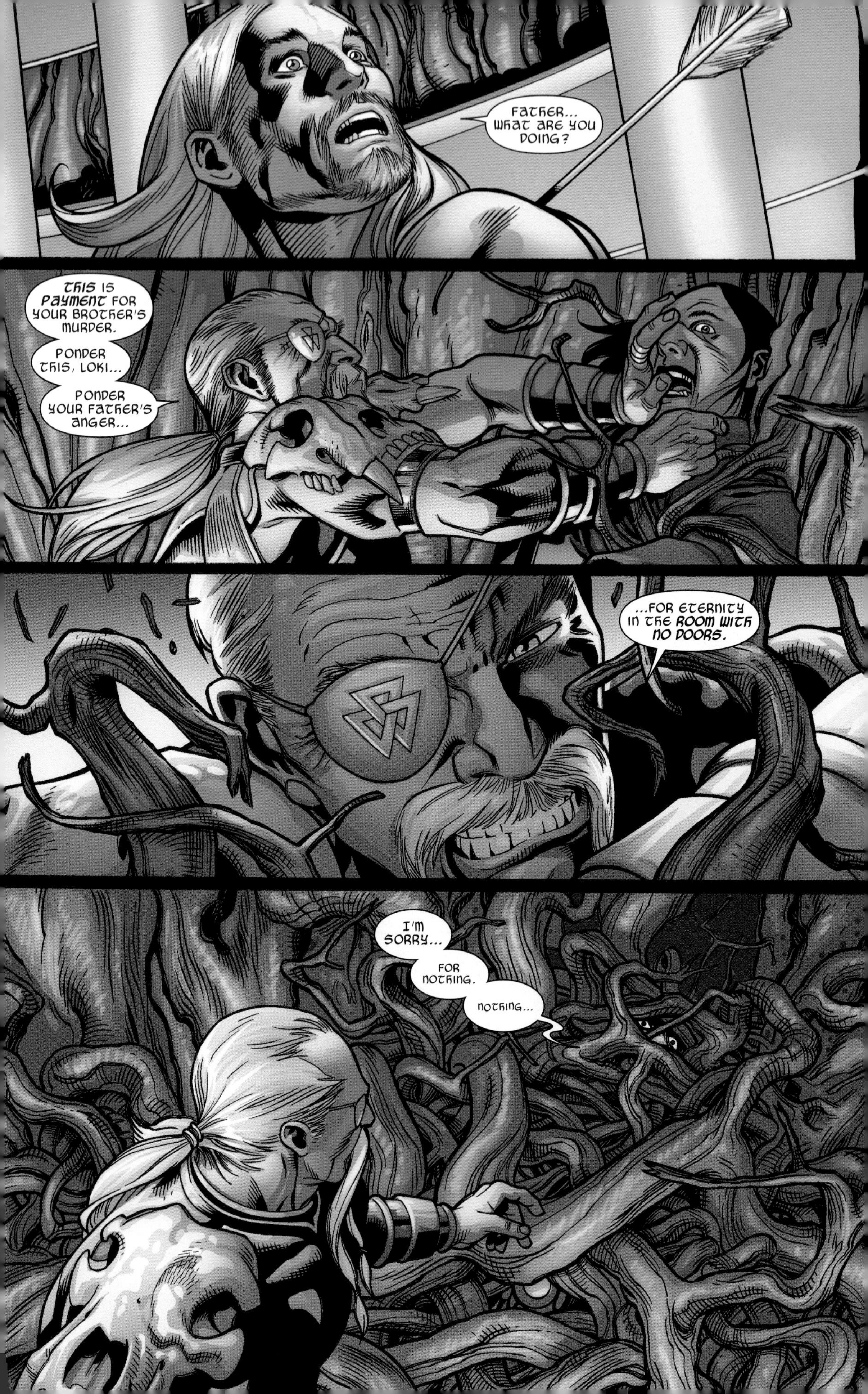
FATHER... WHAT ARE YOU DOING?
THIS IS PAYMENT FOR YOUR BROTHER'S MURDER.
PONDER THIS, LOKI...
PONDER YOUR FATHER'S ANGER...
...FOR ETERNITY IN THE ROOM WITH NO DOORS.
I'M SORRY...
FOR NOTHING.
NOTHING...

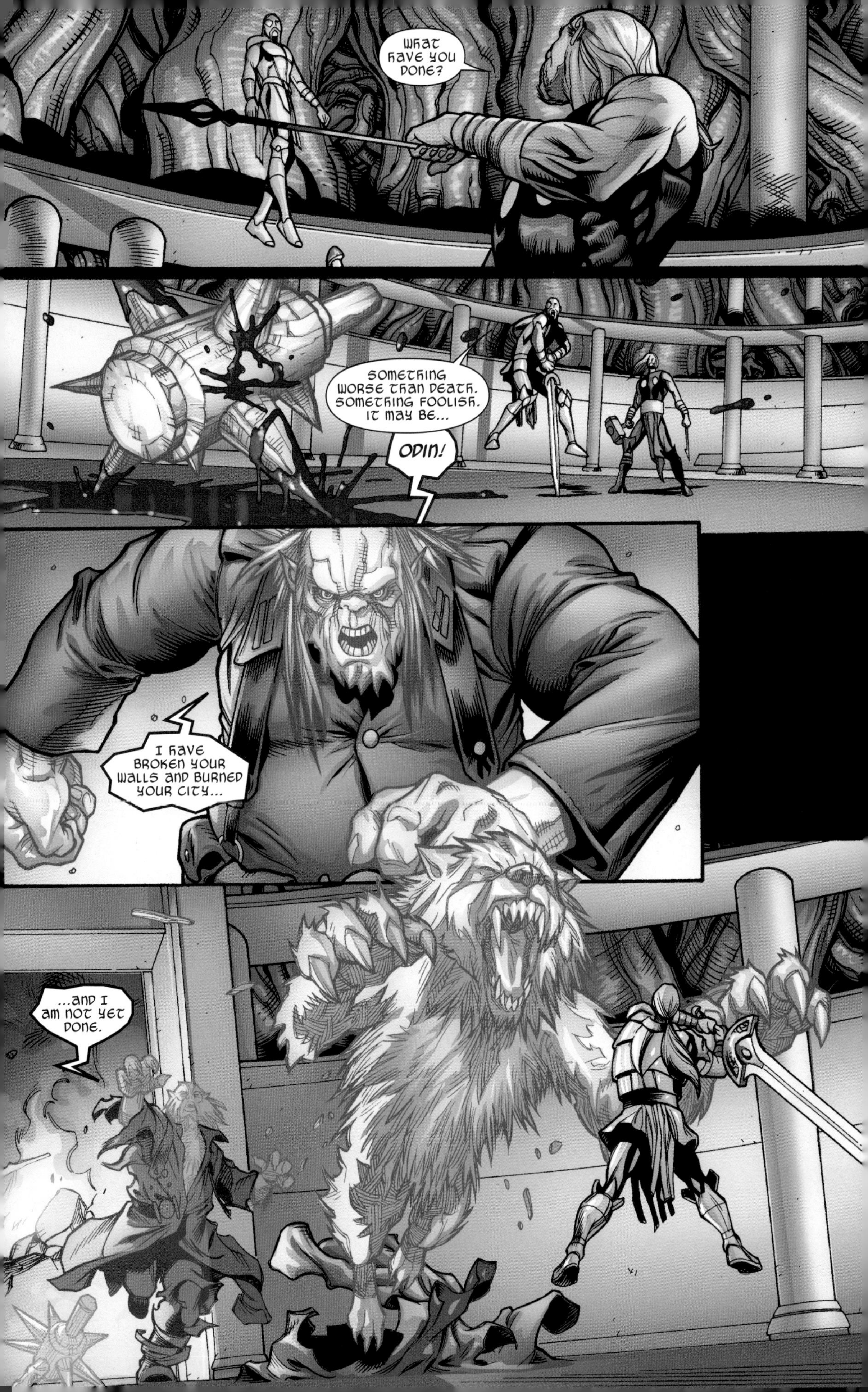
WHAT HAVE YOU DONE?
SOMETHING WORSE THAN DEATH. SOMETHING FOOLISH. IT MAY BE...
ODIN!
I HAVE BROKEN YOUR WALLS AND BURNED YOUR CITY...
...AND I AM NOT YET DONE.

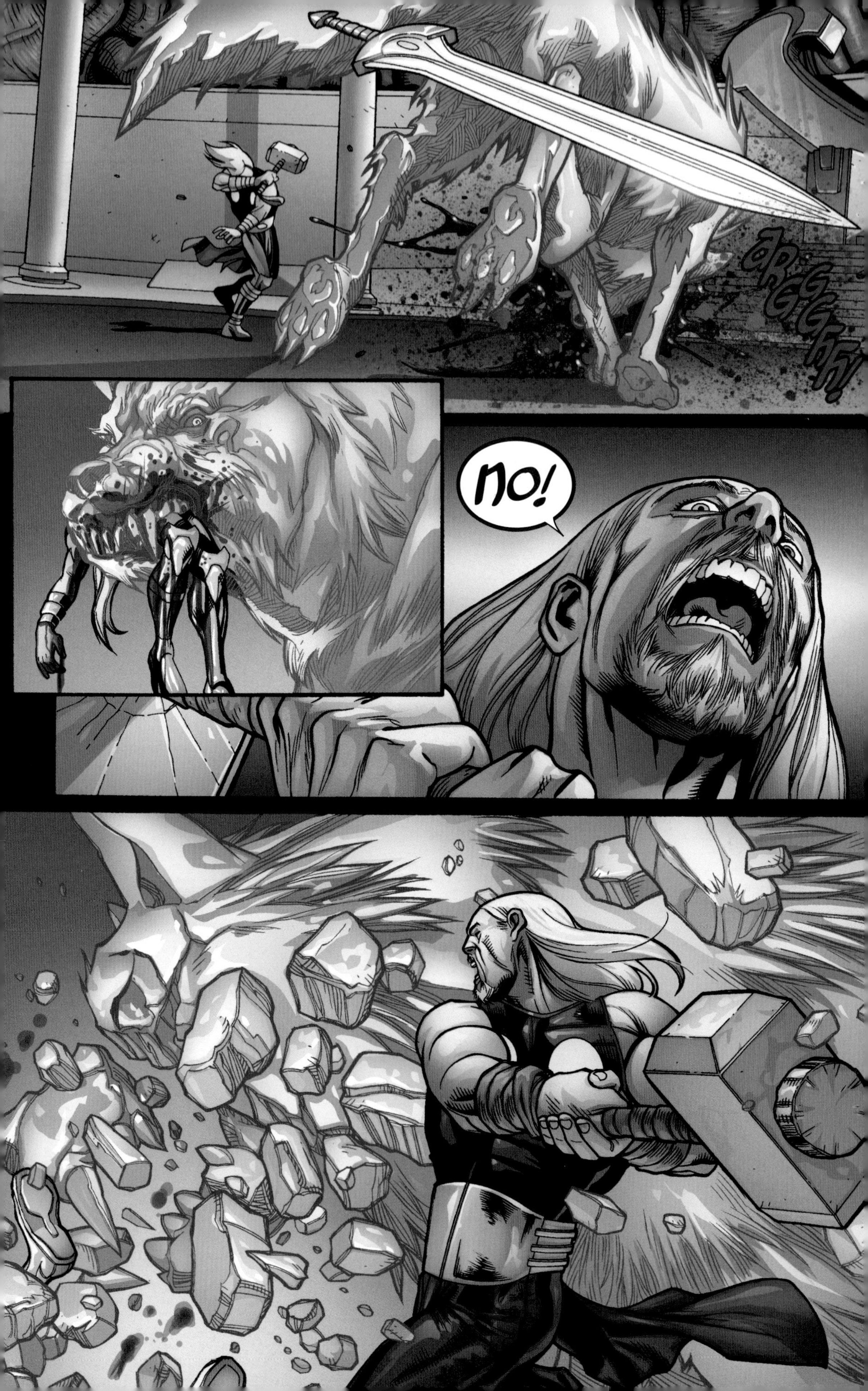
ARGGGHH!
NO!

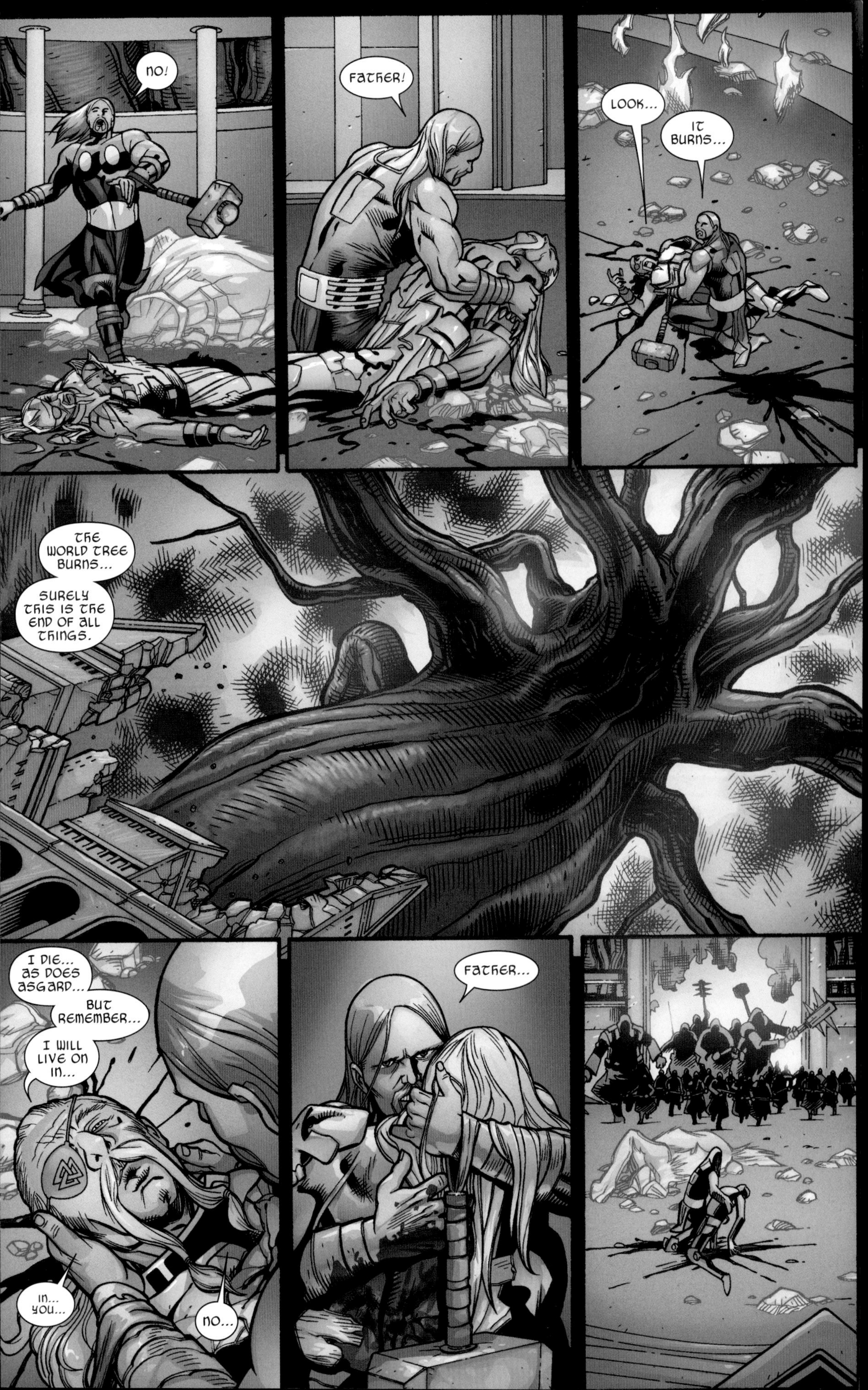
NO!
FATHER!
LOOK...
IT BURNS...
THE WORLD TREE BURNS...
SURELY THIS IS THE END OF ALL THINGS.
I DIE... AS DOES ASGARD...
BUT REMEMBER...
I WILL LIVE ON IN...
IN... YOU...
NO...
FATHER...

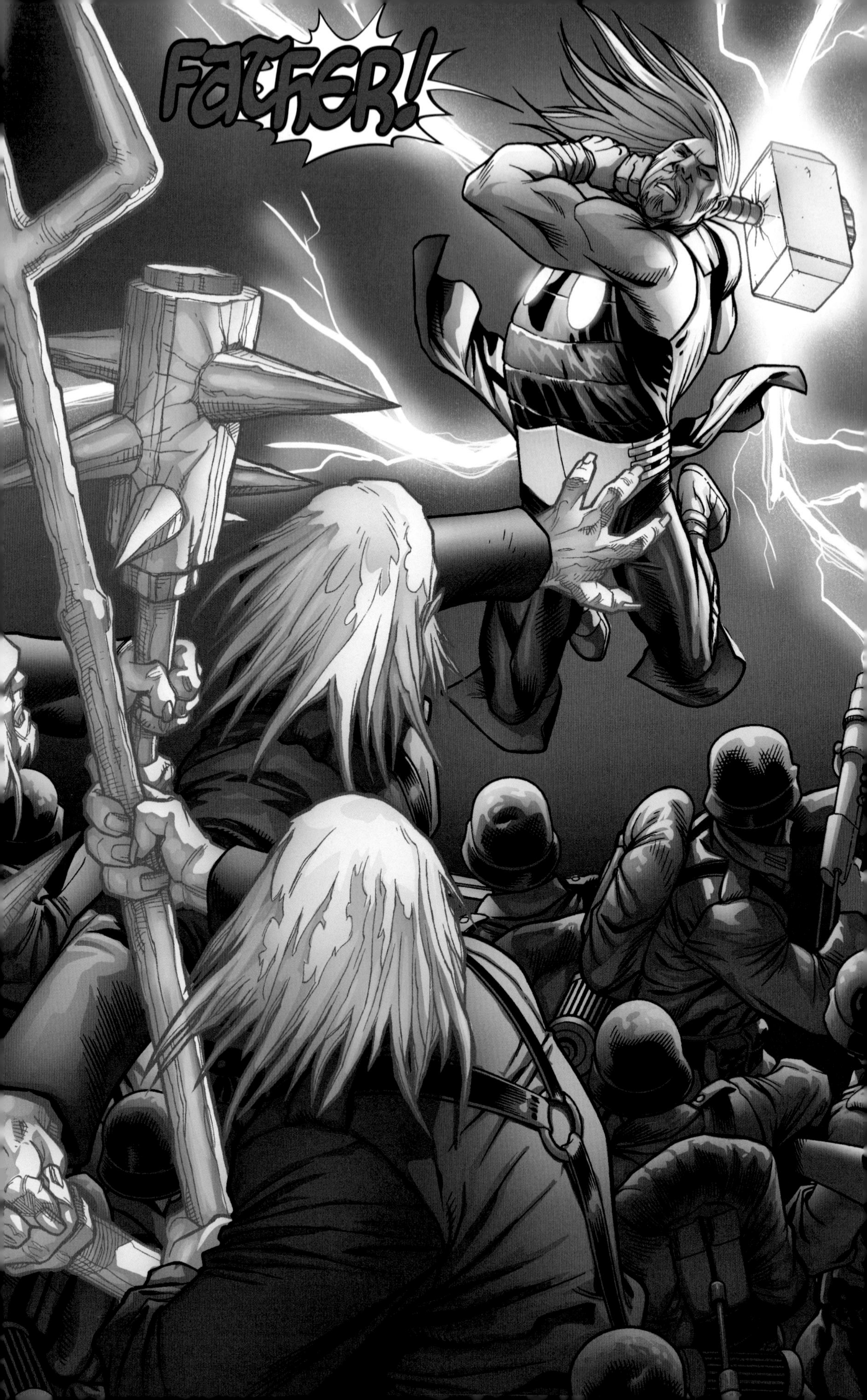
FATHER!

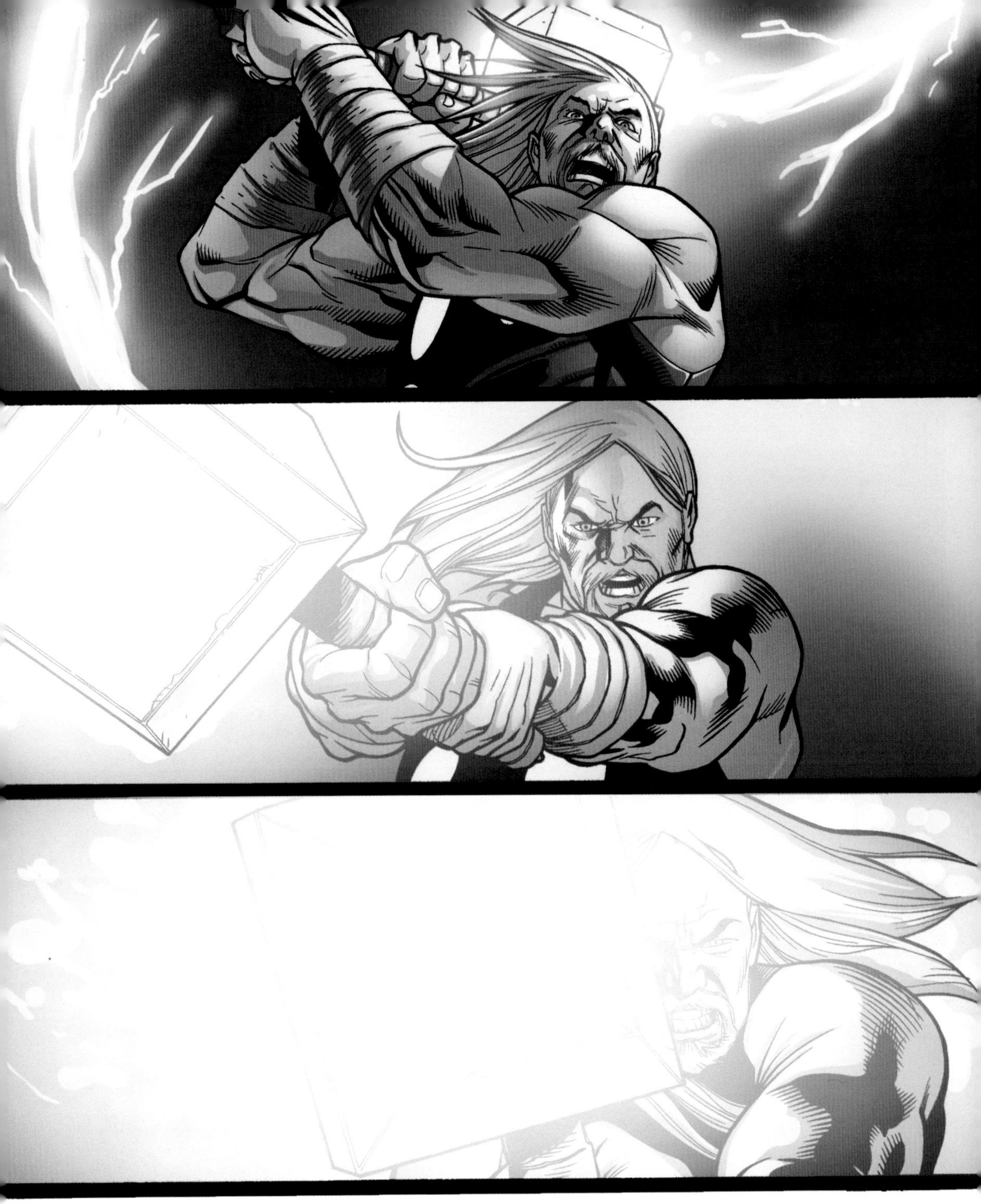

4

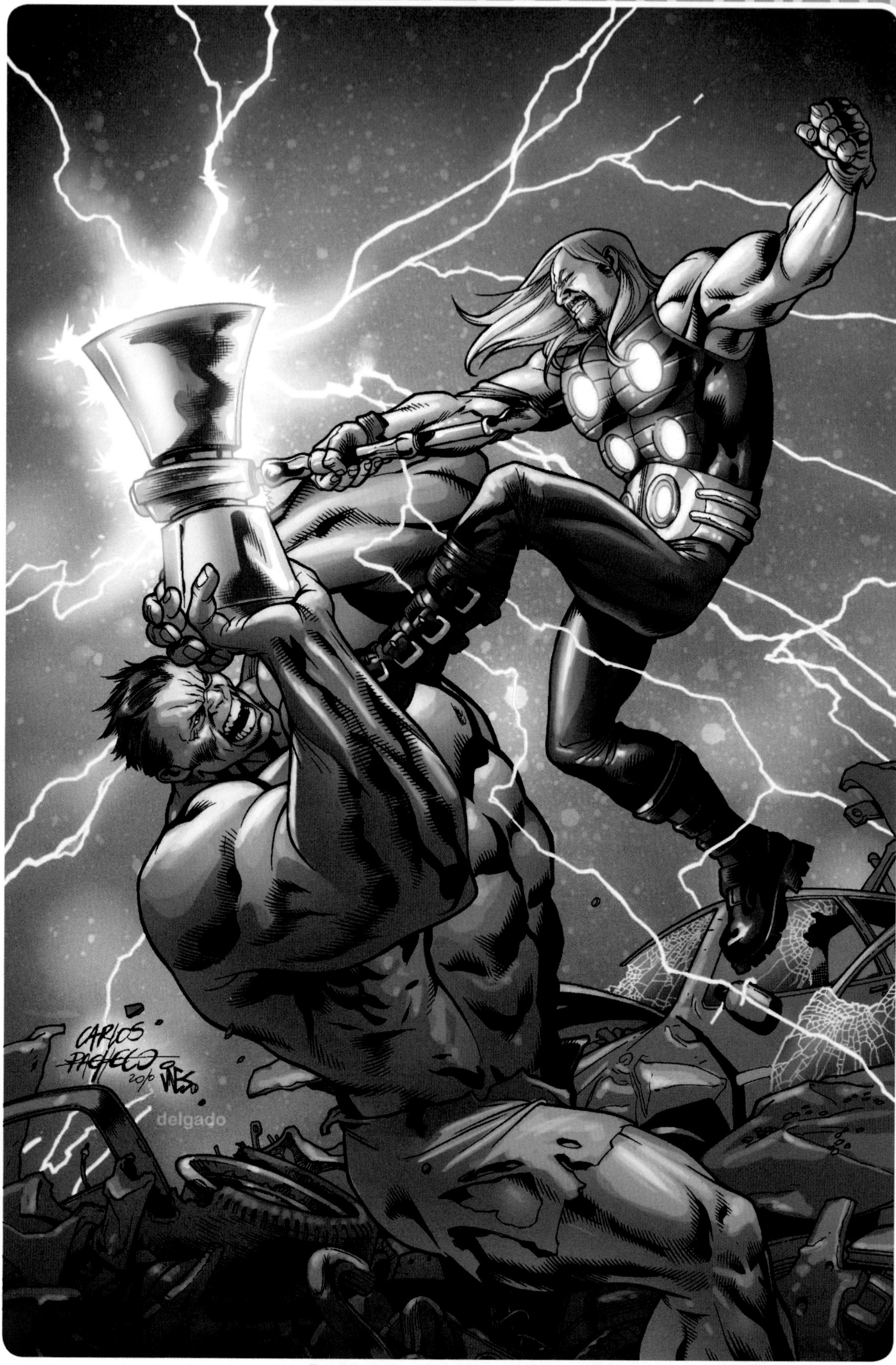
CARLOS
delgado

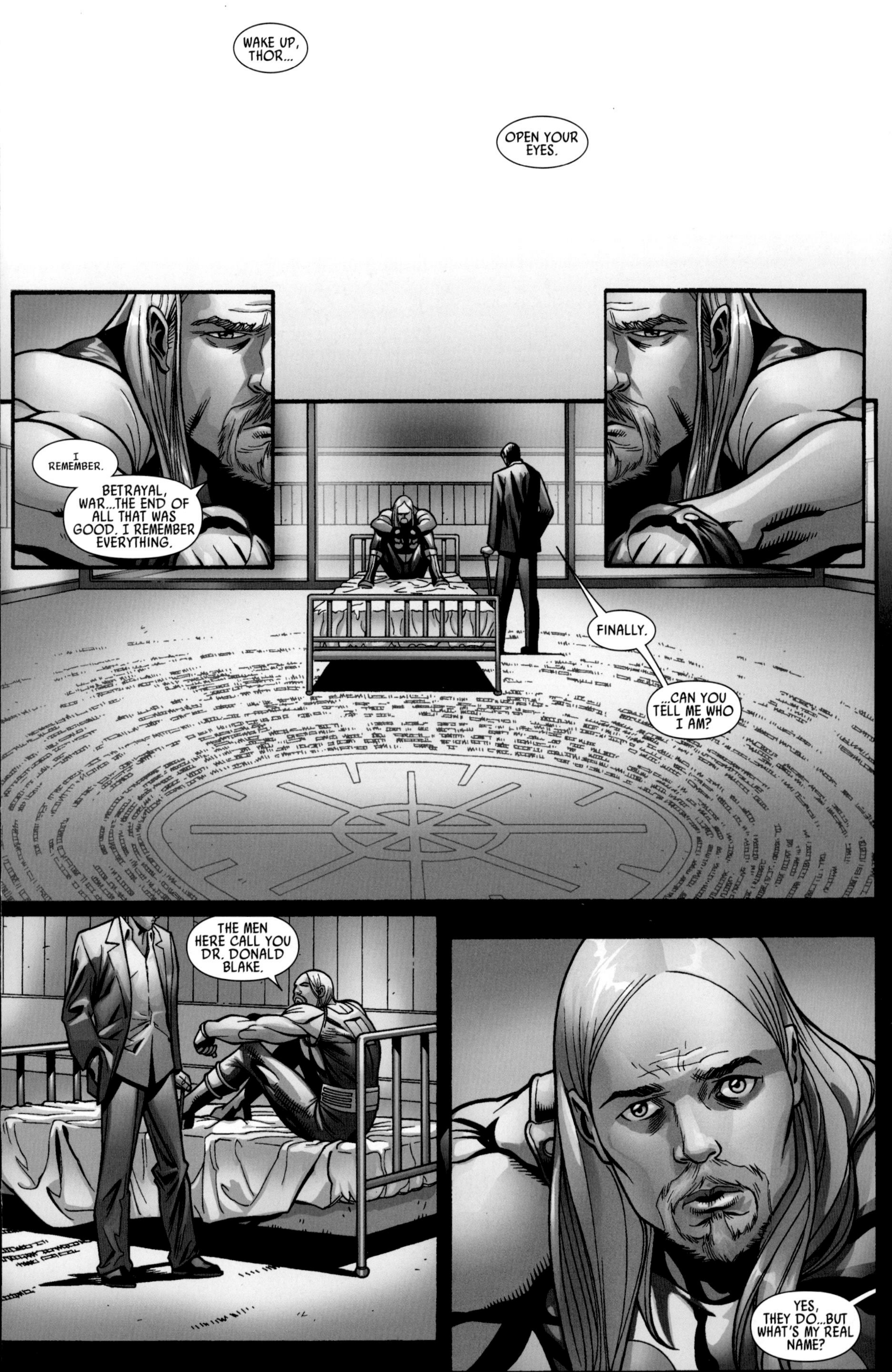
WAKE UP, THOR...
OPEN YOUR EYES.
I REMEMBER.
BETRAYAL, WAR...THE END OF ALL THAT WAS GOOD. I REMEMBER EVERYTHING.
FINALLY.
...CAN YOU TELL ME WHO I AM?
THE MEN HERE CALL YOU DR. DONALD BLAKE.
YES, THEY DO...BUT WHAT'S MY REAL NAME?

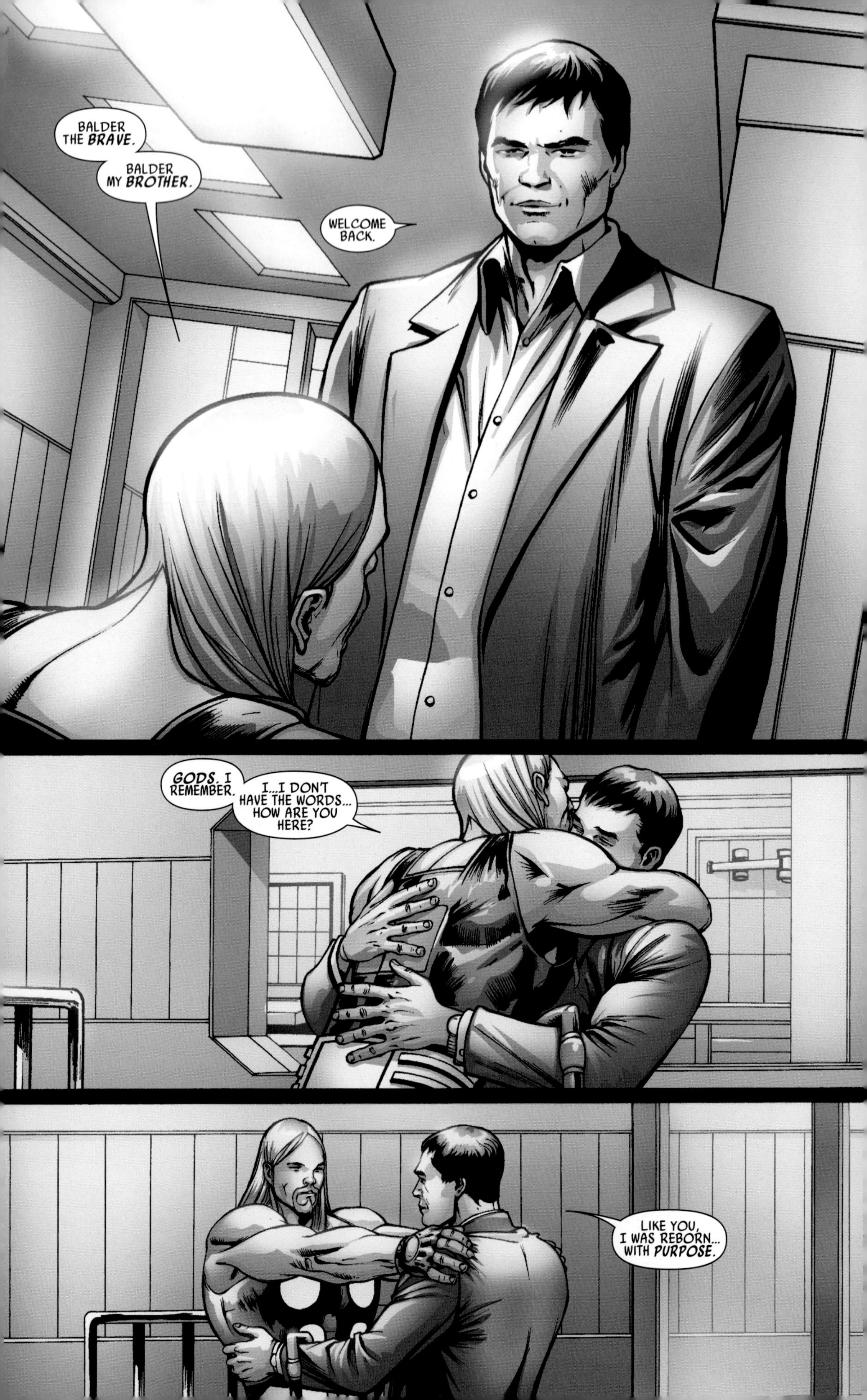
BALDER THE *BRAVE*.
BALDER MY *BROTHER*.
WELCOME BACK.
GODS. I REMEMBER.
I...I DON'T HAVE THE WORDS... HOW ARE YOU HERE?
LIKE YOU, I WAS REBORN... WITH *PURPOSE*.

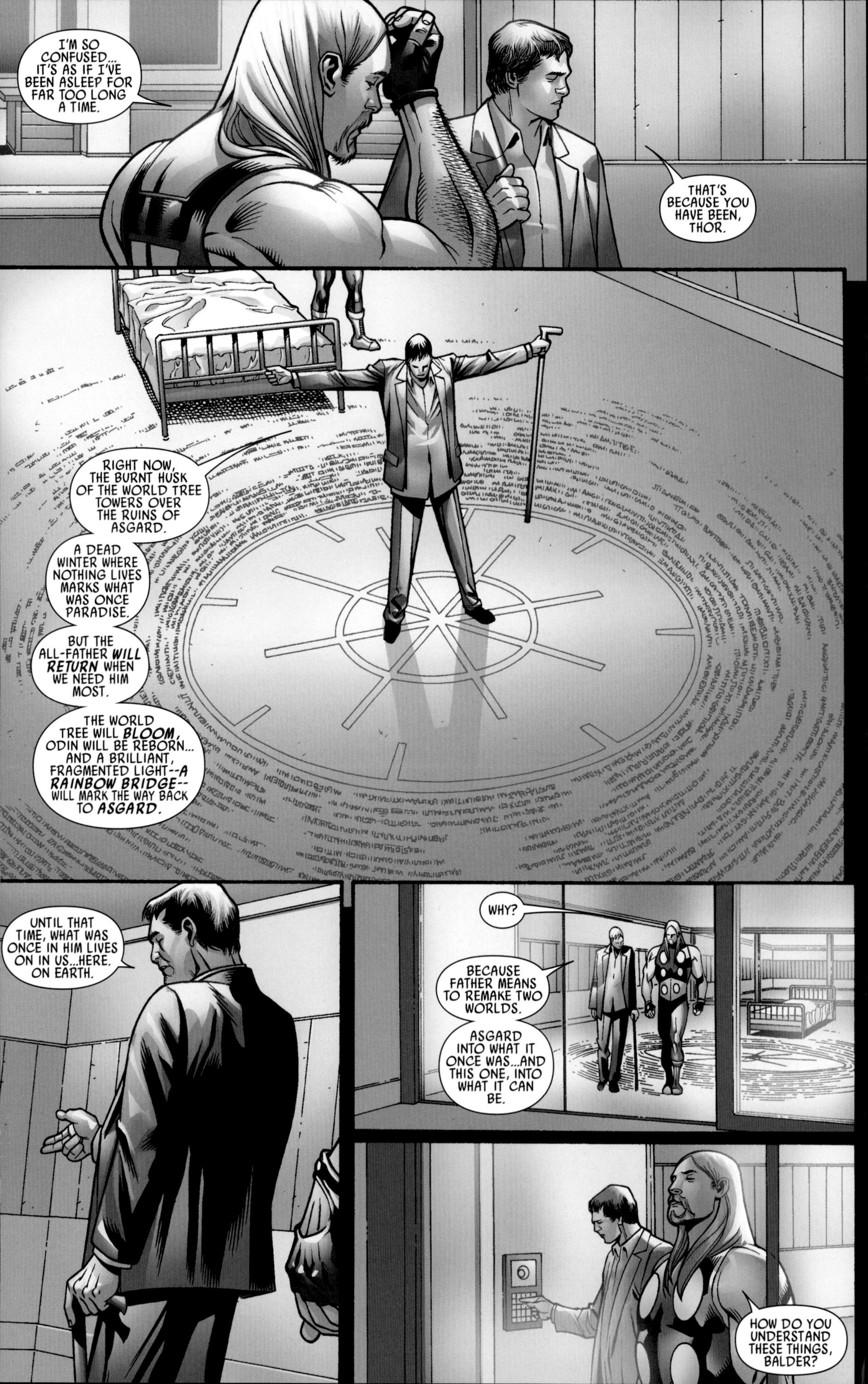
I'M SO CONFUSED... IT'S AS IF I'VE BEEN ASLEEP FOR FAR TOO LONG A TIME.
THAT'S BECAUSE YOU HAVE BEEN, THOR.
RIGHT NOW, THE BURNT HUSK OF THE WORLD TREE TOWERS OVER THE RUINS OF ASGARD.
A DEAD WINTER WHERE NOTHING LIVES MARKS WHAT WAS ONCE PARADISE.
BUT THE ALL-FATHER *WILL RETURN* WHEN WE NEED HIM MOST.
THE WORLD TREE WILL *BLOOM*, ODIN WILL BE REBORN... AND A BRILLIANT, FRAGMENTED LIGHT--*A RAINBOW BRIDGE*--WILL MARK THE WAY BACK TO *ASGARD*.
UNTIL THAT TIME, WHAT WAS ONCE IN HIM LIVES ON IN US...HERE. ON EARTH.
WHY?
BECAUSE FATHER MEANS TO REMAKE TWO WORLDS.
ASGARD INTO WHAT IT ONCE WAS...AND THIS ONE, INTO WHAT IT CAN BE.
HOW DO YOU UNDERSTAND THESE THINGS, BALDER?

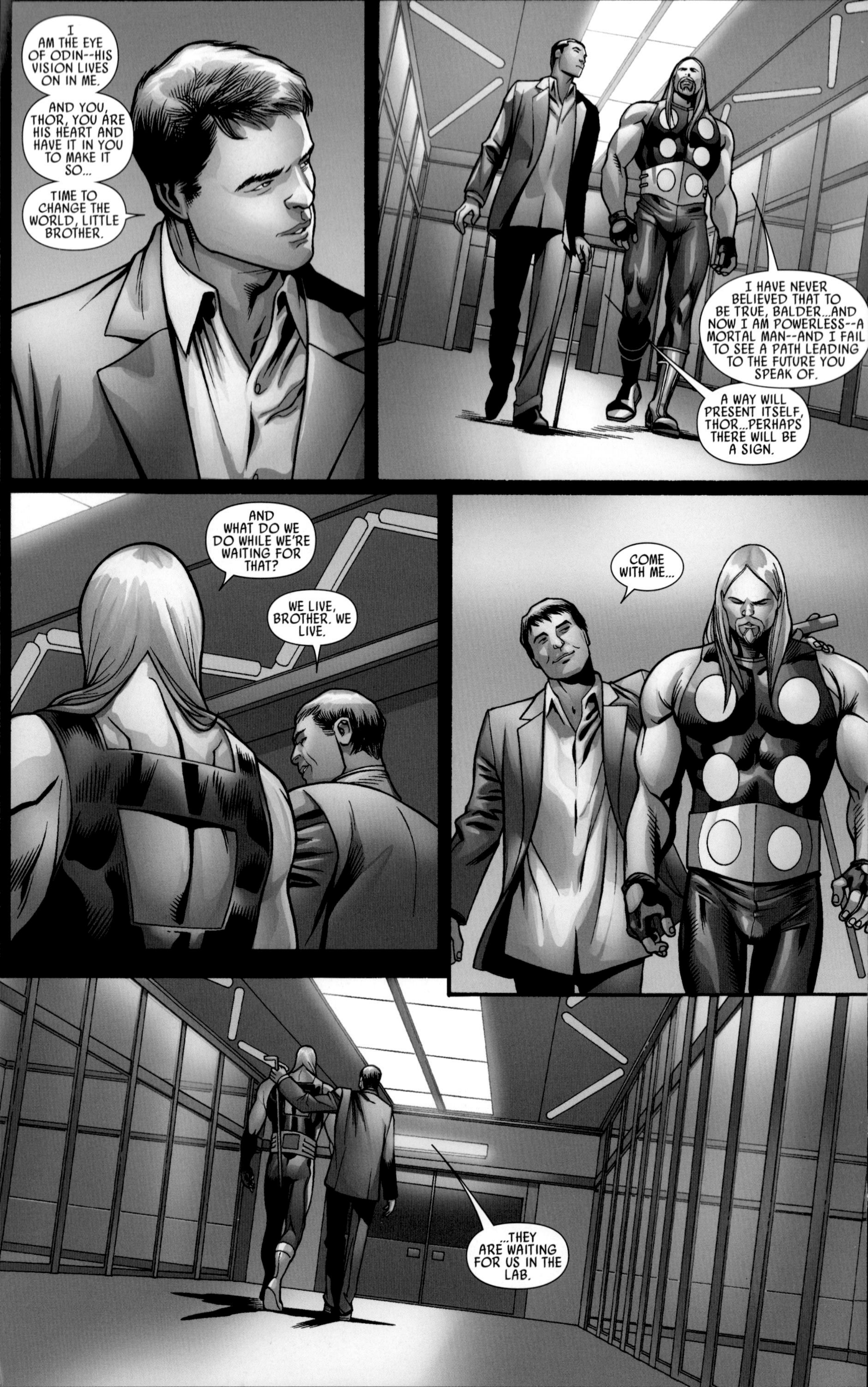
I AM THE EYE OF ODIN--HIS VISION LIVES ON IN ME.
AND YOU, THOR, YOU ARE HIS HEART AND HAVE IT IN YOU TO MAKE IT SO...
TIME TO CHANGE THE WORLD, LITTLE BROTHER.
I HAVE NEVER BELIEVED THAT TO BE TRUE, BALDER...AND NOW I AM POWERLESS--A MORTAL MAN--AND I FAIL TO SEE A PATH LEADING TO THE FUTURE YOU SPEAK OF.
A WAY WILL PRESENT ITSELF, THOR...PERHAPS THERE WILL BE A SIGN.
AND WHAT DO WE DO WHILE WE'RE WAITING FOR THAT?
WE LIVE, BROTHER. WE LIVE.
COME WITH ME...
...THEY ARE WAITING FOR US IN THE LAB.

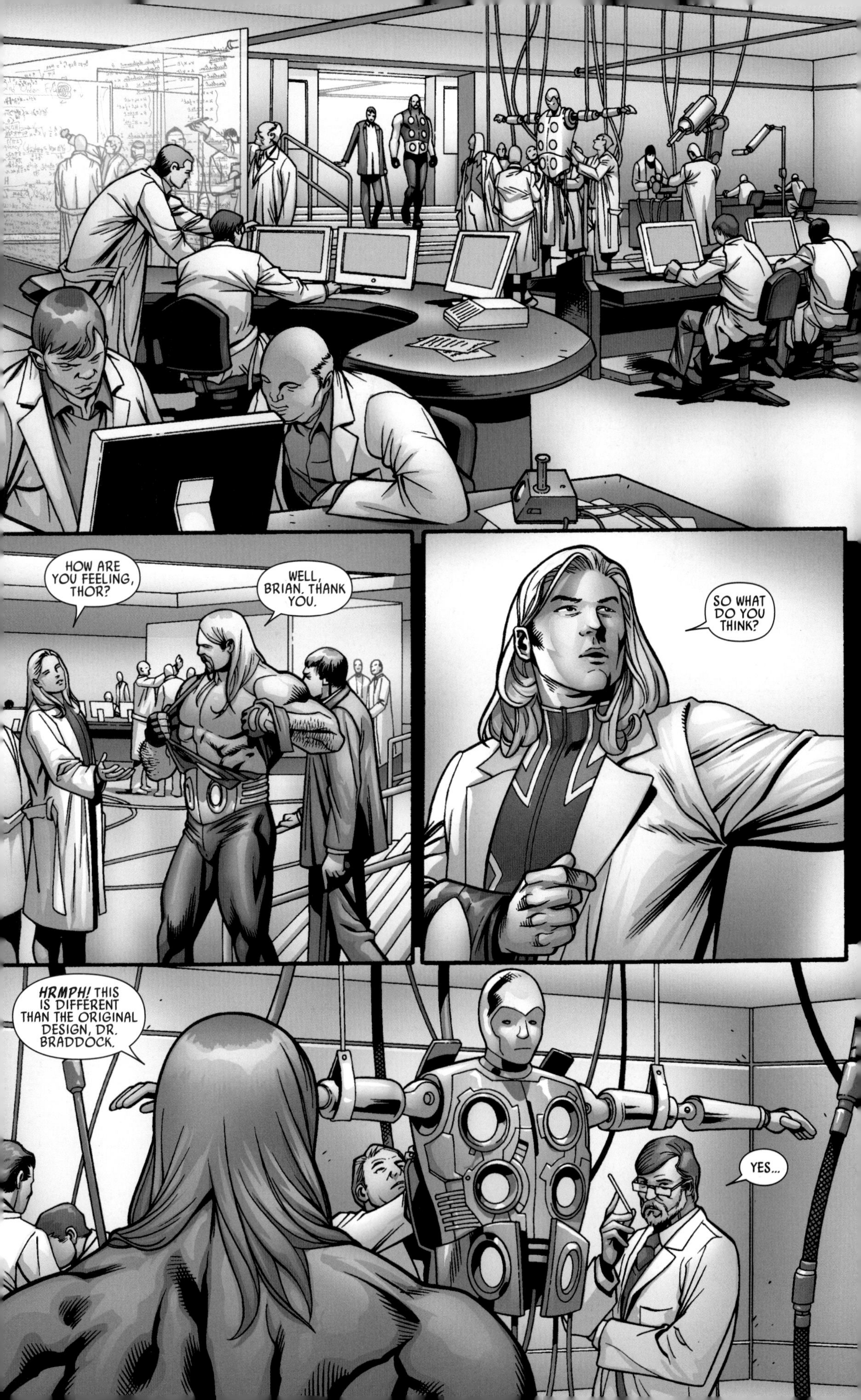
HOW ARE YOU FEELING, THOR?
WELL, BRIAN. THANK YOU.
SO WHAT DO YOU THINK?
HRMPH! THIS IS DIFFERENT THAN THE ORIGINAL DESIGN, DR. BRADDOCK.
YES...

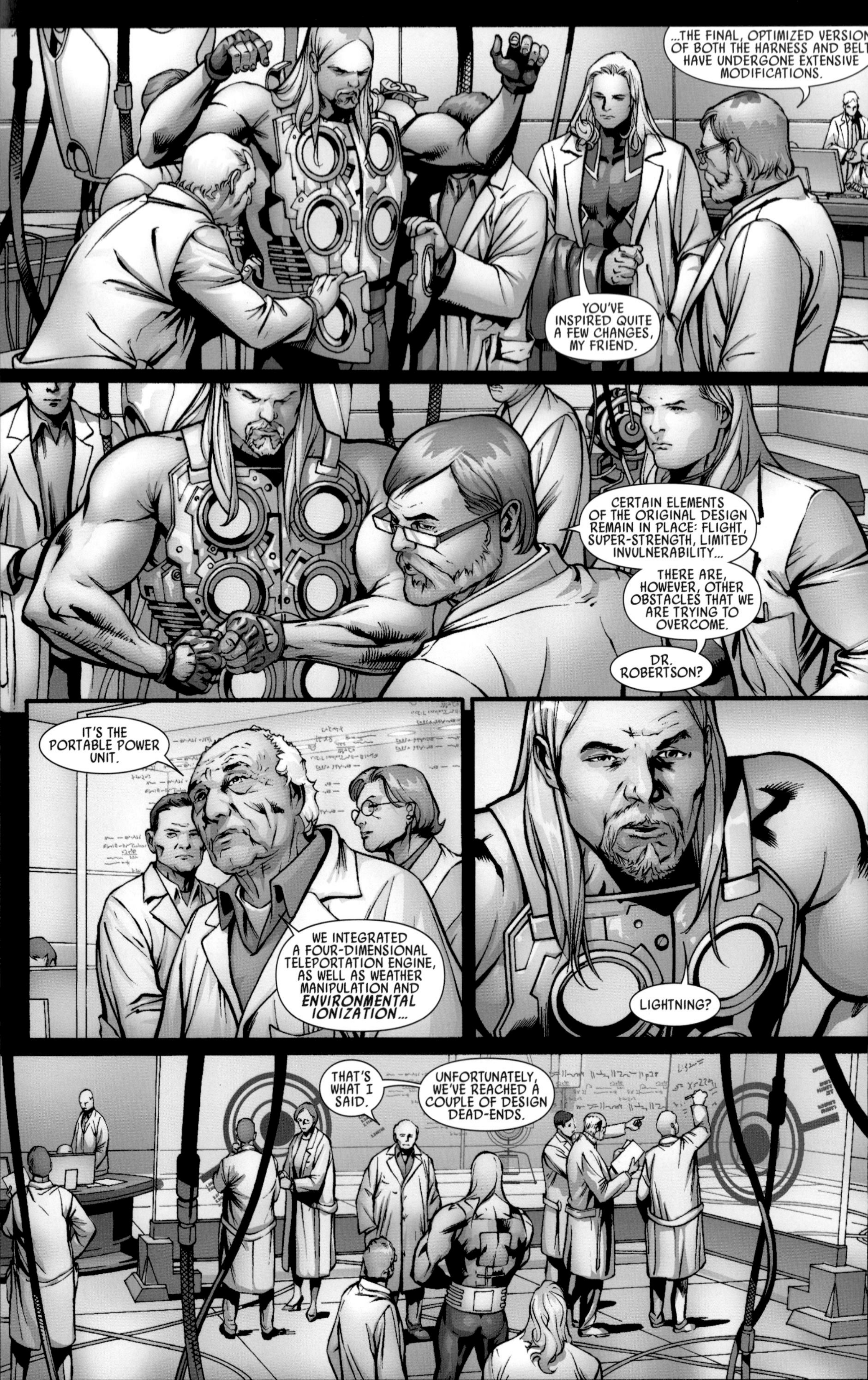
...THE FINAL, OPTIMIZED VERSION OF BOTH THE HARNESS AND BELT HAVE UNDERGONE EXTENSIVE MODIFICATIONS.
YOU'VE INSPIRED QUITE A FEW CHANGES, MY FRIEND.
CERTAIN ELEMENTS OF THE ORIGINAL DESIGN REMAIN IN PLACE: FLIGHT, SUPER-STRENGTH, LIMITED INVULNERABILITY...
THERE ARE, HOWEVER, OTHER OBSTACLES THAT WE ARE TRYING TO OVERCOME.
DR. ROBERTSON?
IT'S THE PORTABLE POWER UNIT.
WE INTEGRATED A FOUR-DIMENSIONAL TELEPORTATION ENGINE, AS WELL AS WEATHER MANIPULATION AND *ENVIRONMENTAL IONIZATION*...
LIGHTNING?
THAT'S WHAT I SAID.
UNFORTUNATELY, WE'VE REACHED A COUPLE OF DESIGN DEAD-ENDS.

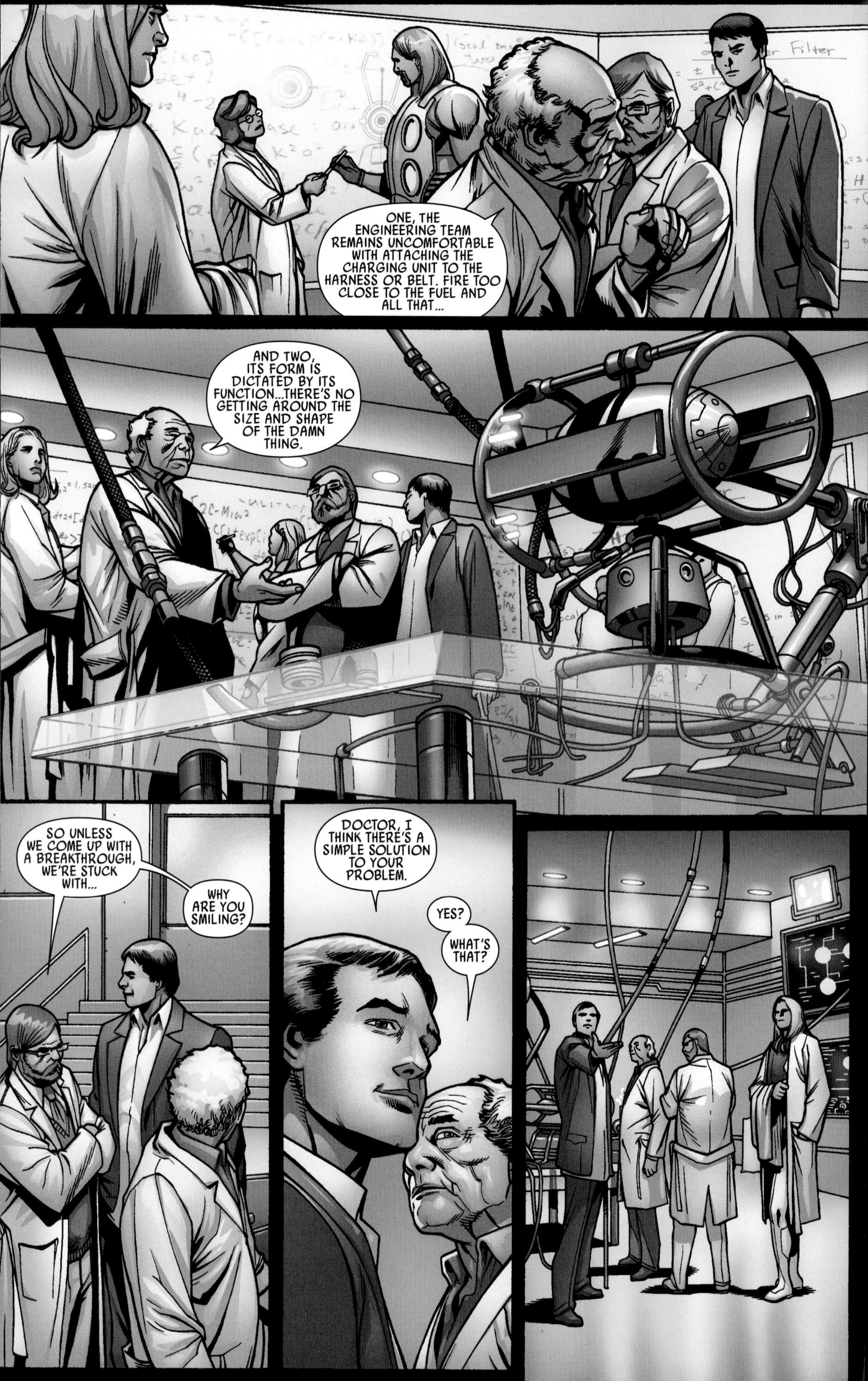
ONE, THE ENGINEERING TEAM REMAINS UNCOMFORTABLE WITH ATTACHING THE CHARGING UNIT TO THE HARNESS OR BELT. FIRE TOO CLOSE TO THE FUEL AND ALL THAT...
AND TWO, ITS FORM IS DICTATED BY ITS FUNCTION...THERE'S NO GETTING AROUND THE SIZE AND SHAPE OF THE DAMN THING.
SO UNLESS WE COME UP WITH A BREAKTHROUGH, WE'RE STUCK WITH...
WHY ARE YOU SMILING?
DOCTOR, I THINK THERE'S A SIMPLE SOLUTION TO YOUR PROBLEM.
YES?
WHAT'S THAT?

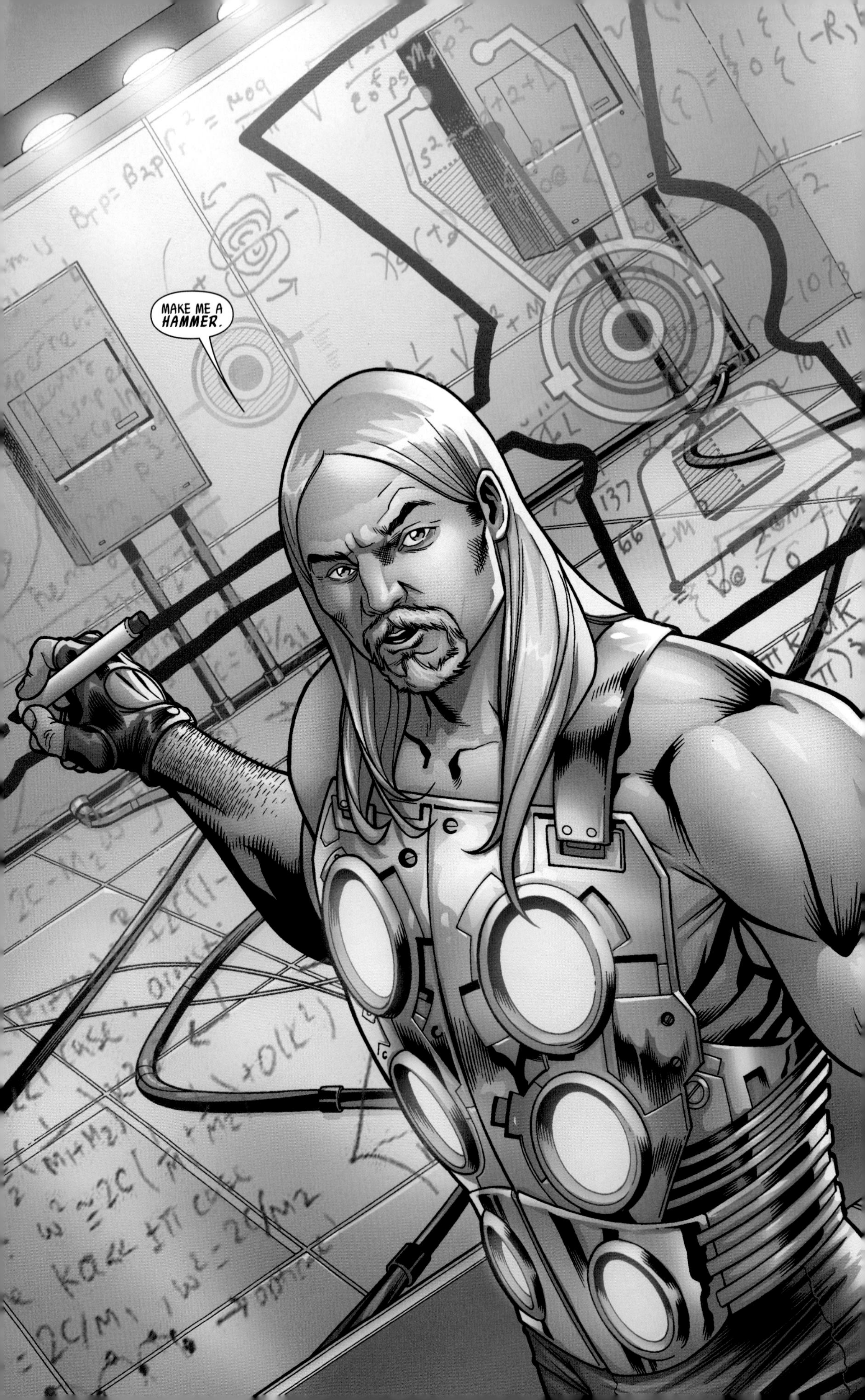
MAKE ME A HAMMER.

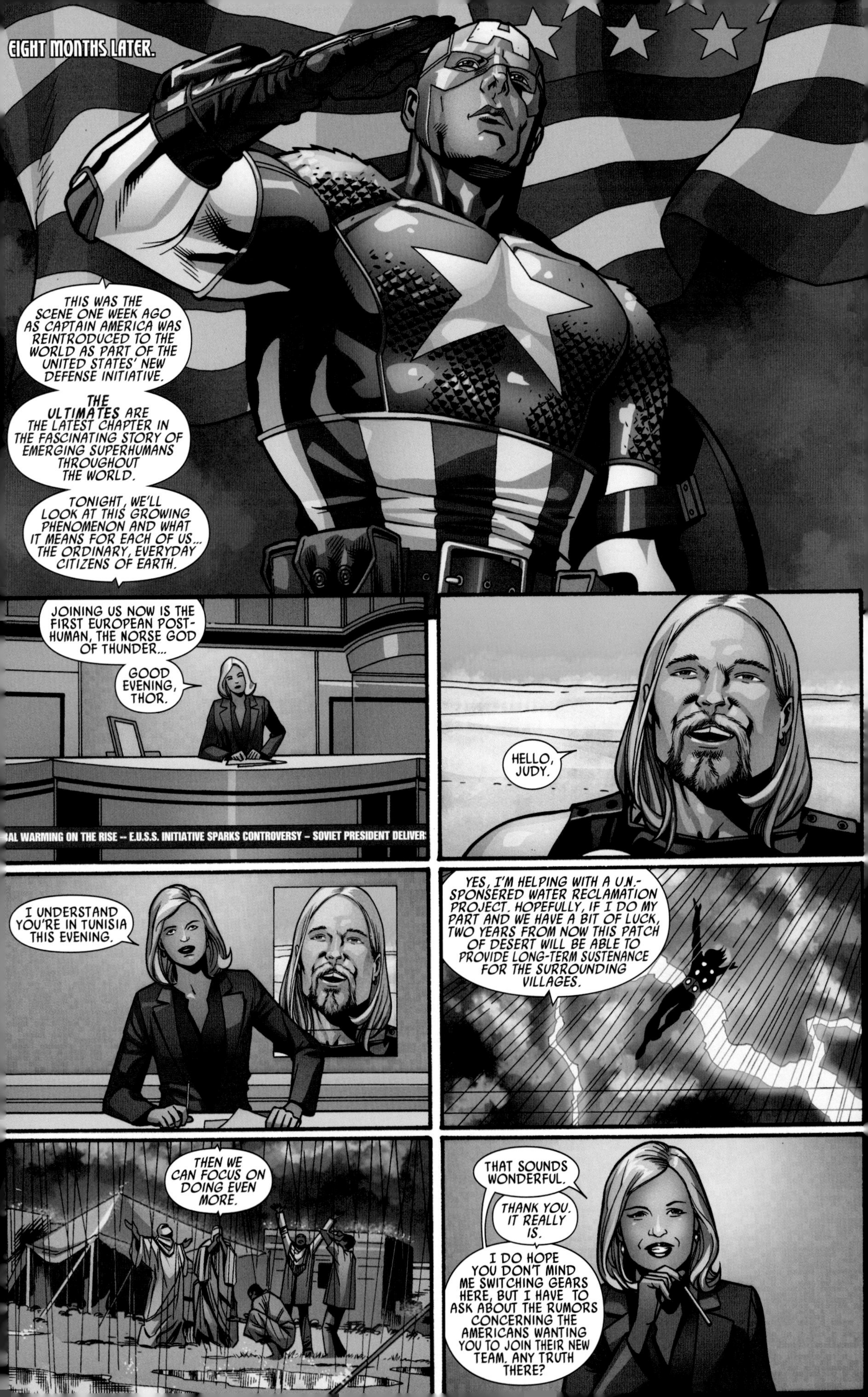
EIGHT MONTHS LATER.
THIS WAS THE SCENE ONE WEEK AGO AS CAPTAIN AMERICA WAS REINTRODUCED TO THE WORLD AS PART OF THE UNITED STATES' NEW DEFENSE INITIATIVE.
THE ULTIMATES ARE THE LATEST CHAPTER IN THE FASCINATING STORY OF EMERGING SUPERHUMANS THROUGHOUT THE WORLD.
TONIGHT, WE'LL LOOK AT THIS GROWING PHENOMENON AND WHAT IT MEANS FOR EACH OF US... THE ORDINARY, EVERYDAY CITIZENS OF EARTH.
JOINING US NOW IS THE FIRST EUROPEAN POST-HUMAN, THE NORSE GOD OF THUNDER...
GOOD EVENING, THOR.
BAL WARMING ON THE RISE -- E.U.S.S. INITIATIVE SPARKS CONTROVERSY -- SOVIET PRESIDENT DELIVER
HELLO, JUDY.
I UNDERSTAND YOU'RE IN TUNISIA THIS EVENING.
YES, I'M HELPING WITH A U.N.-SPONSERED WATER RECLAMATION PROJECT. HOPEFULLY, IF I DO MY PART AND WE HAVE A BIT OF LUCK, TWO YEARS FROM NOW THIS PATCH OF DESERT WILL BE ABLE TO PROVIDE LONG-TERM SUSTENANCE FOR THE SURROUNDING VILLAGES.
THEN WE CAN FOCUS ON DOING EVEN MORE.
THAT SOUNDS WONDERFUL.
THANK YOU. IT REALLY IS.
I DO HOPE YOU DON'T MIND ME SWITCHING GEARS HERE, BUT I HAVE TO ASK ABOUT THE RUMORS CONCERNING THE AMERICANS WANTING YOU TO JOIN THEIR NEW TEAM. ANY TRUTH THERE?

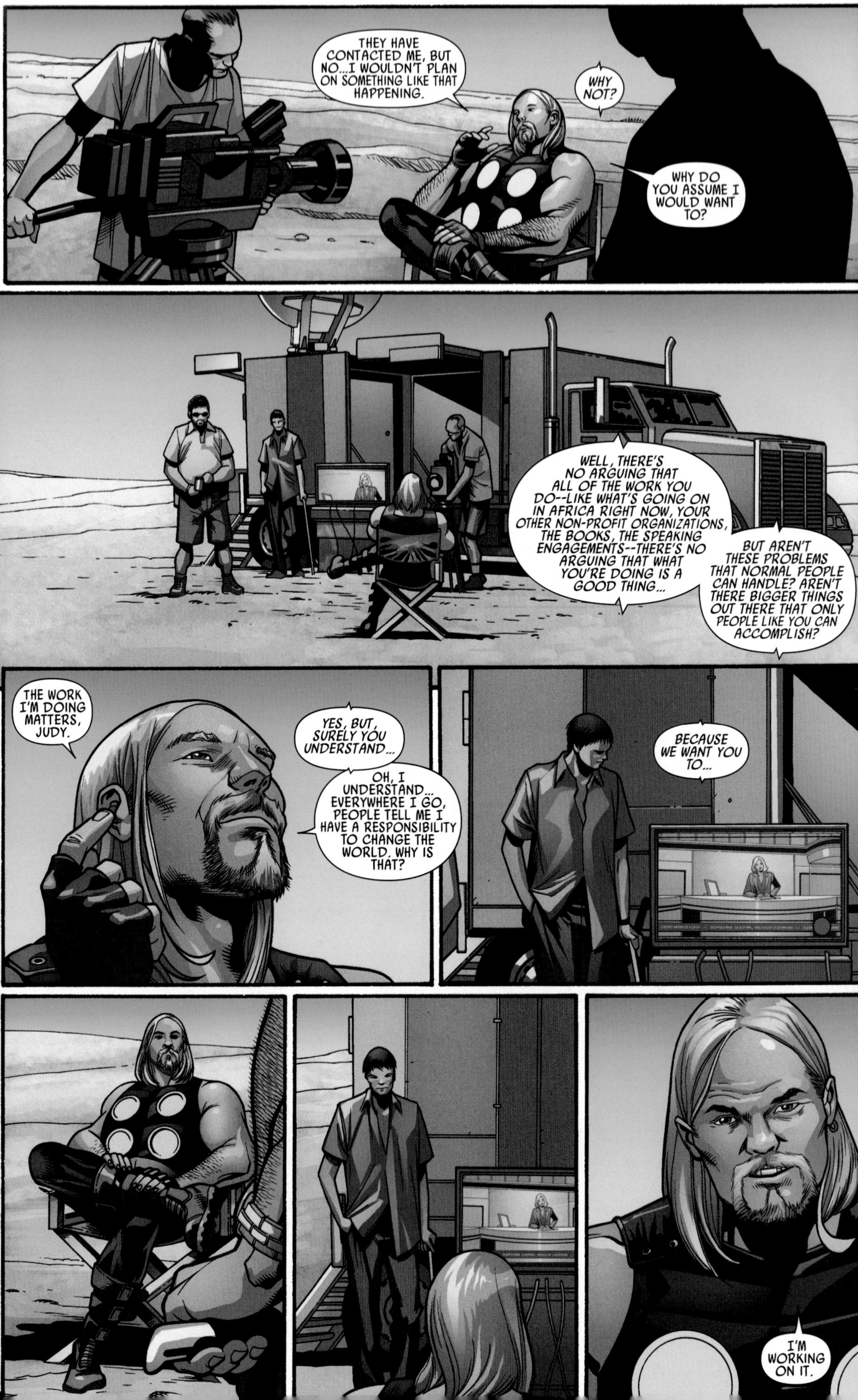
THEY HAVE CONTACTED ME, BUT NO...I WOULDN'T PLAN ON SOMETHING LIKE THAT HAPPENING.
WHY NOT?
WHY DO YOU ASSUME I WOULD WANT TO?
WELL, THERE'S NO ARGUING THAT ALL OF THE WORK YOU DO--LIKE WHAT'S GOING ON IN AFRICA RIGHT NOW, YOUR OTHER NON-PROFIT ORGANIZATIONS, THE BOOKS, THE SPEAKING ENGAGEMENTS--THERE'S NO ARGUING THAT WHAT YOU'RE DOING IS A GOOD THING...
BUT AREN'T THESE PROBLEMS THAT NORMAL PEOPLE CAN HANDLE? AREN'T THERE BIGGER THINGS OUT THERE THAT ONLY PEOPLE LIKE YOU CAN ACCOMPLISH?
THE WORK I'M DOING MATTERS, JUDY.
YES, BUT, SURELY YOU UNDERSTAND...
OH, I UNDERSTAND... EVERYWHERE I GO, PEOPLE TELL ME I HAVE A RESPONSIBILITY TO CHANGE THE WORLD. WHY IS THAT?
BECAUSE WE WANT YOU TO...
I'M WORKING ON IT.

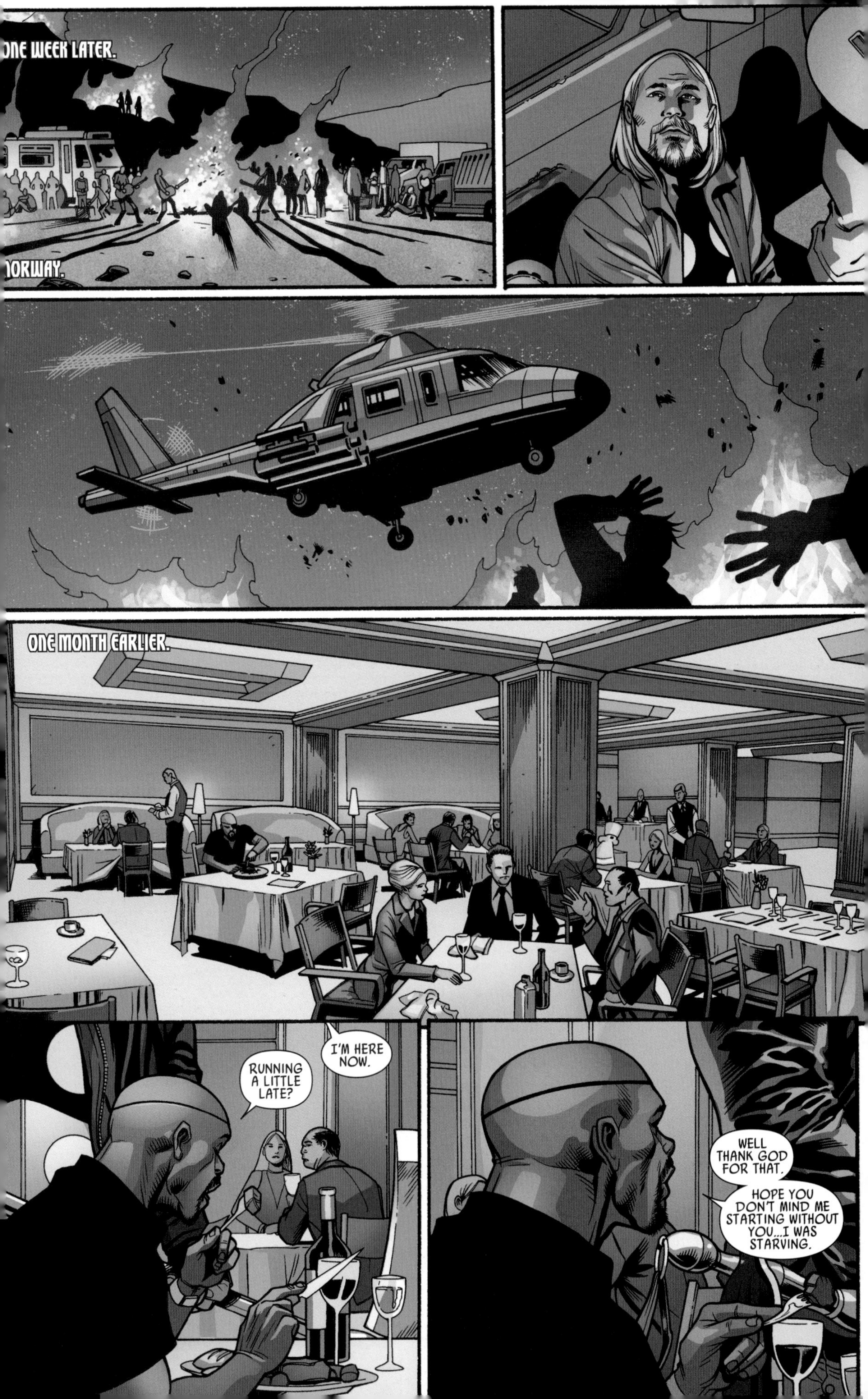

ONE WEEK LATER.
NORWAY.
ONE MONTH EARLIER.
RUNNING A LITTLE LATE?
I'M HERE NOW.
WELL THANK GOD FOR THAT.
HOPE YOU DON'T MIND ME STARTING WITHOUT YOU...I WAS STARVING.

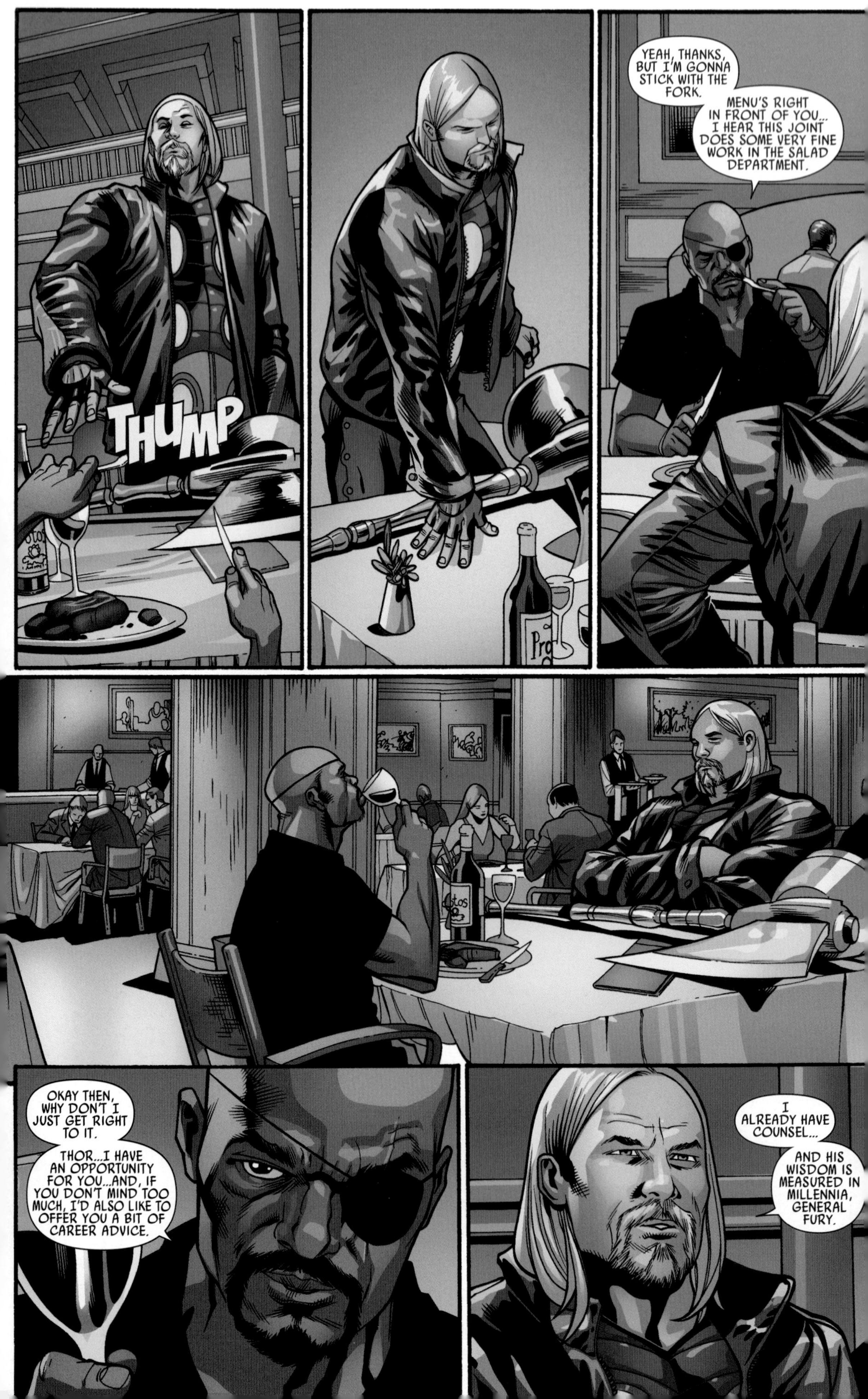
THUMP
YEAH, THANKS, BUT I'M GONNA STICK WITH THE FORK.
MENU'S RIGHT IN FRONT OF YOU... I HEAR THIS JOINT DOES SOME VERY FINE WORK IN THE SALAD DEPARTMENT.
OKAY THEN, WHY DON'T I JUST GET RIGHT TO IT.
THOR...I HAVE AN OPPORTUNITY FOR YOU...AND, IF YOU DON'T MIND TOO MUCH, I'D ALSO LIKE TO OFFER YOU A BIT OF CAREER ADVICE.
I ALREADY HAVE COUNSEL...
AND HIS WISDOM IS MEASURED IN MILLENNIA, GENERAL FURY.

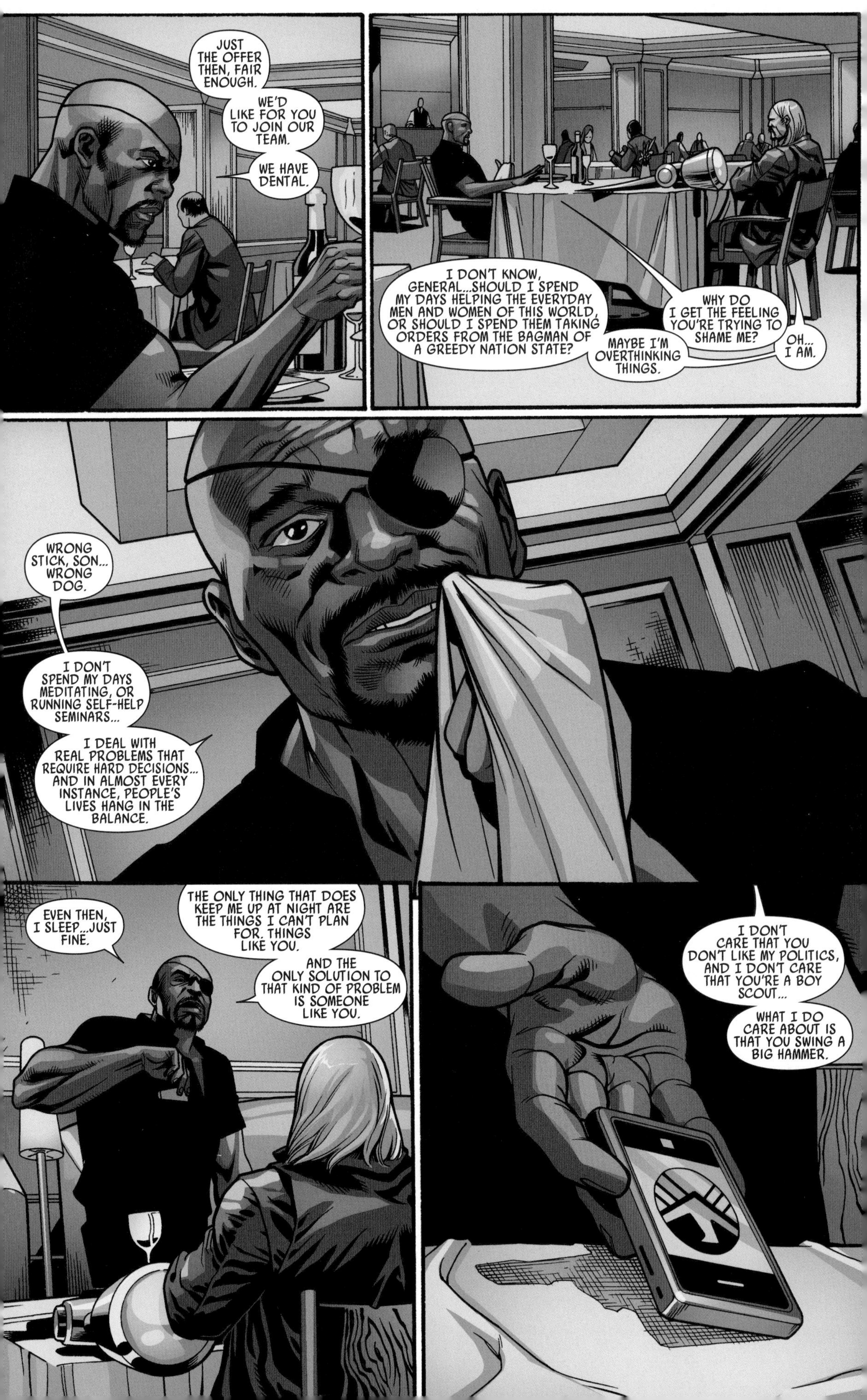
JUST THE OFFER THEN, FAIR ENOUGH.
WE'D LIKE FOR YOU TO JOIN OUR TEAM.
WE HAVE DENTAL.
I DON'T KNOW, GENERAL...SHOULD I SPEND MY DAYS HELPING THE EVERYDAY MEN AND WOMEN OF THIS WORLD, OR SHOULD I SPEND THEM TAKING ORDERS FROM THE BAGMAN OF A GREEDY NATION STATE?
WHY DO I GET THE FEELING YOU'RE TRYING TO SHAME ME?
MAYBE I'M OVERTHINKING THINGS.
OH... I AM.
WRONG STICK, SON... WRONG DOG.
I DON'T SPEND MY DAYS MEDITATING, OR RUNNING SELF-HELP SEMINARS...
I DEAL WITH REAL PROBLEMS THAT REQUIRE HARD DECISIONS... AND IN ALMOST EVERY INSTANCE, PEOPLE'S LIVES HANG IN THE BALANCE.
EVEN THEN, I SLEEP...JUST FINE.
THE ONLY THING THAT DOES KEEP ME UP AT NIGHT ARE THE THINGS I CAN'T PLAN FOR. THINGS LIKE YOU.
AND THE ONLY SOLUTION TO THAT KIND OF PROBLEM IS SOMEONE LIKE YOU.
I DON'T CARE THAT YOU DON'T LIKE MY POLITICS, AND I DON'T CARE THAT YOU'RE A BOY SCOUT...
WHAT I DO CARE ABOUT IS THAT YOU SWING A BIG HAMMER.

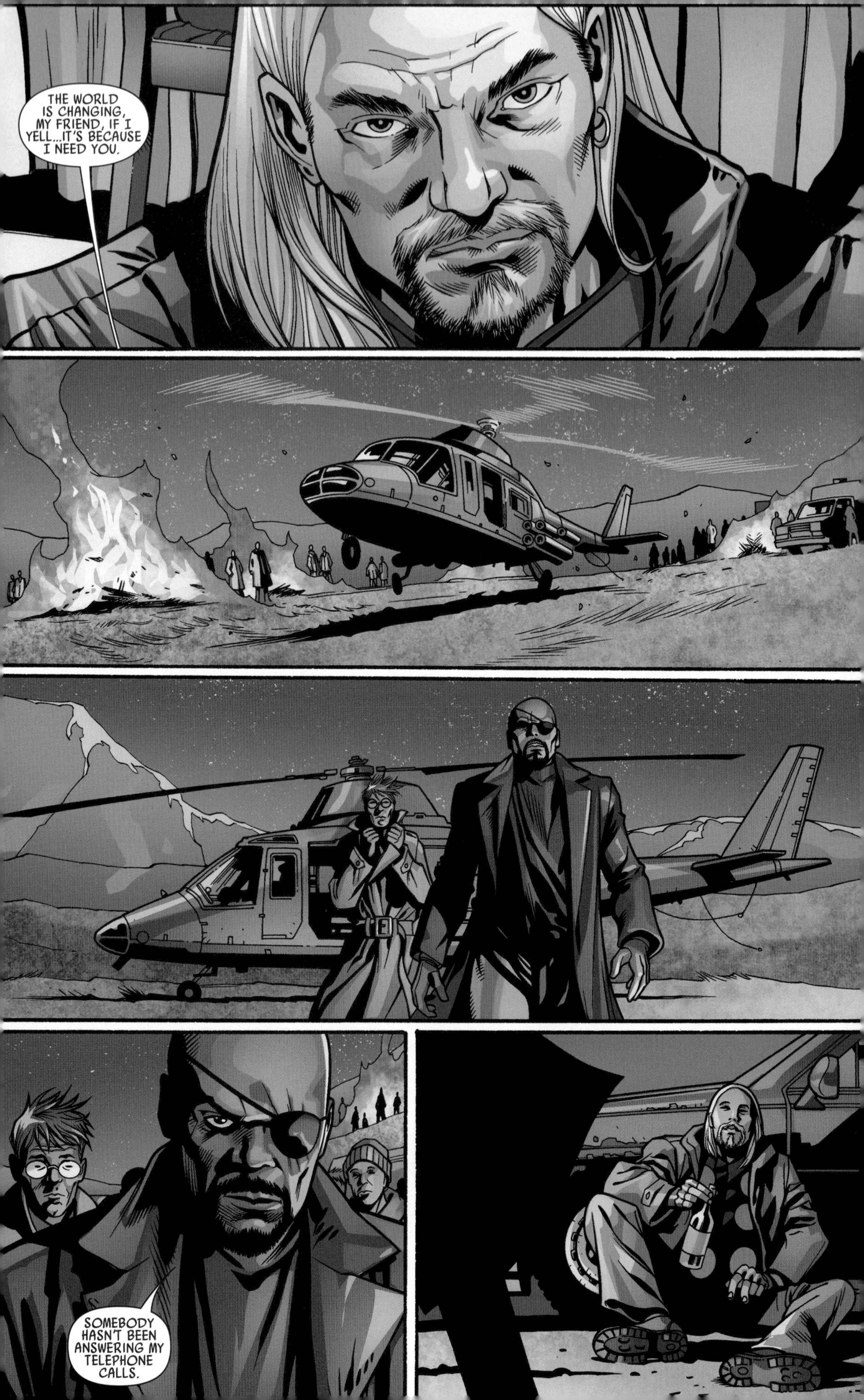
THE WORLD IS CHANGING, MY FRIEND, IF I YELL...IT'S BECAUSE I NEED YOU.
SOMEBODY HASN'T BEEN ANSWERING MY TELEPHONE CALLS.

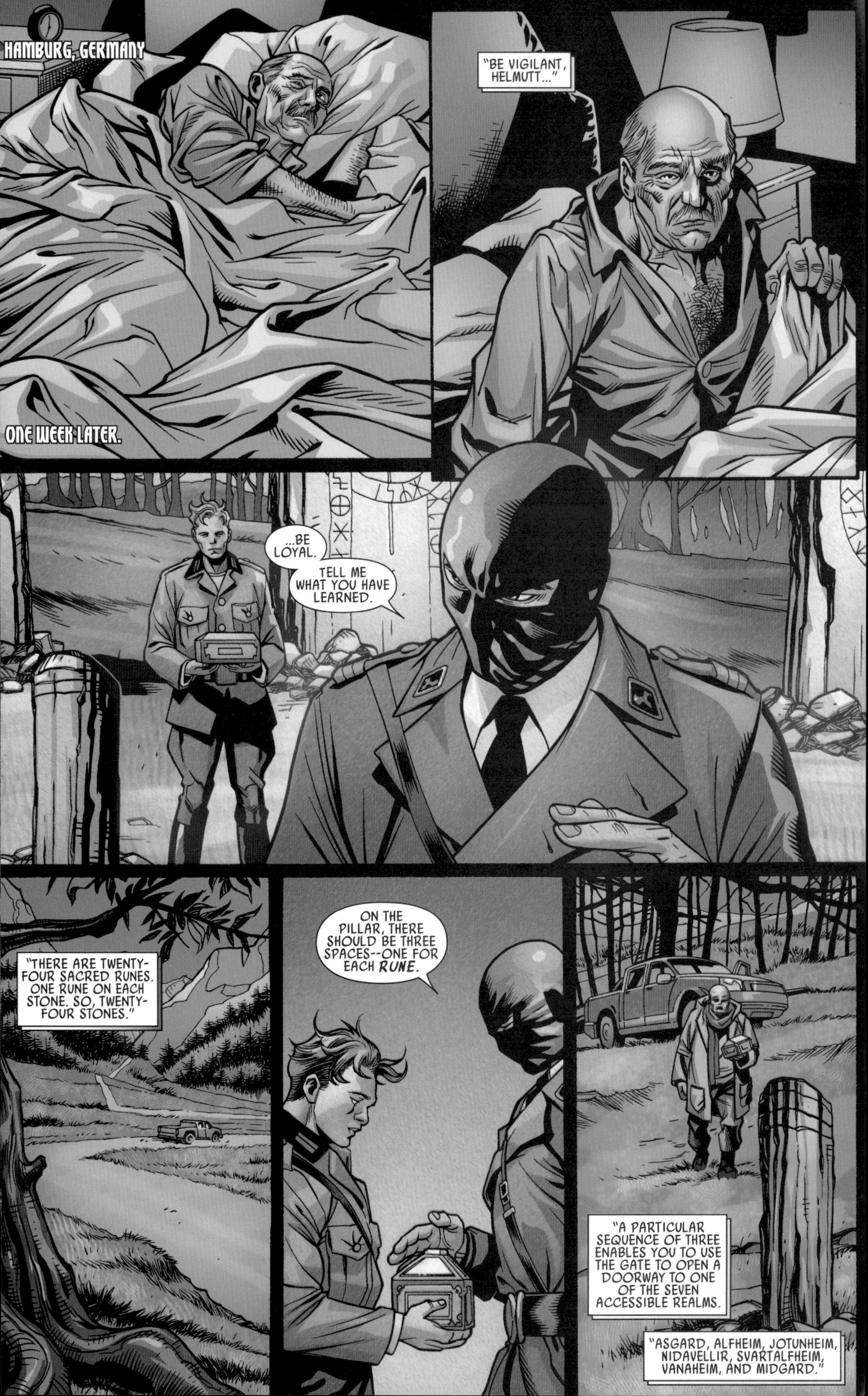
HAMBURG, GERMANY
ONE WEEK LATER.
"BE VIGILANT, HELMUTT..."
...BE LOYAL.
TELL ME WHAT YOU HAVE LEARNED.
"THERE ARE TWENTY-FOUR SACRED RUNES. ONE RUNE ON EACH STONE. SO, TWENTY-FOUR STONES."
ON THE PILLAR, THERE SHOULD BE THREE SPACES--ONE FOR EACH RUNE.
"A PARTICULAR SEQUENCE OF THREE ENABLES YOU TO USE THE GATE TO OPEN A DOORWAY TO ONE OF THE SEVEN ACCESSIBLE REALMS.
"ASGARD, ALFHEIM, JOTUNHEIM, NIDAVELLIR, SVARTALFHEIM, VANAHEIM, AND MIDGARD."

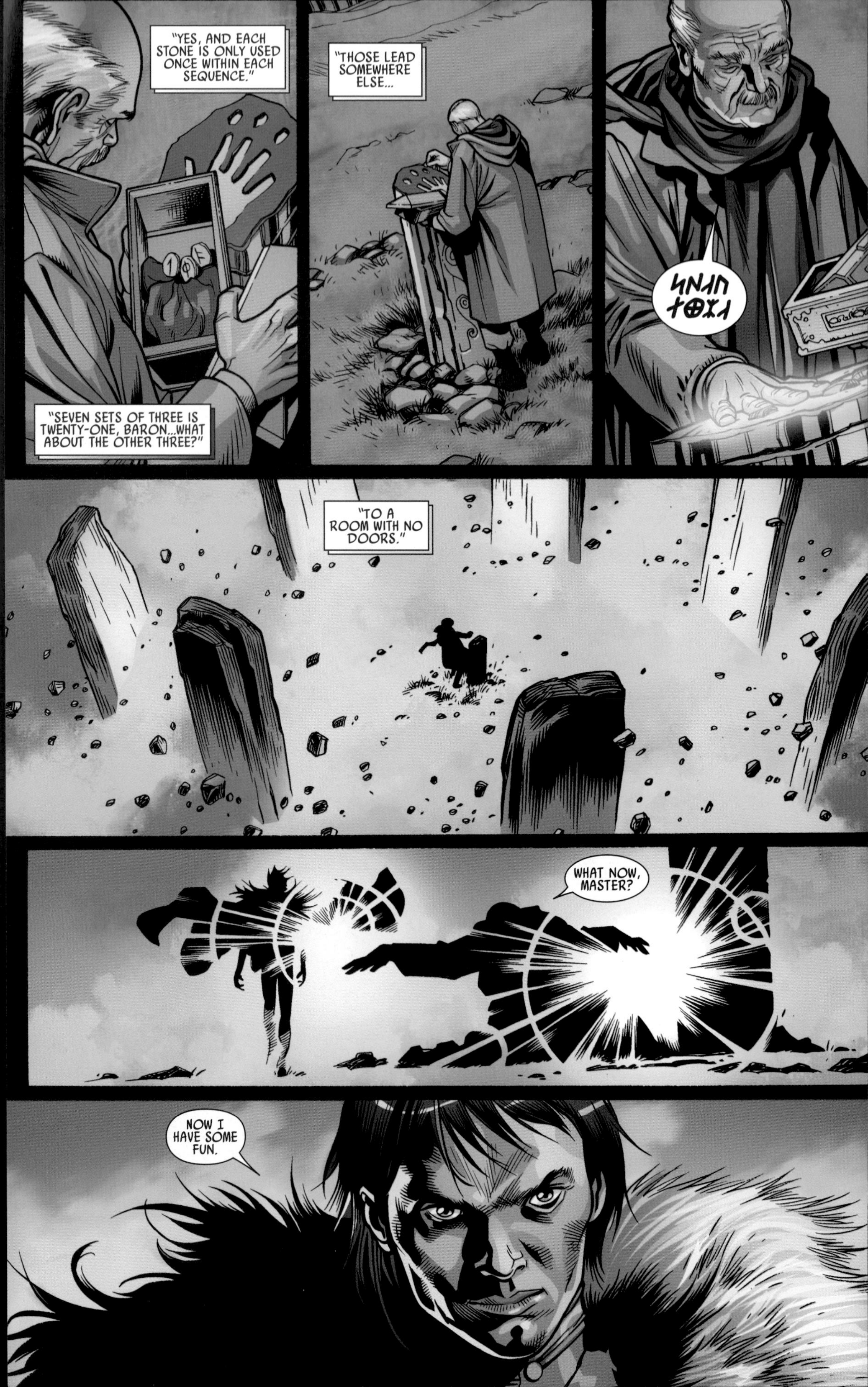
"YES, AND EACH STONE IS ONLY USED ONCE WITHIN EACH SEQUENCE."
"SEVEN SETS OF THREE IS TWENTY-ONE, BARON...WHAT ABOUT THE OTHER THREE?"
"THOSE LEAD SOMEWHERE ELSE...
"TO A ROOM WITH NO DOORS."
WHAT NOW, MASTER?
NOW I HAVE SOME FUN.

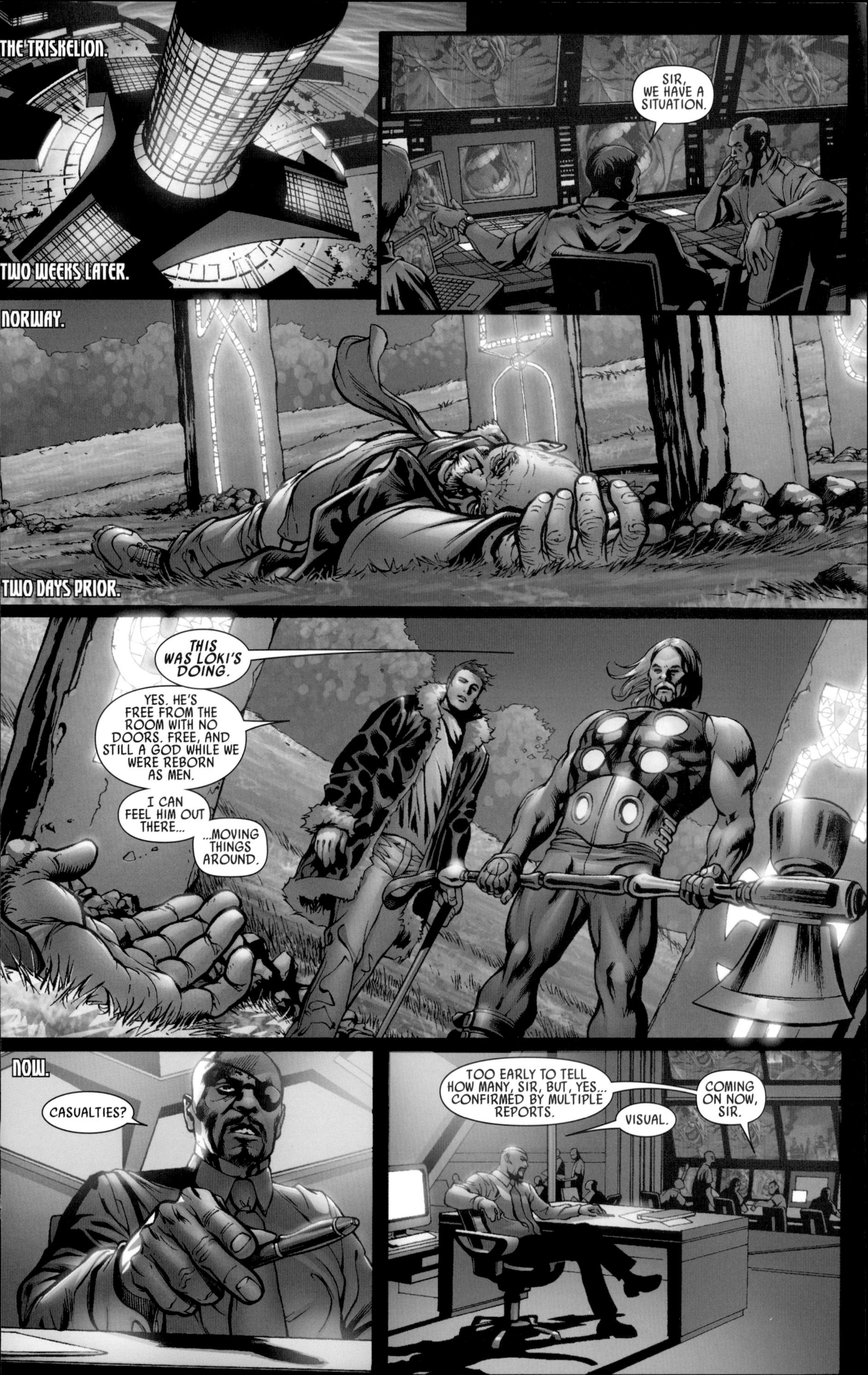
THE TRISKELION.
TWO WEEKS LATER.
SIR, WE HAVE A SITUATION.
NORWAY.
TWO DAYS PRIOR.
THIS WAS LOKI'S DOING.
YES. HE'S FREE FROM THE ROOM WITH NO DOORS. FREE, AND STILL A GOD WHILE WE WERE REBORN AS MEN.
I CAN FEEL HIM OUT THERE...
...MOVING THINGS AROUND.
NOW.
CASUALTIES?
TOO EARLY TO TELL HOW MANY, SIR, BUT, YES... CONFIRMED BY MULTIPLE REPORTS.
VISUAL.
COMING ON NOW, SIR.

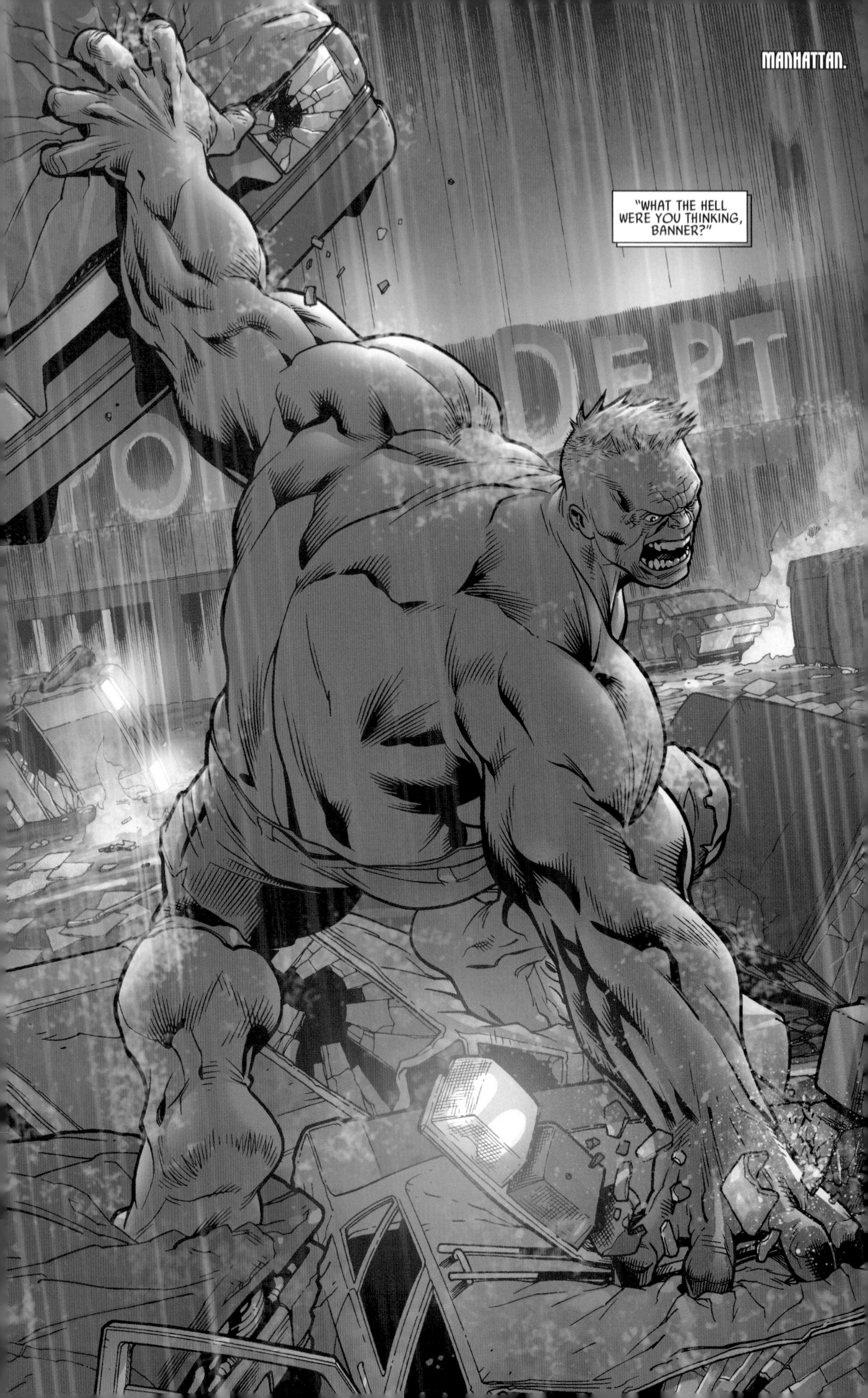
MANHATTAN.
"WHAT THE HELL WERE YOU THINKING, BANNER?"
DEPT

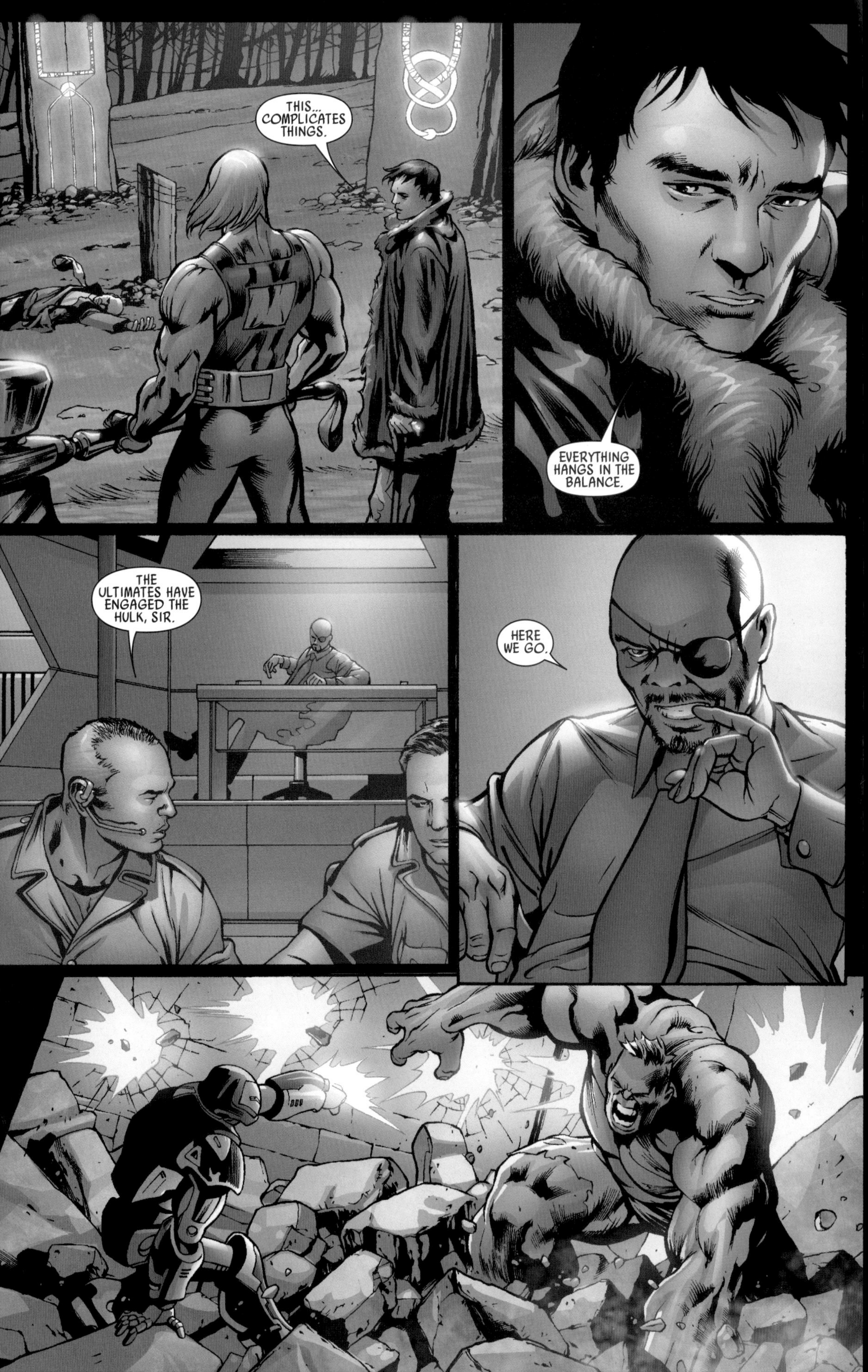
THIS... COMPLICATES THINGS.
EVERYTHING HANGS IN THE BALANCE.
THE ULTIMATES HAVE ENGAGED THE HULK, SIR.
HERE WE GO.

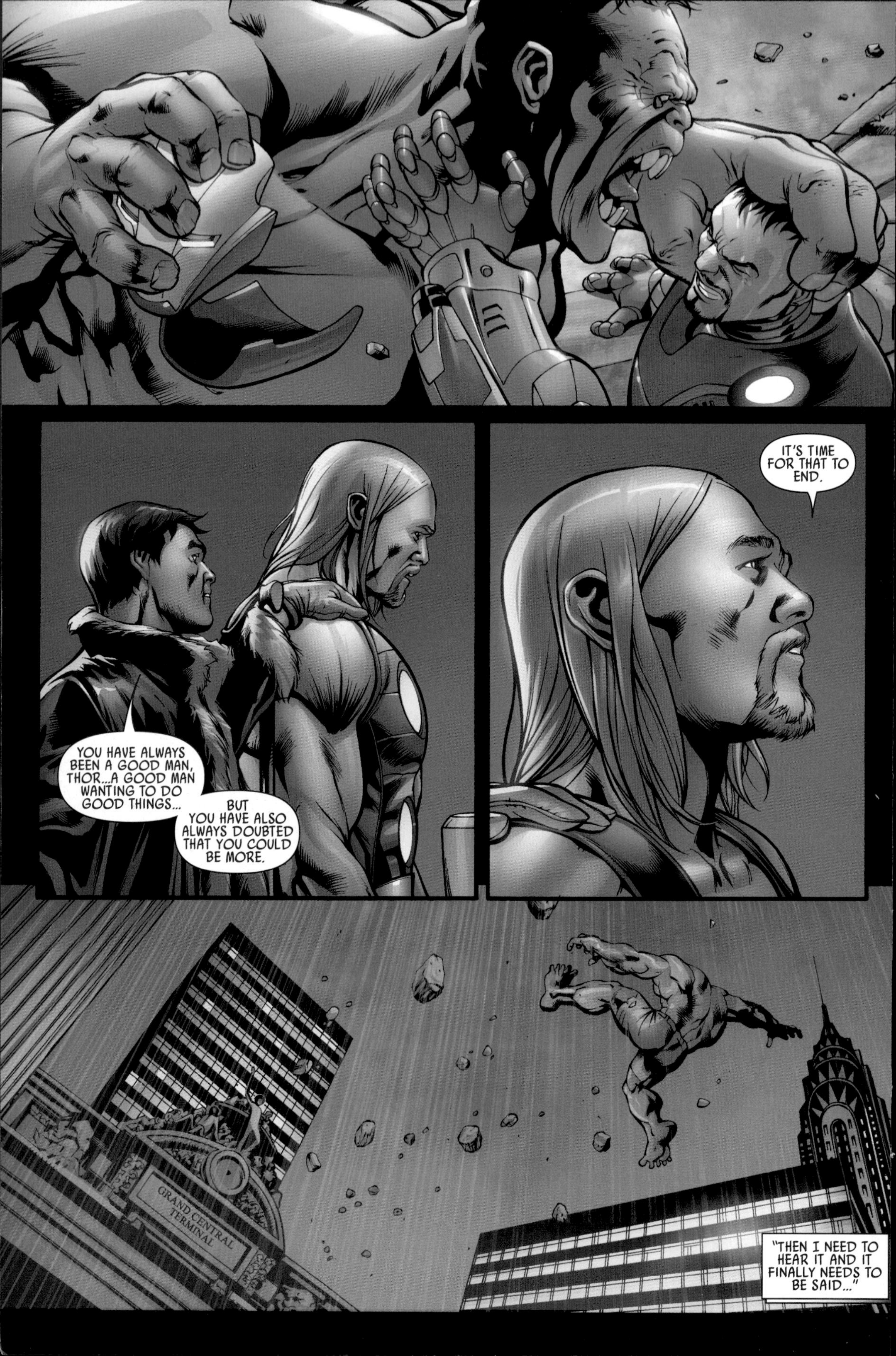
YOU HAVE ALWAYS BEEN A GOOD MAN, THOR...A GOOD MAN WANTING TO DO GOOD THINGS...
BUT YOU HAVE ALSO ALWAYS DOUBTED THAT YOU COULD BE MORE.
IT'S TIME FOR THAT TO END.
GRAND CENTRAL TERMINAL
"THEN I NEED TO HEAR IT AND IT FINALLY NEEDS TO BE SAID..."

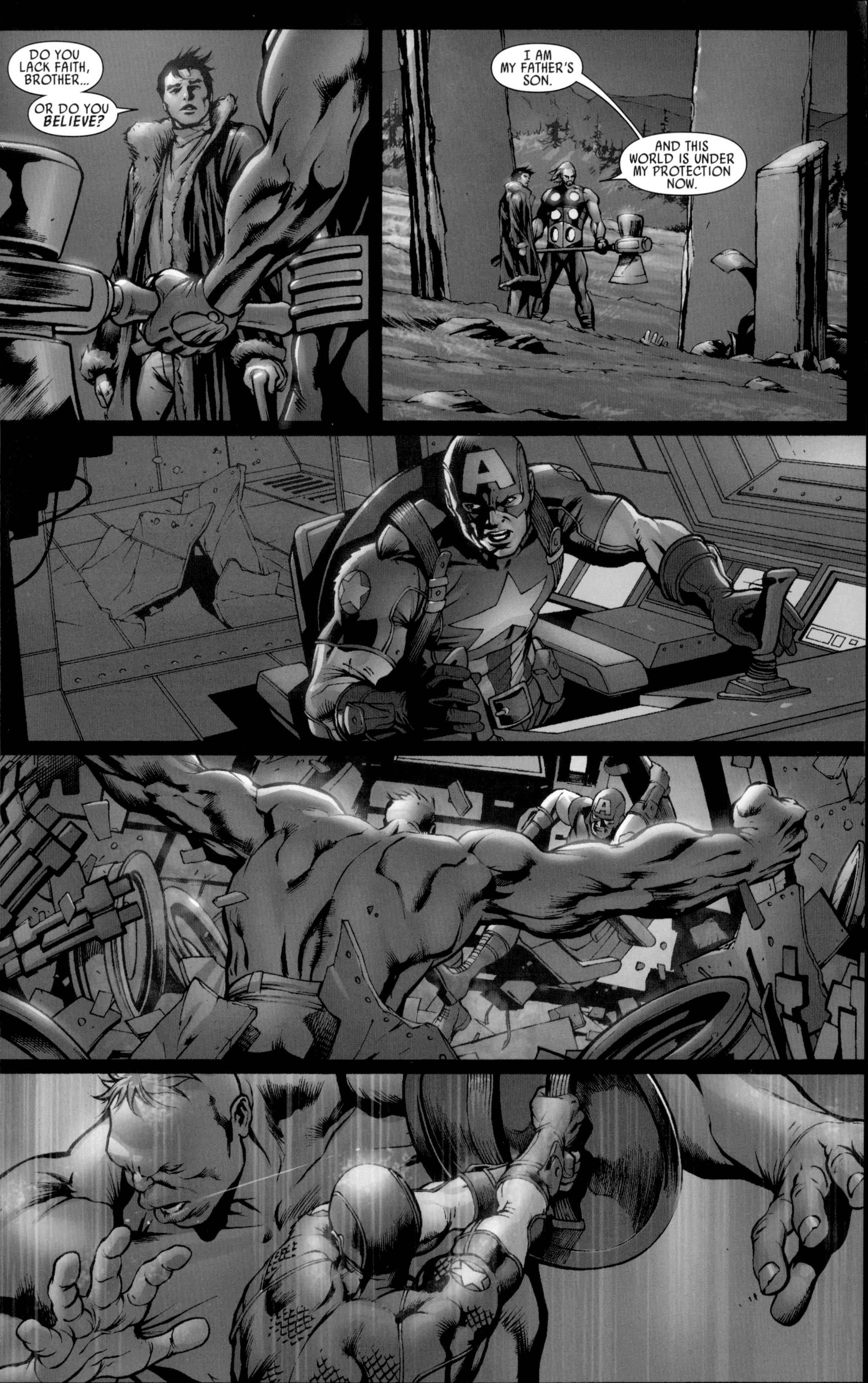
DO YOU LACK FAITH, BROTHER...
OR DO YOU BELIEVE?
I AM MY FATHER'S SON.
AND THIS WORLD IS UNDER MY PROTECTION NOW.

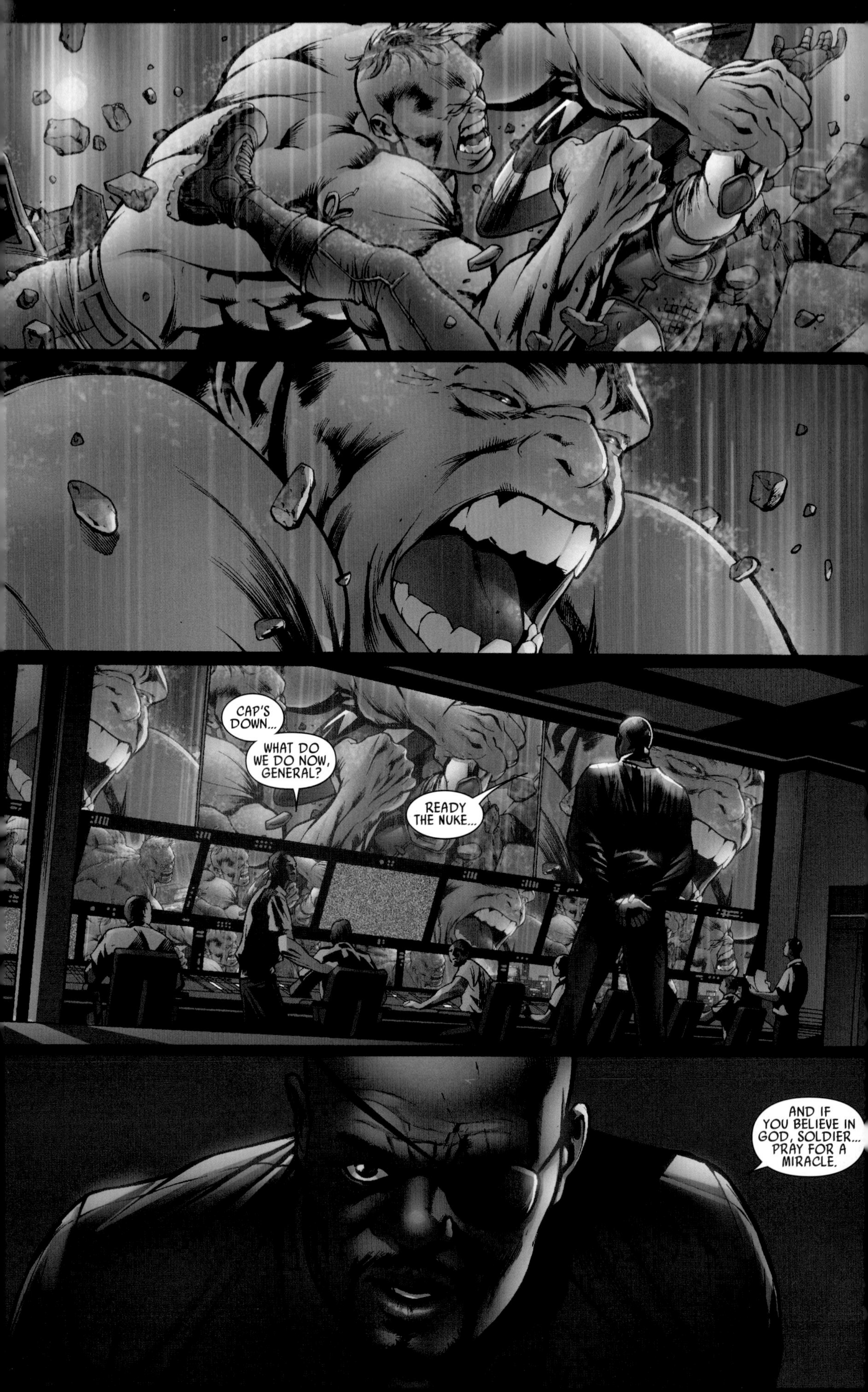
CAP'S DOWN...
WHAT DO WE DO NOW, GENERAL?
READY THE NUKE...
AND IF YOU BELIEVE IN GOD, SOLDIER... PRAY FOR A MIRACLE.

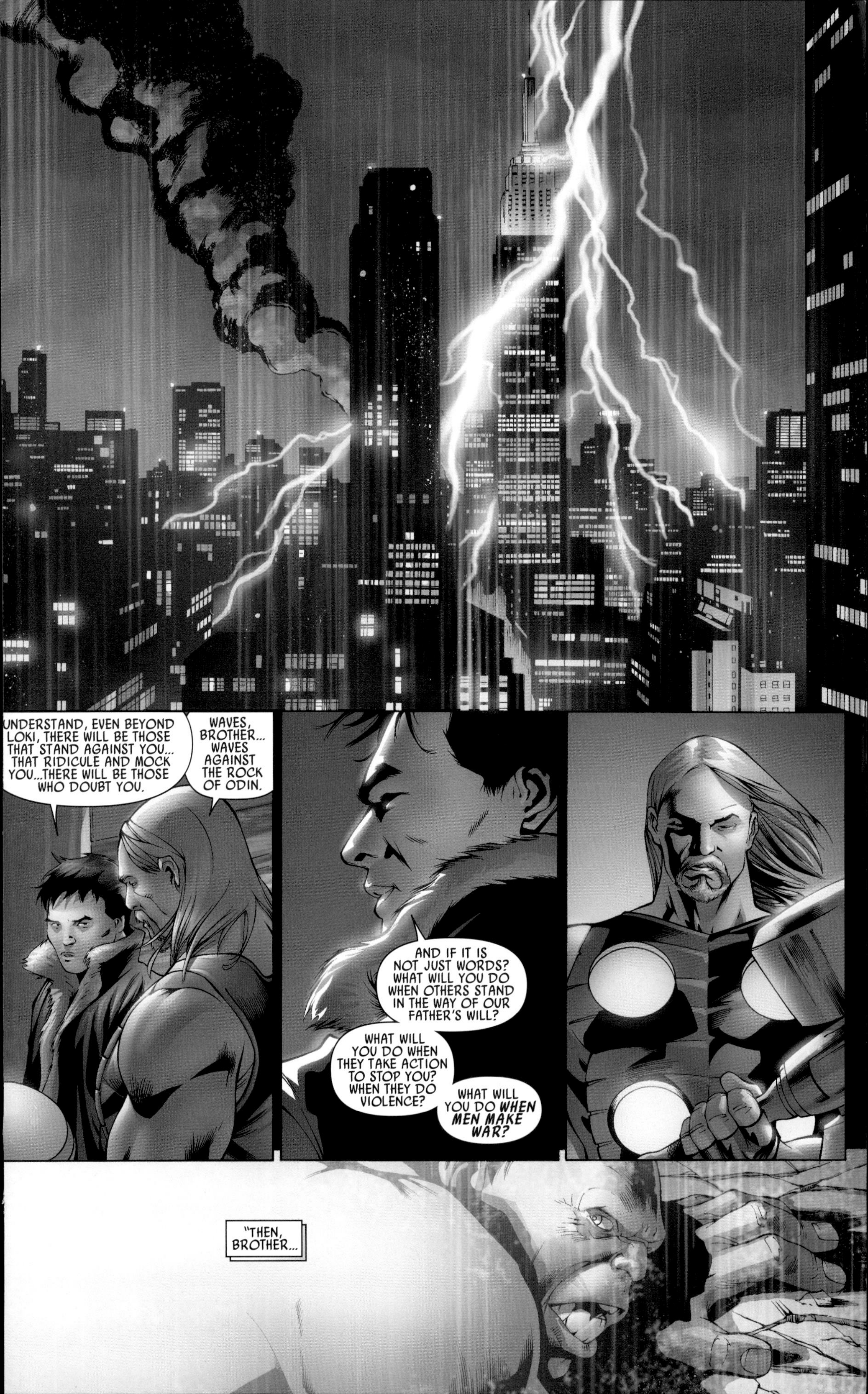
UNDERSTAND, EVEN BEYOND LOKI, THERE WILL BE THOSE THAT STAND AGAINST YOU... THAT RIDICULE AND MOCK YOU...THERE WILL BE THOSE WHO DOUBT YOU.
WAVES, BROTHER... WAVES AGAINST THE ROCK OF ODIN.
AND IF IT IS NOT JUST WORDS? WHAT WILL YOU DO WHEN OTHERS STAND IN THE WAY OF OUR FATHER'S WILL?
WHAT WILL YOU DO WHEN THEY TAKE ACTION TO STOP YOU? WHEN THEY DO VIOLENCE?
WHAT WILL YOU DO WHEN MEN MAKE WAR?
"THEN, BROTHER...

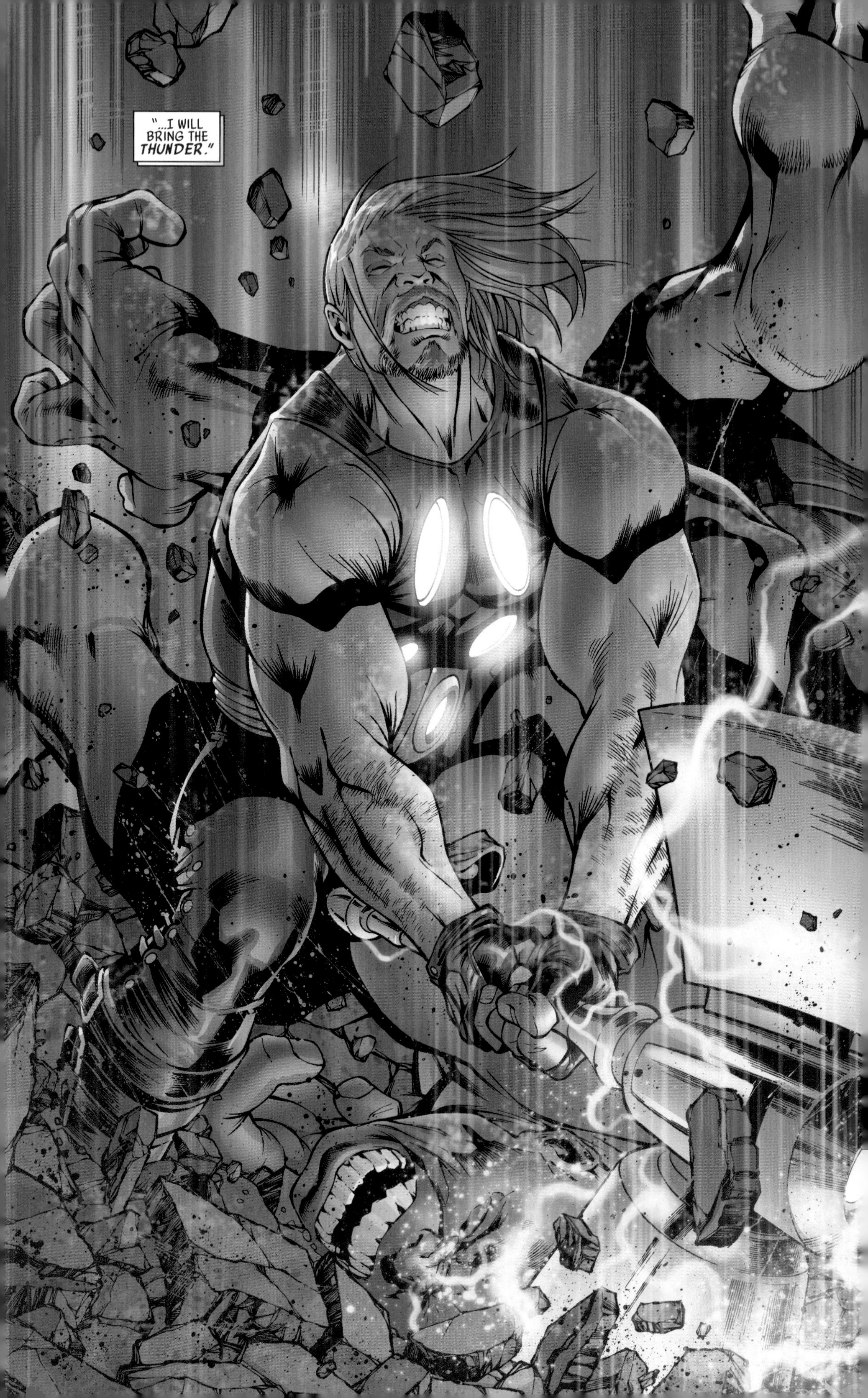
"...I WILL BRING THE *THUNDER*."

BELIEVE.

#1 VARIANT
BY MIKE CHOI & MORRY HOLLOWELL

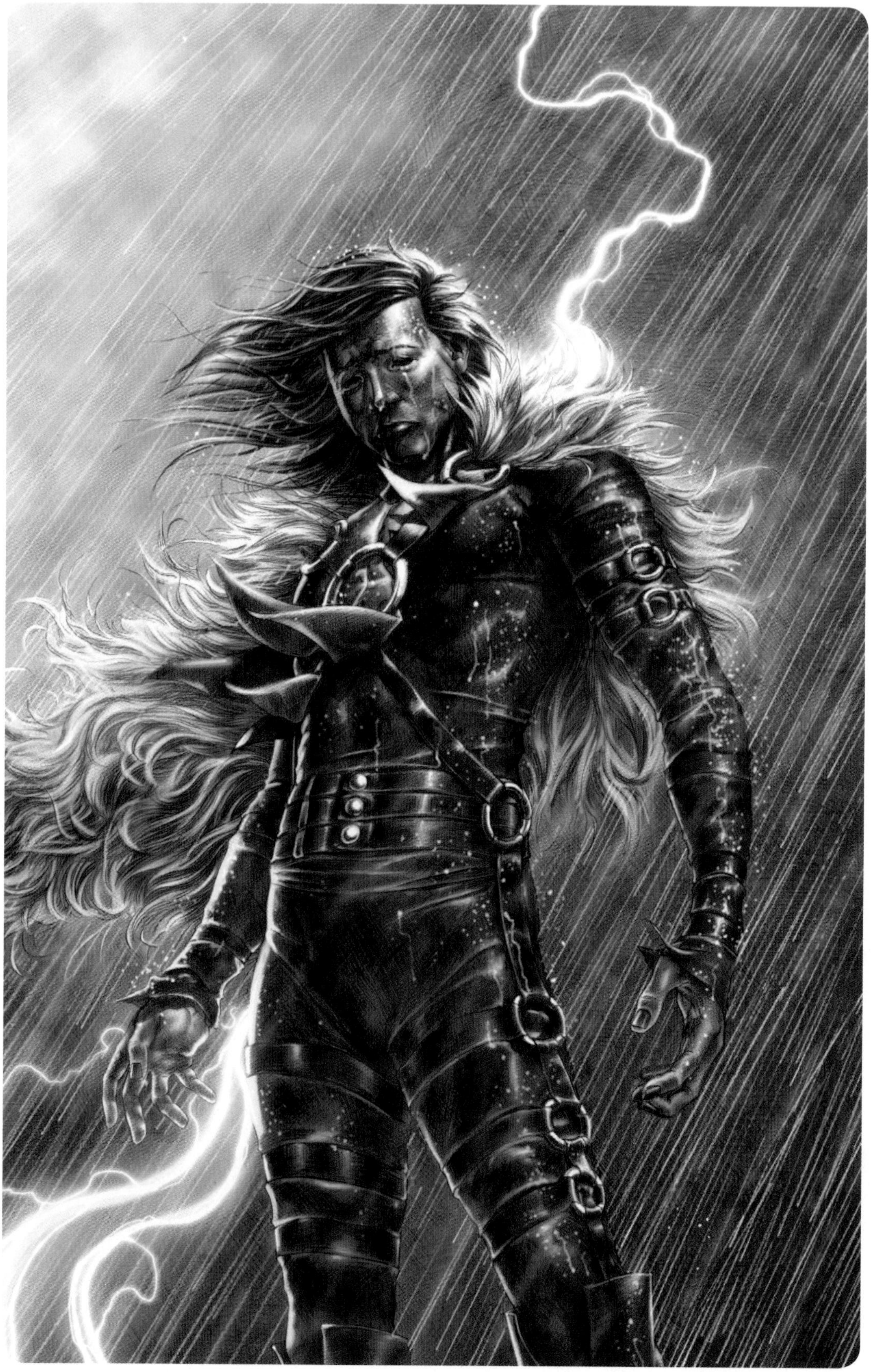

1 VARIANT

BY J. SCOTT CAMPBELL & NEI RUFFINO

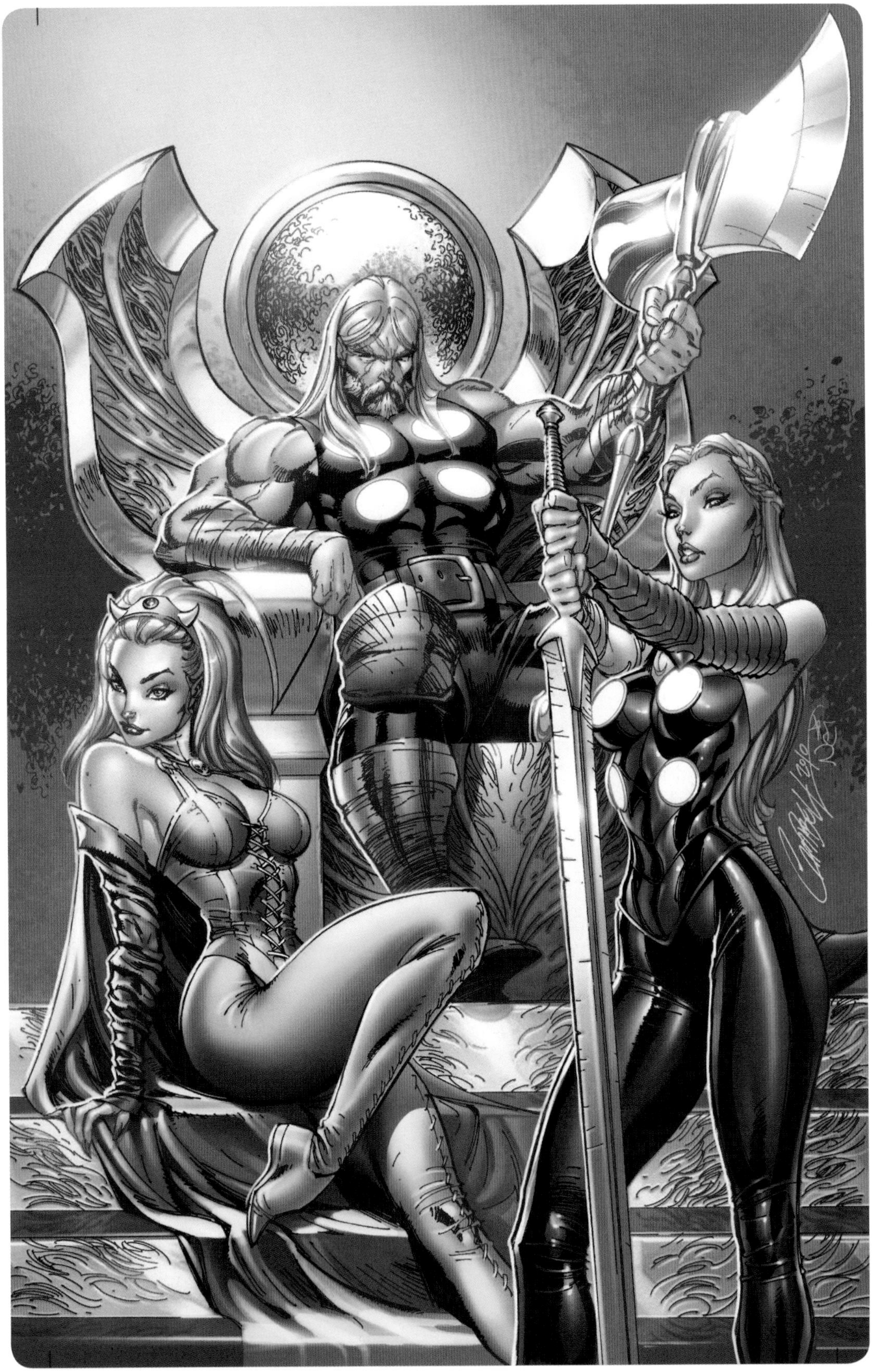

CHARACTER DESIGNS
BY CARLOS PACHECO

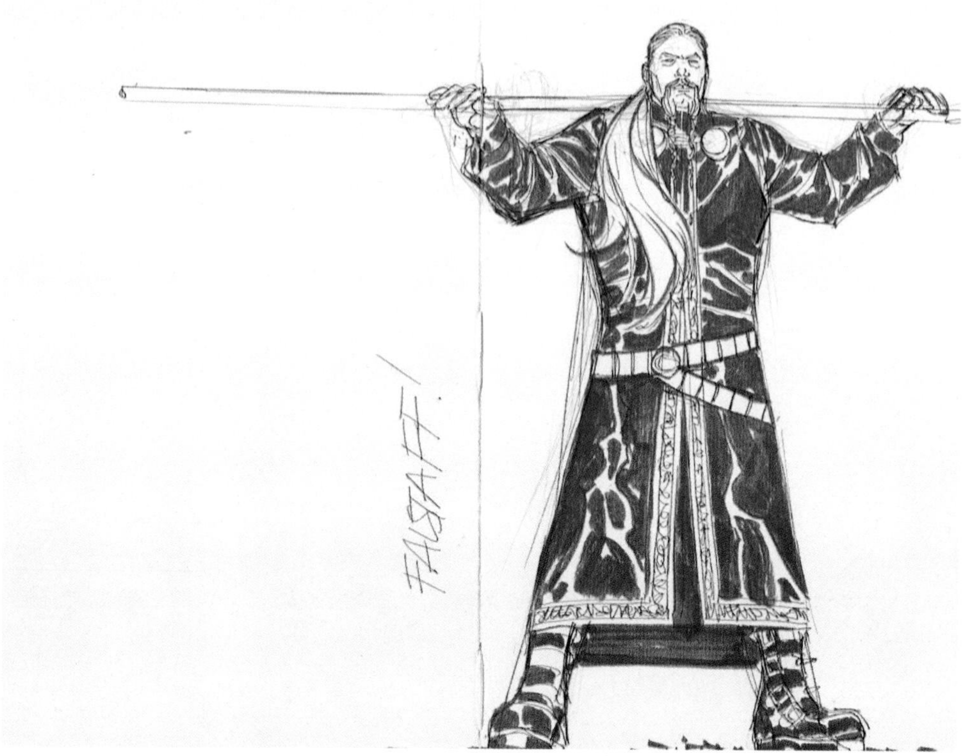
FALSTAFF!

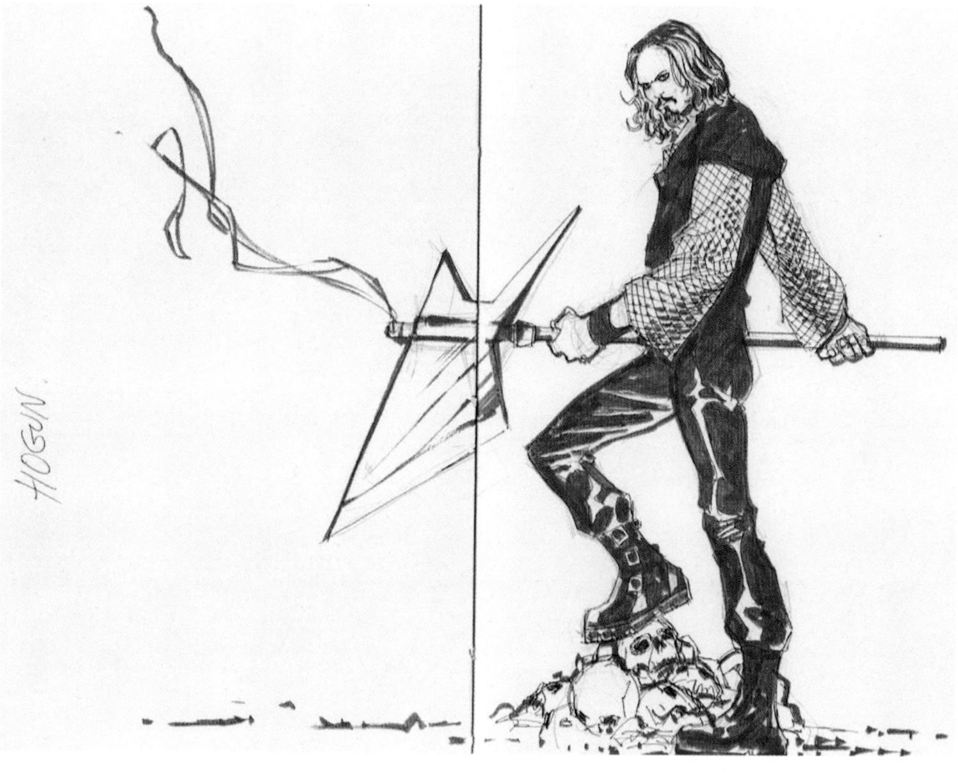
HOGUN

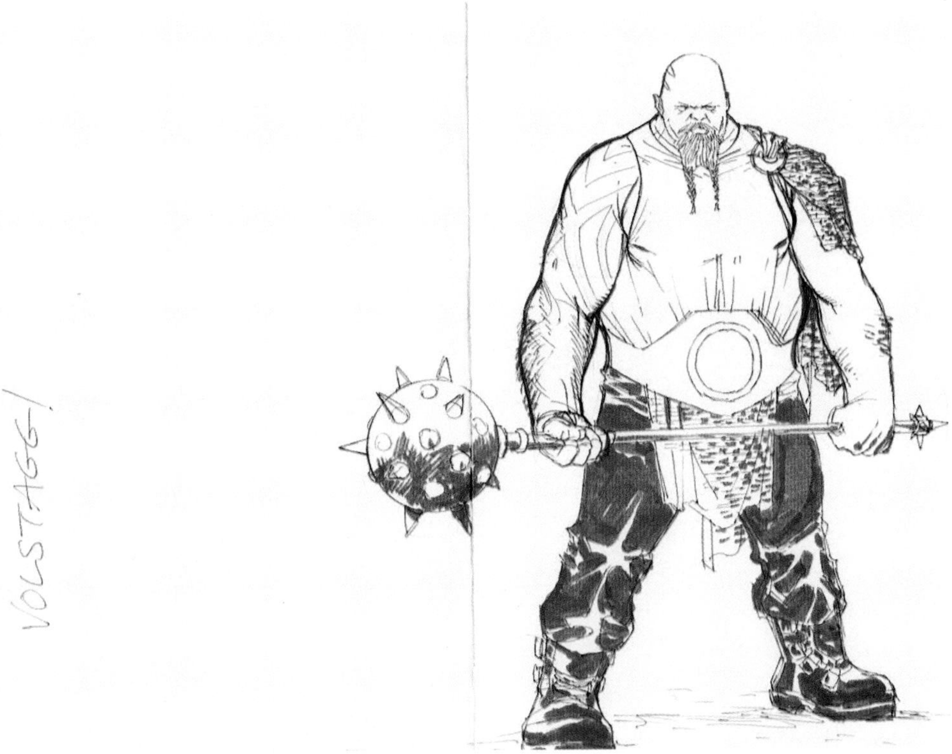
VOLSTAGG!

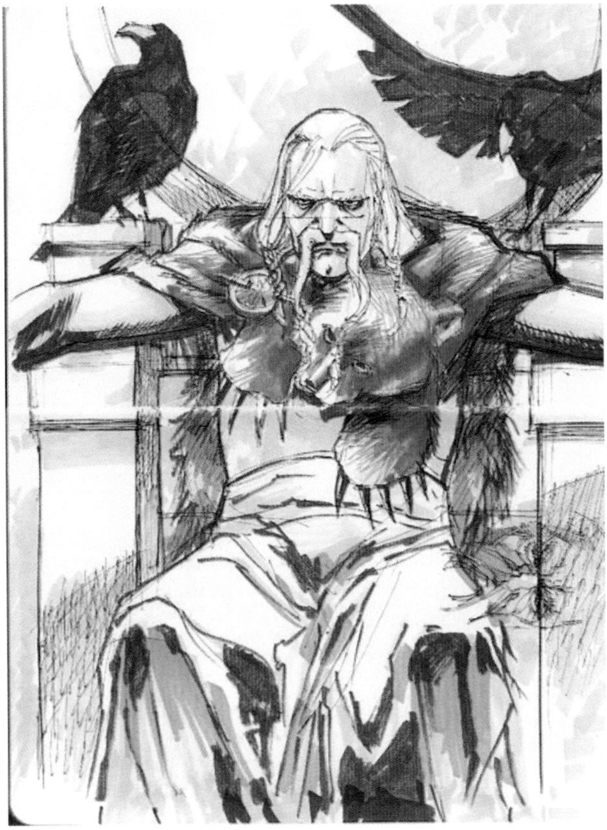

COVER SKETCHES
BY CARLOS PACHECO

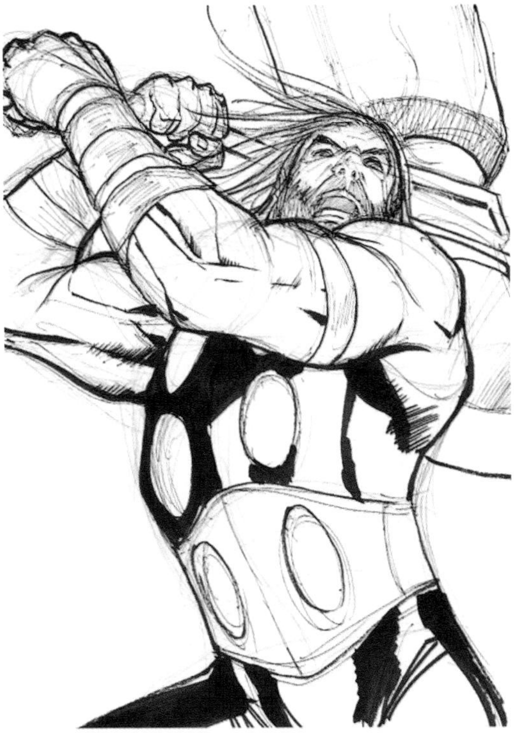

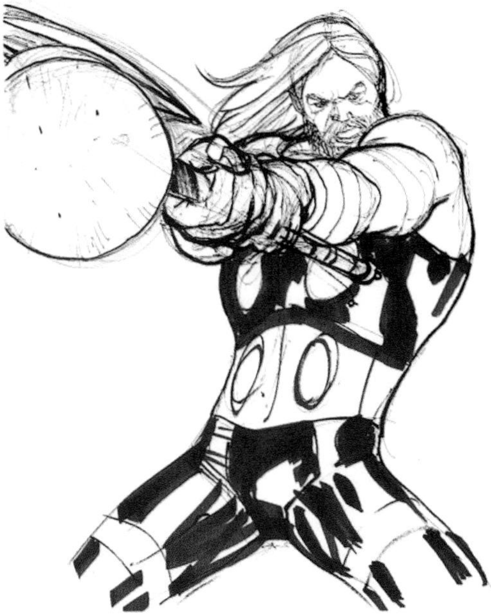

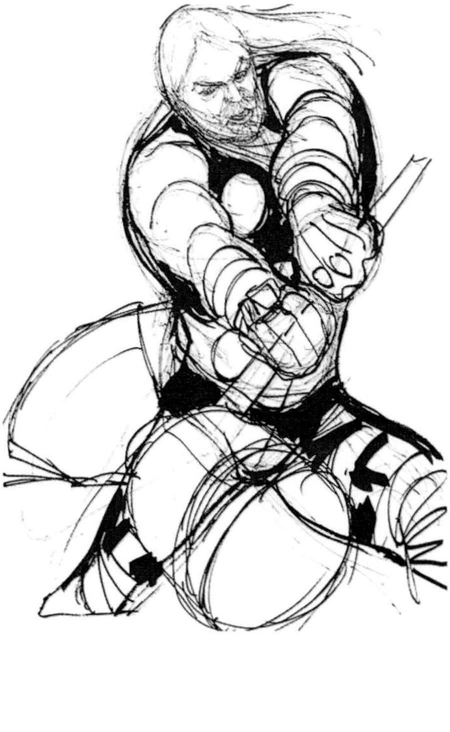

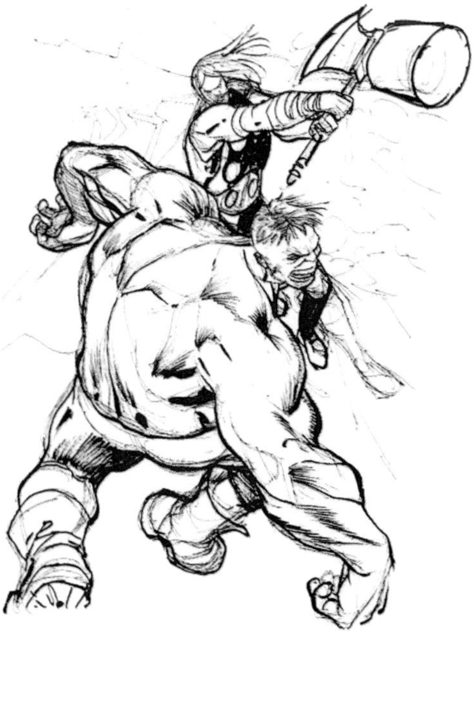

#1 PAGES 4-5 INKS
BY CARLOS PACHECO & DEXTER VINES

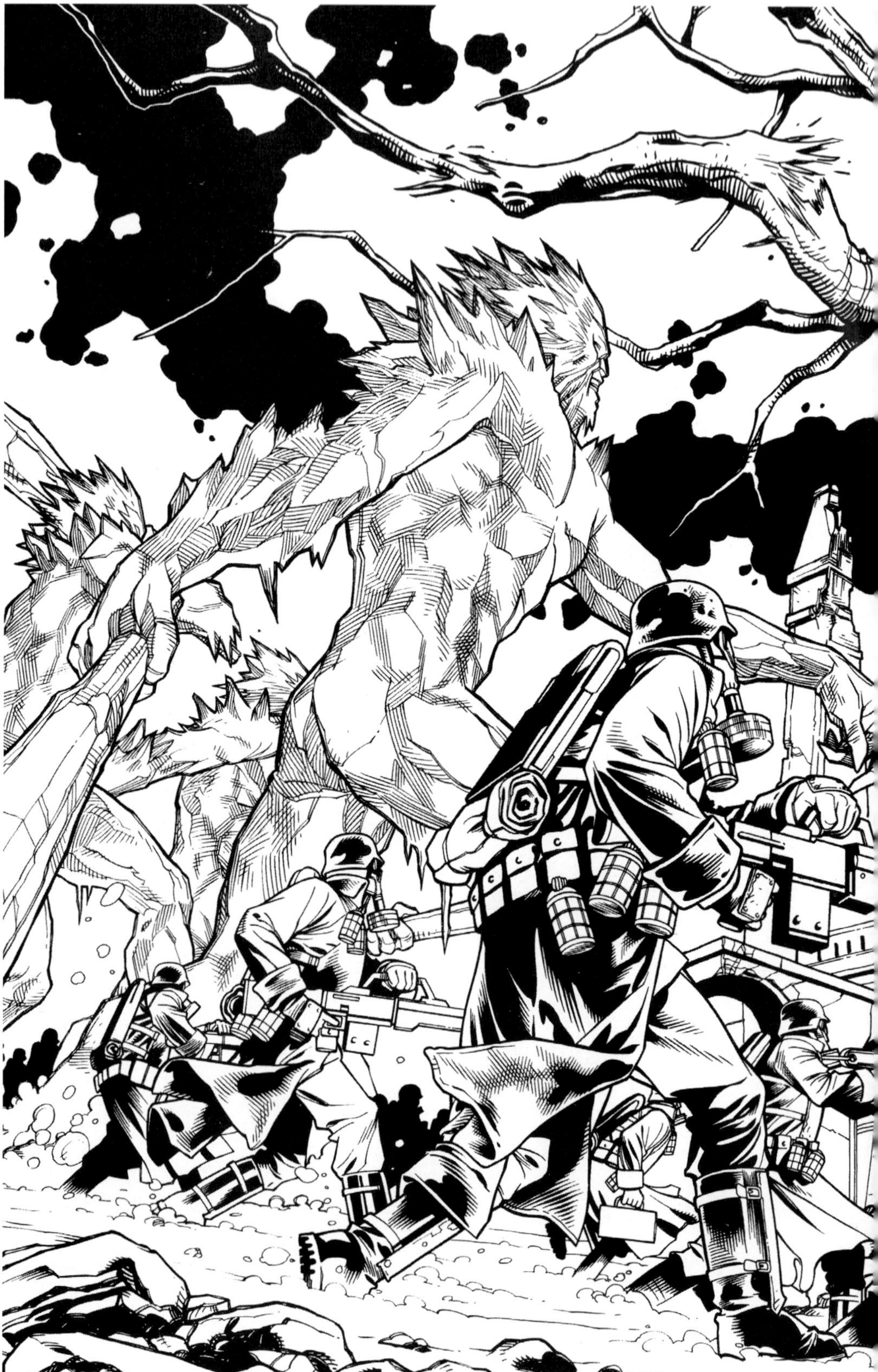

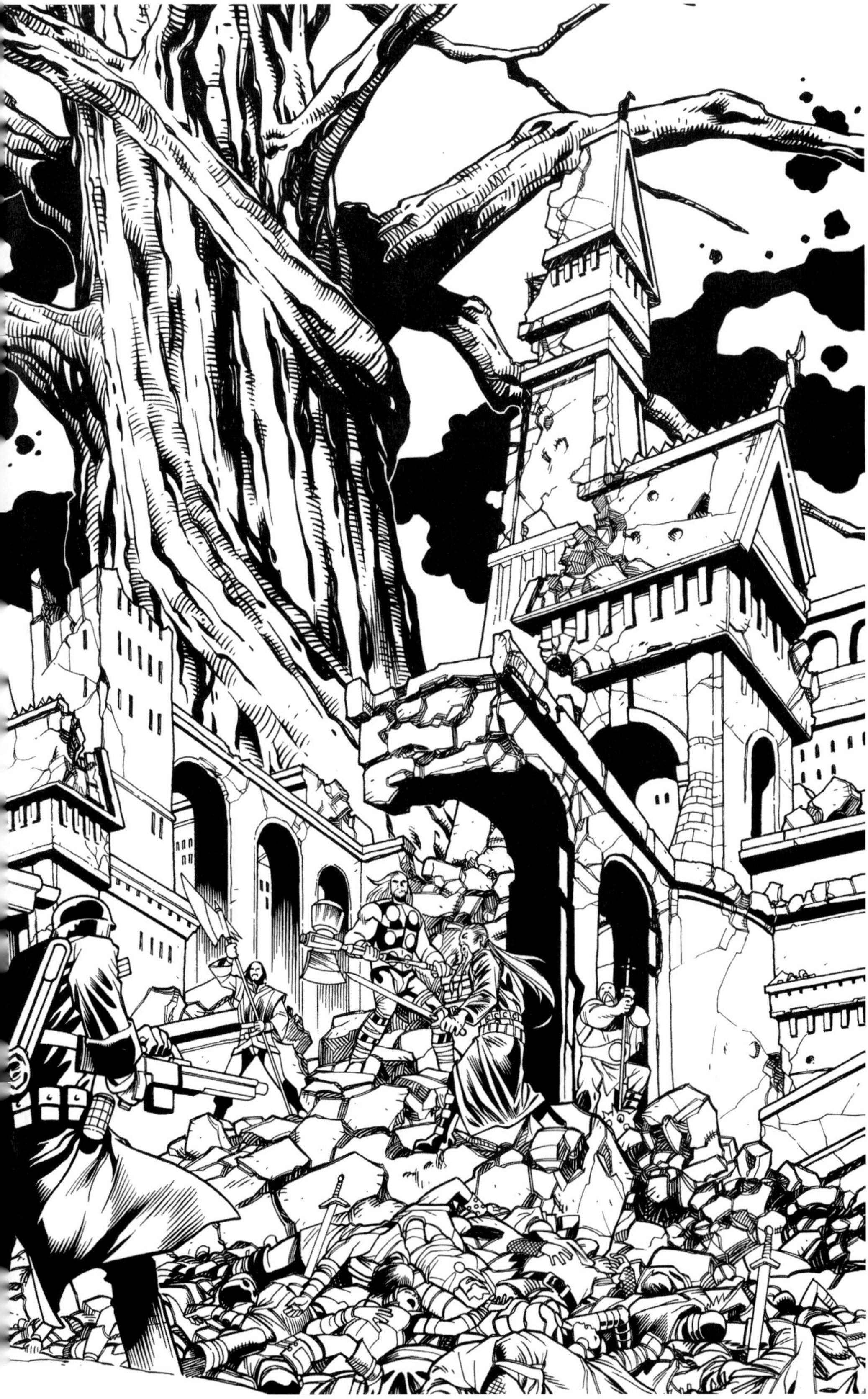

1 PAGE 15 INKS

BY CARLOS PACHECO & DEXTER VINES

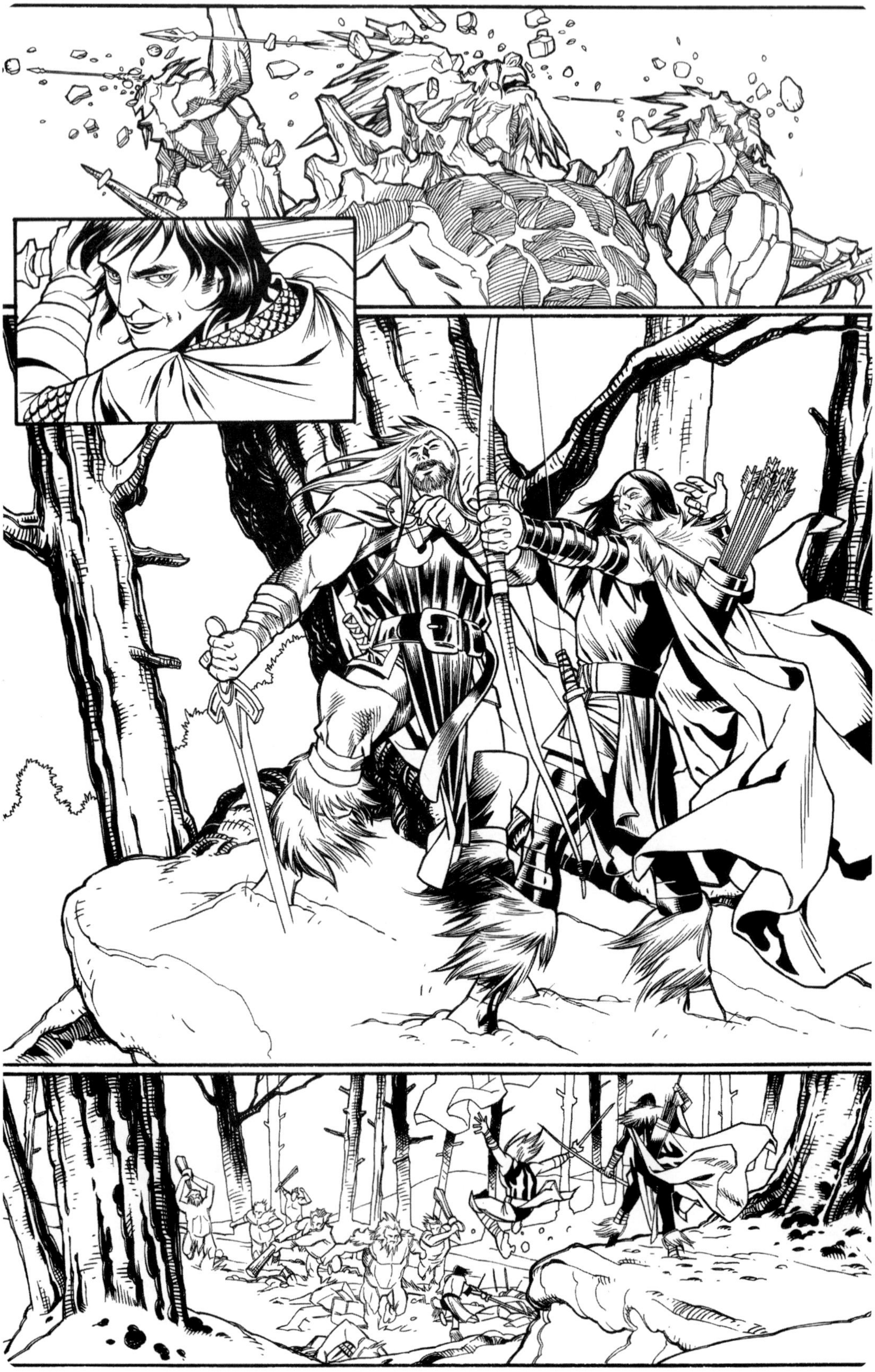

#3 PAGE 21 INKS

BY CARLOS PACHECO & DEXTER VINES

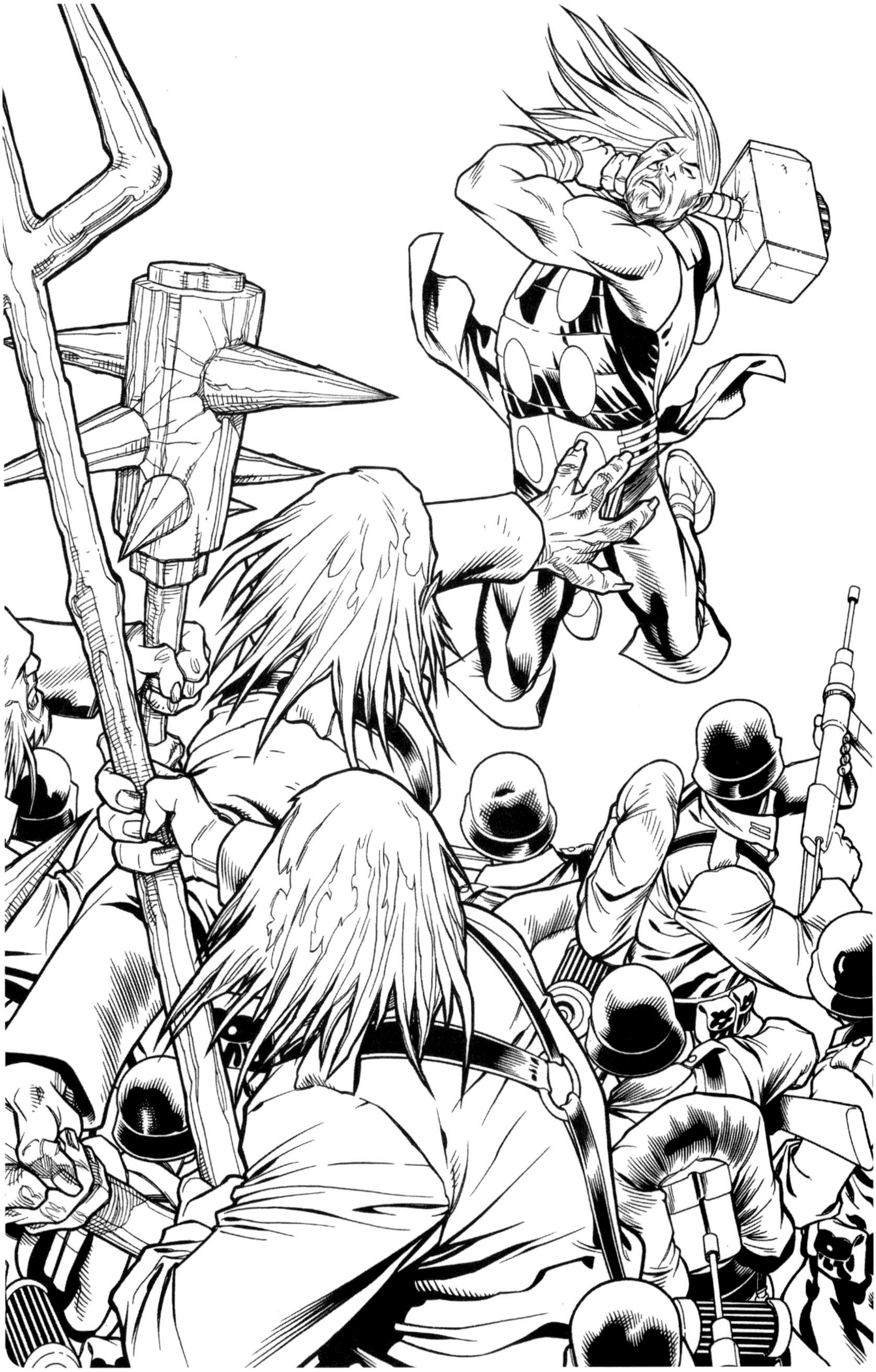

#4 PAGE 24 INKS
BY CARLOS PACHECO & DEXTER VINES

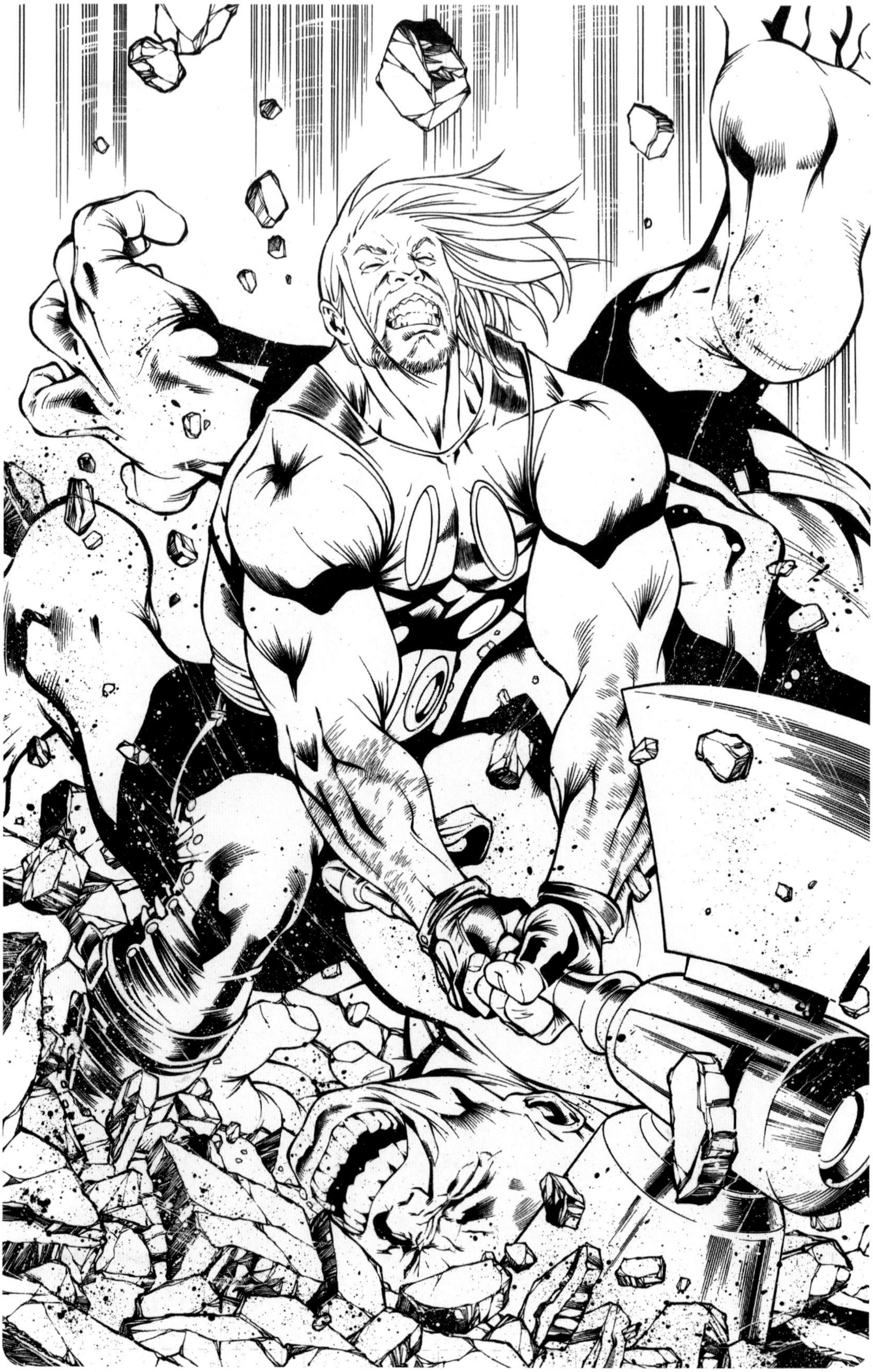